NIETZSCHE AS AFFIRMATIVE THINKER

MARTINUS NIJHOFF PHILOSOPHY LIBRARY

VOLUME 13

For a complete list of volumes in this series see final page of the volume.

Nietzsche as Affirmative Thinker

Papers Presented at the Fifth Jerusalem Philosophical Encounter, April 1983

edited by

Yirmiyahu Yovel
(Professor of Philosophy at the Hebrew University of Jerusalem)

1986 **MARTINUS NIJHOFF PUBLISHERS**
a member of the KLUWER ACADEMIC PUBLISHERS GROUP
DORDRECHT / BOSTON / LANCASTER

Distributors

for the United States and Canada: Kluwer Academic Publishers, 190 Old Derby Street, Hingham, MA 02043, USA
for the UK and Ireland: Kluwer Academic Publishers, MTP Press Limited, Falcon House, Queen Square, Lancaster LA1 1RN, UK
for all other countries: Kluwer Academic Publishers Group, Distribution Center, P.O. Box 322, 3300 AH Dordrecht, The Netherlands

Library of Congress Cataloging in Publication Data

```
Jerusalem Philosophical Encounter (5th : 1983)
   Nietzsche as affirmative thinker.

   (Martinus Nijhoff philosophy library ; v. 13)
   Includes index.
   1. Nietzsche, Friedrich Wilhelm, 1884-1900--
Congresses.  I. Yovel, Yirmiahu.  II. Title.
III. Series.
B3317.J39  1983        193           85-26019
ISBN 90-247-3269-7
```

ISBN 90-247-3269-7 (this volume)

Copyright

© 1986 by Martinus Nijhoff Publishers, Dordrecht.

All rights reserved. No part of this publication may be reproduced, stored in a retrieval system, or transmitted in any form or by any means, mechanical, photocopying, recording, or otherwise, without the prior written permission of the publishers,
Martinus Nijhoff Publishers, P.O. Box 163, 3300 AD Dordrecht,
The Netherlands.

PRINTED IN THE NETHERLANDS

Walter Kaufmann in Memoriam

Contents

Preface ix
List of Abbreviations xi

I. *Nietzsche and the Method of Philosophy*

Richard Schacht:	Nietzsche on Philosophy, Interpretation, and Truth	1
David C. Hoy:	Nietzsche, Hume, and the Genealogical Method	20
Bernd Magnus:	Nietzsche and the Project of Bringing Philosophy to an End	39
Gianni Vattimo:	Nietzsche and Contemporary Hermeneutics	58

II. *Varieties of Nietzsche's Affirmation*

Robert C. Solomon:	A More Severe Morality: Nietzsche's Affirmative Ethics	69
Alexander Nehamas:	Will to Knowledge, Will to Ignorance, and Will to Power in *Beyond Good and Evil*	90
Ran Sigad:	The Socratic Nietzsche	109
Eliyahu Rosenow:	Nietzsche's Concept of Education	119
Eric Blondel:	Nietzsche's Style of Affirmation: The Metaphors of Genealogy	132
Shlomo Pines:	Nietzsche: Psychology vs. Philosophy, and Freedom	147
Jacob Golomb:	Nietzsche's Enticing Psychology of Power	160

III. *Nietzschean Affinities and Confrontations*

Yirmiyahu Yovel:	Nietzsche and Spinoza: *amor fati* and *amor dei*	183
Eugen Biser:	Nietzsche und Heine. Kritik des christlichen Gottesbegriffs	204
Mazzino Montinari:	Nietzsche—Wagner im Sommer 1878	219
Index		229

Preface

The full century that has elapsed since Nietzsche was at the height of his work did not obliterate his impact. In many ways he is still a contemporary philosopher, even in that sense of 'contemporary' which points to the future. We may have outgrown his style (always, however, admirable and exciting to read), his sense of drama, his creative exaggeration, his sometimes flamboyant posture of a rebel wavering between the heroic and the puerile. Yet Nietzsche's critique of transcendental values and, especially, his attack on the inherited conceptions of rationality remain pertinent and continue to provoke anew cultural critique or dissent.

Today Nietzsche is no longer discussed apologetically, nor is his radicalism shunned or suppressed. That his work remains the object of extremely diverse readings is befitting a philosopher who replaced the concept of truth with that of interpretation. It is, indeed, around the concept of interpretation that much of the renewed interest in Nietzsche seems to center today. Special emphasis is being laid on his manner of doing philosophy, and his views on interpretation and the genealogical method are often re-read in the context of contemporary hermeneutics and "deconstructionist" positions.

Even more significantly, the need is growingly felt to consider Nietzsche not as a critic or a "negative" reformer merely, but to take his role as an *affirmative* thinker more seriously. Nietzsche insists that his Dionysian message is fundamentally an affirmation, a new kind of "yes." What is sometimes improperly called his "nihilism" was rather, on Nietzsche's own program, a call for a new affirmative position, free of the self-deceptive images of permanence, transcendental grounding, eternal truth, and value. Nietzsche was groping for a "revaluation of all values" whose axis was to lie in the rejoicing acceptance of immanent existence as all there is, an existence marked by "will to power" and lacking inherent order, value, or permanence. What philosophical tradition had always abhorred — the flux, the transience, and indeterminacy which govern existence — was made into the cornerstone of a new culture and evaluative approach to life. This difficult affirmation even held for Nietzsche a sober promise of emancipation and indicated an avenue for human perfectibility.

Yet Nietzsche did not spell out his new affirmation and, to most readers, it remained obscured by the more noticeable blows of his critical hammer.

The aim of this volume is to help reassess Nietzsche's work from a contemporary viewpoint while throwing the affirmative dimension of his thought into stronger relief.

The essays in this book were first presented at the Fifth Jerusalem Philosophical Encounter, held in April 1983 in memory of the late Walter Kaufmann. The *Jerusalem Philosophical Encounters* is a series of bi-annual symposia in which philosophers of different backgrounds meet in Jerusalem to discuss a common theme. The Encounters are organized by the S.H. Bergman Center for Philosophical Studies of the Hebrew University of Jerusalem. Former Encounters were concerned with the philosophy of history, the philosophy of language (meaning and use), the works of Spinoza, and Franz Rosenzweig.[1] (As this volume goes to print, a Sixth Jerusalem Philosophical Encounter has taken place, devoted to Maimonides and medieval philosophy).

Cordial thanks are due to the Van Leer Jerusalem Foundation for its cooperation in organizing the Nietzsche Encounter, along with the S.H. Bergman Center of the Hebrew University. Mrs. Rivka Raam of the Van Leer staff has particularly contributed to the success of the Encounter by ably attending to all its organizational needs. Ms. Eva Shorr, managing editor of the Hebrew philosophical quarterly *Iyyun*, has supervised the editing of the present volume with her usual care and dedication.

In dedicating this volume to the memory of Walter Kaufmann, I wish to pay hommage to a courageous and independent thinker whose premature death deprived the contemporary intellectual scene of an avid critic and Nietzsche studies of a prominent scholar and translator. Kaufmann had also been an adviser or a senior colleague of some of the participants in the present volume, and helped produce a new generation of Nietzsche students who, even when taking other paths than his, will recognize his merit and pioneering contribution.

Yirmiyahu Yovel

The S.H. Bergman Center for Philosophical Studies
The Hebrew University of Jerusalem

---

[1] (1) *Philosophy of History and Action,* ed. Y. Yovel, Reidel, 1978 (with papers by P. Ricoeur, C. Taylor, D. Davidson, I. Berlin, J. D'Hondt, N. Rotenstreich, and others). (2) *Meaning and Use,* ed. A. Margalit, Reidel, 1979 (with papers by W.V. Quine, D. Davidson, J. Hintikka, M. Dummett, J. Searle, H. Putnam, P. Strawson, E.M. Zemach, S. Kripke, and others). (3) *Spinoza — His Thought and Work,* ed. N. Rotenstreich, The Israel Academy of Sciences and Humanities, 1983 (with papers by R. McKeon, P. Strawson, S. Hampshire, G. Funke, R. Barcan-Marcus, S. Pines, L. Kolakowski, Y. Yovel, and others). (4) *The Philosophy of Franz Rosenzweig,* ed. P. Mendes-Flohr, New England University Press, forthcoming (with papers by E. Fackenheim, O. Pöggeler, N. Glatzer, E. Levinas, and others).

List of Abbreviations

Unless otherwise noted, citations from Nietzsche's writings are identified by the use of the acronyms of their English titles, by Arabic numbers referring to the paragraphs or sections in which the passages appear, and, where appropriate, by Roman numerals indicating the parts of the works in which they are to be found.

As a convenience to English-speaking readers, most of the contributors have followed Walter Kaufmann's renderings in the translations he published.

Citations from the other works listed are based on the texts as they appear in the Colli-Montinari *Kritische Gesamtausgabe* (KGA) or the *Kritische Studienausgabe* (KSA), unless otherwise noted.

PTA — Philosophy in the Tragic Age of the Greeks
BT — The Birth of Tragedy, in: *The Basic Writings of Nietzsche* (New York: Random House, 1968)
SE — Schopenhauer as Educator
HH — Human, All-Too-Human
D — Dawn (or Daybreak)
GS — The Gay Science (New York: Random House, 1974)
Z — Thus Spoke Zarathustra, in: *The Portable Nietzsche* (New York: Viking, 1968)
BGE — Beyond Good and Evil, in: *The Basic Writings*
GM — On the Genealogy of Morals, in: *The Basic Writings*
TI — Twilight of the Idols, in: *The Portable Nietzsche*
A — The Antichrist, in: *The Portable Nietzsche*
EH — Ecce Homo, in: *The Basic Writings*
WP — The Will to Power (New York: Random House, 1968)

Richard Schacht

Nietzsche on Philosophy, Interpretation and Truth[1]

"Interpretation," according to Nietzsche, has always been the actual — if generally unacknowledged — activity of philosophers and other thinkers, at least to the extent that they have been more than mere philosophical and intellectual "laborers" content to work within and with the framework of interpretations developed by others. And it is his further contention that genuine philosophers — including the "new philosophers" he envisions and calls for — will not and should not abandon interpretation in favor of some more "exact" form of thinking and reasoning, but rather must engage more self-consciously and deliberately and less dogmatically in it. So he characterizes his own philosophical activity as interpretive, despite the fact that this would appear to place his own positions on a par with those he rejects and brands as "lies," "errors," and "fictions." "Supposing that this also is only interpretation — and you will be eager enough to make this objection? — well, so much the better" (BGE 22).

This might lead one to wonder whether, by allowing and indeed insisting that "interpretation" (or more fully, the devising and making of cases for and against various "interpretations") is at the heart of all genuine philosophical activity, Nietzsche does not in fact lower philosophy as he conceives and commends it to the level of the mere mongering of *Weltanschauungen,* thus reducing it to a kind of quasi-literary enterprise of little or no cognitive significance. Some interpreters and many readers have in fact taken this to be precisely his intention, or at any rate the upshot of his treatment of the matter;

---

[1] For a much more extensive treatment of issues dealt with in this paper, and of others related to them, see the Introduction and first two chapters of my *Nietzsche* (London: Routledge & Kegan Paul, 1983), from which several paragraphs in this paper have been taken. See also my "Nietzsche and Nihilism," *Journal of the History of Philosophy* 11 (January, 1973), which appears as Chapter 8 of my *Hegel and After* (Pittsburgh: University of Pittsburgh Press, 1975).

and they have then proceeded to praise or condemn him, as this conclusion agrees or conflicts with their own sentiments. This is especially common among those inclined to suppose that "interpretation" is a very subjective sort of affair; and that, to the extent that it can be shown to be involved in the development of a position being advanced, its presence undermines any appearance the positions may have of credibility. Once something becomes a matter of one interpretation against another, the idea runs, "it is all relative" — relative to the feelings and attitudes of those advancing the conflicting interpretations; and thus the discussion has left the ground on which serious argument can alone be based and cognitively significant conclusions reached. *Incipit Zarathustra, exit scientia.*

As I read him, however, this is not at all Nietzsche's view of the matter. "Interpretation" as he understands it is by no means an affair so hopelessly "relative" and "subjective" that to construe philosophical activity in terms of it is tantamount to depriving it of all cognitive import. Indeed, it seems to me that he is on to something important in taking the enterprise of philosophy — properly understood and carried on — to be fundamentally (although perhaps not exclusively) a matter of engaging in the complementary activities of critically examining received or proposed interpretations and developing (and making cases for) others which might improve upon them. And if this is so, the question of what constitutes and counts as a philosophical argument largely becomes the question of what is involved in the establishment of the relative soundness and adequacy of such interpretations.

To be sure, Nietzsche does take the *value* of different interpretations in most human contexts to be primarily a function of considerations of other sorts relating above all to the preservation and enhancement of life. He also suggests that interpretations are of considerable *symptomatic* significance, serving to reveal a great deal about those who advance them. It by no means follows, however, that he holds the relative soundness or tenability of different interpretations to be conceivable only along one or both of these lines. Indeed, an attentive reading of him reveals that he not only allows but moreover insists that some interpretations may be better than others, where "better" is construed not in terms of such cognitively neutral notions as that of "value for life," but rather in terms of soundness and adequacy. This is a matter of considerable importance for the understanding of his entire philosophical enterprise; and so I shall offer some comments upon it, before turning to a fuller characterization of that enterprise as he conceives and engages in it.

I

Can some interpretations conceivably be "better" than others, in the sense of being more illuminating, more adequate, more insightful, and more just than others are? In approaching this question, consider first the "interpretation" of works of art and literature. Here, particularly in the case of the performing arts, it often refers to what performers do with the works being performed — in short, to their adaptions. "Interpretations" of this sort may be considered works of art in their own right, to be evaluated and judged on their own terms, rather than in terms of strict fidelity to a "text" and intentions of its creator. To ask whether one is better than another would thus be to ask something like whether one is aesthetically superior to another. This question, however, is not the sort of question presently under consideration. Nietzsche admittedly does at times suggest that a kind of quasi-aesthetic perspective (from which a premium is placed, e.g., on elegance) is *one* perspective from which the superiority of some "interpretations" to others may be determined — one differing, it may be noted, from that of "value for life." But he quite clearly does not wish to collapse the distinction between truth and beauty (or, more judiciously put, between cognitive and aesthetic significance), as is shown, among other things, by his frequent acknowledgment of the aesthetically repellent features of many matters as he interprets them.

More to the point is another use of "interpretation" in connection with the arts, and also (quite significantly, in view of Nietzsche's training and early career), in philology insofar as it is concerned with the analysis of texts. It refers to the examination of a work with a view to establishing something about its nature that goes beyond the level of what is sufficiently obvious in it to require no comment. Such interpretations, while sometimes offered merely in an attempt to affect the receptivity of others to a work in such a way that they will get something new and different out of their future encounters with it, are often serious attempts to enhance the *understanding* of a work — to show that it has certain features which require to be recognized if one is properly to construe it. Different interpreters, however, will often seize upon different aspects of a work, and sometimes proceed to construe the whole in terms of the part that they have brought to light. And some are only too ready to read their own concerns and commitments into and out of anything that is of interest to others already, thereby to win a wider and more sympathetic audience than they might be able to attract on their own. For these and other such reasons, observers of the fray are commonly inclined to conclude that where interpretations of works of art and literature are concerned, it is pointless to raise the issue of soundness. Interpretations of *Hamlet,* for example, are legion; how could one begin to settle the question of which of them, if any, is to be preferred?

On the other hand, it should be obvious to anyone who has read a fair number of interpretations of such a work that, while none of them may be definitive and completely adequate, some do less justice to the work than others; even though it may be difficult to determine which of several apt and insightful interpretations does more. And this can be so even though there may be important respects in which it is simply ambiguous, and admits of different "takings" or readings (or "interpretations" in the sense mentioned previously). Indeed, it may be so constituted as to require — or at least to invite — something of this sort on the part of those who encounter it. And part of what "interpretation" in the sense presently under consideration involves is the ascertainment of the ways and extent to which this sort of thing constitutes part of the nature of the work, when it does.

It further may be that the work has been available and interpreted in various ways for so long that, as Nietzsche remarks with reference to the world we live in, the text has virtually disappeared beneath the interpretations. But it does not follow that nothing on the order of a text remains beneath them — that they as it were float suspended in the void — and that interpretations are all that other interpretations have to deal with, and probe for. It may also be that it is only by developing an interpretation oneself that one can attempt to say anything about a text otherwise interpreted by others. But it does not follow that any new interpretation thus proposed is *merely* "another interpretation," in principle no more adequate to the text than any other. No new interpretation, simply by virtue of its being new (let alone one's own), may legitimately be held superior in point of adequacy or validity to every other; but it cannot be assumed that any standing interpretation, however hallowed by tradition or popular acceptance, is as sound or more so than any other which might be opposed to it could possibly be. There likewise may never be an interpretation of a work so completely adequate to it that the possibility of another more illuminating and doing greater justice to it would be foreclosed. But that does not mean that nothing more is understood of the nature of a work when it is interpreted in one way than when it is interpreted in another.

It is Nietzsche's view that the parallel between this situation and that which obtains in the cases of most other forms of inquiry (philosophy included), while undoubtedly not exact, is at any rate quite close, even though the latter generally do not have to do with things produced as works of art and literature are. Interpretation may quite properly be considered the task of the historian, for example, notwithstanding the fact that it is human events rather than works of this kind with which the historian concerns himself; and the same sorts of remarks would be appropriate in connection with historical interpretation as were made above with respect to the interpretation of such works. Scientific theories too may be considered "interpretations" the status of which is not so radically different from that of literary and historical interpretations as to brook no comparison, despite the evident differences in the relation of the matters with which they respectively deal to the aims and purposes of men. This is a point Nietzsche himself makes much of, insisting that most of what passes for explanation in a science like physics is actually only redescription within an interpretive framework; and that even an idea as basic to it as that of "nature's conformity to law" is "no matter of fact," but rather "is interpretation not text" (BGE 22).

These reflections suggest that many forms of inquiry often taken to be widely disparate in character actually display a kinship — as kinds of interpretation — which is overlooked only at the cost of misunderstanding their actual status and significance, the possible cognitive import of the views advanced by those engaging in them being underestimated in some cases and overestimated in others. And they at least lend greater plausibility to the idea that philosophy may be conceived in terms of "interpretation" without thereby relegating it to the outer darkness of cognitive indifference — analogous to the "night in which all cows are black" disparaged by Hegel — and banishing it from the company of disciplines pursued in sufficient light to render the growth of understanding a possibility.

A different perspective upon what it means (and does not mean) to associate philosophy with the notion of "interpretation" is achieved by considering several of the most important cognitive claims of a *positive* nature of which this association is intended by Nietzsche to be a denial. There are two such claims in particular with which he wishes to take issue; and it is important to see what they are, because they are such strong claims that their rejection, far from stranding one with no coherent alternative position short of a nihilism involving the repudiation of all cognitive aspirations, actually leaves one with a good deal of ground to occupy. One is the claim that the kind of accurate and complete comprehension and conceptual articulation of reality to which metaphysicians long have aspired is a genuine possibility. The other is the claim that the ascertainment of certain irreducible, incontrovertible, unadorned and unadulterated states of affairs, commonly styled pure *facts,* is such a possibility.

Philosophers convinced of one or both of these possibilities, joined in this instance by many of their critics, are inclined to disparage the cognitive import (at least where substantive philosophical questions are at issue) of anything that might be said which upon examination turns out to be unassignable to — or at any rate not intimately connected with — either category. This disparagement is to some extent understandable; for if it is assumed that only "knowledge" which is either purely factual or "absolute" is truly deserving of the name, it would appear reasonable to hold that what is neither the one nor the other is not entitled to it — at first "strictly speaking," but eventually *tout court*.

Nietzsche emphatically rejects both claims: and one reason why his position concerning the cognitive status of some of what falls into neither category (but is in our power to achieve) is frequently misunderstood is that, in the spirit of one who has discovered value in something others have disparaged, he combatively employs the language used to disparage it in his own references to it even as he lays claim to its actual cognitive significance; while he likewise often uses the terms preempted by those to whom he is opposed in his references to their cherished myths. Thus he maintains that there can be no "absolute knowledge," and that there are no pure "facts"; and that, rather than either, there are *only* "interpretations" — or (even more pugnaciously) only "beliefs." For example: "Against positivism, which halts at phenomena — 'There are only *facts*' — I would say: No, facts is precisely what there is not, only interpretations" (WP 481). And he contends that anything on the order of "'knowledge-in-itself' is as impermissible a concept as is 'thing-in-itself'" (WP 608).

At first reading, such passages as these might seem to have sweepingly nihilistic implications. Upon closer consideration, however, it becomes clear that what Nietzsche is rejecting is the existence of "facts" *as positivists* understand them — a rejection amounting to a good deal less than a denial of any way of distinguishing between what is the case and what is not in various situations. And he likewise is rejecting the possibility of "knowledge" *as absolutists* (and especially as rationalistic metaphysicians) envision it — a rejection falling far short of a repudiation of the possibility of any cognitively significant difference between various alternative accounts of some object of inquiry.

In this connection notice should also be taken of the language Nietzsche employs in remarks of the following sort: "The sense of truthfulness...is nauseated by the falseness and mendaciousness of all Christian interpretations of the world and of history; rebound from 'God is truth' to the fanatical faith 'All is false'..." (WP 1). And again: "One interpretation has collapsed; but because it was considered *the* interpretation it now seems as if there were no meaning at all in existence..." (WP 55). Here he both commits himself to the appropriateness of characterizing a *particular* interpretation as "untenable," "false," and "mendacious," and at the same time quite clearly suggests the illegitimacy of concluding, from the "collapse" of one interpretation discovered to be thus unworthy of acceptance, that any other must be equally objectionable. Indeed, his derisive reference to "the fanatical faith 'All is false'" shows that he is by no means disposed to lump all "interpretations" together as equally "false."

Nietzsche employs similar language in speaking of certain other interpretations as well. Here I shall take note only of something he says with respect to one in particular. He questions

> ...the faith with which so many materialistic natural scientists rest content nowadays, the faith in a world that is supposed to have its equivalent and its measure in human thought and human valuations... That the only justifiable interpretation of the world should be...an interpretation that permits counting, calculating, weighing, seeing, and touching, and nothing more — that is a crudity and naivete... (GS 373)

Several points about Nietzsche's many remarks along these lines may be noted. One is that he considers the various interpretations he singles out for attention — from the "Christian-moral" to the "natural-scientific" — to have a definite utility, in the sense of performing a significant practical function in relation to the needs and limitations of various sorts of human beings. And the second is that, this utility notwithstanding, he expressly terms each of them not merely perspectival but *erroneous,* or at any rate naive and superficial. He does suggest that the practical value of an interpretation endows it with a certain sort of validity, and even that it may thus be accorded a kind of (pragmatic) "truth." The fact that he also considers it appropriate to characterize interpretations enjoying this status in these other ways, however, clearly indicates that he not only envisions the possibility of attaining a vantage point from which their contingency can be discerned, but moreover takes it to be one of his accomplishments to have reached a position from which the untenability or inadequacy of such interpretations may be grasped. That he countenanced this possibility, and what he takes its realization to involve, may further be seen in the following passage, which sheds considerable light on much of what he says and tries to do:

> But precisely because we seek knowledge, let us not be ungrateful to such resolute reversals of accustomed perspectives and valuations which the spirit has, with apparent mischievousness and futility, raged against itself for so long: to see differently in this way for once, to *want* to see differently, is no small discipline and preparation of the intellect for its future 'objectivity' — the latter understood not as 'contemplation without interest' (which is nonsensical absurdity), but as the ability to *control* one's Pro and Con and to dispose of them, so that one knows how to employ a *variety* of

perspectives and affective interpretations in the service of knowledge.

Henceforth, my dear philosophers, let us be on guard against the dangerous old conceptual fiction that posited a 'pure, will-less, painless, timeless knowing subject'; let us guard against the snares of such contradictory concepts as 'pure reason,' 'absolute spirituality,' 'knowledge in itself': these always demand that we should think of an eye that is completely unthinkable, an eye turned in no particular direction, in which the active and interpreting forces, through which alone seeing becomes *something*, are supposed to be lacking; these always demand of the eye an absurdity and a nonsense. There is *only* a perspective 'knowing'; and the *more* affects we allow to speak about one thing, the *more* eyes, different eyes, we can use to observe one thing, the more complete will our 'concept' of this thing, our 'objectivity,' be. (GM III:12)

Notwithstanding his insistence that there is "*only* a perspective 'knowing'" (as opposed to a knowing that would be absolute and independent of all "perspective seeing"), Nietzsche thus is concerned to distinguish "knowledge" from "perspectives and affective interpretations" merely as such, and suggests that it is something which can be sought and can in some measure be achieved. It, no less than that which is employed "in the service" of its attainment, has the character of "interpretation" — but it is "interpretation" with a difference. It has an "objectivity" that is lacking in the cases of the various "perspectives and affective interpretations" it employs and upon which it draws. For when the latter are played off against each other, one ceases to be locked into any one of them; and so it becomes possible to achieve a meta-level perspective, from which vantage point various lower-order interpretations may be superseded in favor of others less narrow and distorting than they. The endeavor Nietzsche describes in this passage may not elevate one to the position of "pure, will-less, painless, timeless, knowing subjects," capable of taking a God's-eye view of reality; but it can at least place one in a position to "seek knowledge," and to "employ in the service of knowledge" many of the very factors which impede understanding under most circumstances. And this is so even if that "knowing" which is thus possible can never be "absolute," but rather only provisional, and even if the "knowledge" which is thus obtainable inevitably has the character of a relation between an interpreter and that which is interpreted.

II

In conceiving of philosophy as a fundamentally interpretive affair, therefore, and in practicing what he preaches, Nietzsche may thus be seen neither to cut the ground from under his own feet, nor to place himself beyond the pale of serious discussion. Yet he remains very difficult to reckon with. He often simply says what he thinks, presenting his interpretations of various matters without making cases for them beyond showing that and how they enable one to make sense of the matters in question. He does not subscribe to the view that a philosopher is permitted to say what he believes to be true and advance what he supposes to be an illuminating and sound interpretation only when he can come up with a line of reasoning by which it is (more or less strictly) entailed. Insight and understanding matter more in philosophy as he conceives of it than does the ability to provide this sort of justification; and he further believes them to be attainable where it is wanting or impossible no less than when it can be managed, even though certainty of their attainment may not be. Such certainty might in principle be desirable; but to insist upon it, for Nietzsche, is to blinker and shackle oneself to the point that comprehension in most matters of moment will escape one. And so in his own philosophizing he often follows the lead of certain thinkers to whom he was most strongly drawn from the start, and whom he celebrates in his earliest writings on philosophy: Heraclitus and Schopenhauer.

It is instructive, in this connection, to consider certain of his remarks about each of them. In his early essay *Philosophy in the Tragic Age of the Greeks,* he singles out Heraclitus for special praise, as "a type of prophet of truth" who "knows but does not reckon," having looked deeply into the world and discerned its nature more clearly and profoundly than any of his contemporaries: "In each word of Heraclitus the pride and majesty of truth are expressed — but truth grasped in intuitions, not truth reached by the rope ladder of logic" (PTA 9). To see and give expression to "the truth" is held to have been all he deemed it important and necessary to do, and to be something requiring insight rather than calculation or "rope-ladder" reasoning. Nietzsche's own subsequent philosophical practice is by no means confined entirely within these limits; but it often undeniably has this general character.

While he remained convinced of the indispensability of this sort of thinking, however, and indeed of the impossibility of any other at certain points in philosophical inquiry, he also came to have a strong sense of the importance of supplementing it in several respects. He indicates one of them in the very same passage, associating it with Heraclitus' opposite number, Parmenides. "In his contemporary Parmenides there stands by his side a counter-part to him, likewise representing a type of prophet of truth, but formed of ice and not of fire, pouring cold, piercing light around him" (*ibid.*). This "cold, piercing light" is that of reason rather than of intuition; and in its absence Nietzsche recognizes that philosophy is bound to fare poorly. Thus, in *Schopenhauer as Educator,* he laments the neglect of intellectual rigor among his philosophical contemporaries, and even goes so far as to remark that "without doubt what now goes on in the various sciences is more logical, cautious, modest, inventive, in short more philosophical than what is done among the so-called philosophers" (SE 8).

It is not primarily on this count, however, that he lauds Schopenhauer in this essay. He does not consider him to suffer from the above-mentioned general defect; but he conceives Schopenhauer's "greatness" in other terms. It is held to be owing to the fact that he was not overly fastidious on this point, but rather "confronts the picture of life as a whole, in order to construe it as a whole." He did not succumb to the tendency — to which "the most acute minds" are suggested so often to be prone — to "exhaust themselves in conceptual scholasticism," to become preoccupied with "those places in great philosophical edifices where scholarly reckoning and counter-reckoning, rumination, doubt and contradiction are permitted," and to fall victim to the "error" that "painstaking investigations" of various phenomena will yield the best understanding obtainable of the world's nature. On this last point, Nietzsche urges that "only he who has the general portrait of life and existence clearly in view can draw upon the various sciences without any harm," either to himself or to philosophical understanding; for "in the absence of such a guiding total picture they are threads leading nowhere," and having the effect merely of increasing confusion concerning "life's course" and the world's fundamental nature (SE 3).

In taking "Schopenhauer's greatness" as a philosopher to consist in his having "pursued this picture...without allowing himself to be diverted, as scholars do," Nietzsche reveals something further about the conception of philosophy with which he began, and which influenced the course and nature of his own subsequent philosophical activity. Much of his later effort went into his own attempt to bring "life and existence clearly in view," and to construe them and the world "as a whole" in a manner doing justice to them. In the course of working out his interpretation of them, he has a great deal to say about many different things. Since what he has to say so often involves simultaneously elaborating this interpretation and bringing these specific matters within its compass, however, extending his line of thinking rather than presenting a line of reasoning, his points frequently admit of no piecemeal assessment.

At times, in his philosophizing, Nietzsche thinks and writes rather in the spirit of a Heraclitean "truth-sayer"; at other times, in the manner of an analytic philosopher. At others still, and most commonly and fundamentally, however, he is most like the sort of philosopher he here suggests Schopenhauer to have been — without, however, ever attempting anything on the order of Schopenhauer's systematic and comprehensive elaboration of his interpretation of *der Welt als Wille und Vorstellung*. One may to some extent approach and assess him in the manner appropriate to previous and subsequent philosophers in the tradition most familiar to us; but in the end one must adapt one's treatment of him to the character and aims of philosophy as he conceives and practices it. To do otherwise is to deal with him in the untoward manner of Procrustes, and to fail to take him seriously enough. It is ultimately as an interpreter of "life and existence," concerned to reorient our thinking about the world, ourselves and value, that Nietzsche confronts us, and would have us reckon with him.

III

"I do not wish to persuade anyone to philosophy," Nietzsche writes; for "it is inevitable, it is perhaps also desirable, that the philosopher should be a *rare* plant" (WP 420). The hazards of genuinely philosophical thinking constitute one of his reasons for taking this position; and his recognition of the fact that he has "set up the most difficult idea of the philosopher" ("Learning is not enough!") is another (WP 421). Few people possess the many qualities he takes to be required if one is to be able to measure up to the intellectual standard he sets forth. And fewer are capable of withstanding the rigors of philosophy as he "understood and lived it." For it involves "living voluntarily among ice and high mountains — seeking out everything strange and questionable in existence" — and requires that one be able to "dare" and "endure" much more "truth" than most people can (EH P:3).

It means, moreover, that one must "take his stand *beyond* good and evil" (TI VII:1), abandoning all reliance upon customary modes of evaluation, and dispensing with the guidance and security afforded by belief in the indisputability of certain moral principles. Indeed, it demands that one take nothing for granted, and question even one's most cherished assumptions. One must be most wary, and hardest toward oneself, precisely where one may be inclined to "remain stuck" — whether "to a person" or "a fatherland" or "a science," or to "some pity" or "one's own detachment" or even "one's own virtues" (BGE 41). And one must strive relentlessly to escape "from the musty agreeable nooks into which preference and prejudice, youth, origin, the accidents of people and books or even exhaustion from wandering seemed to have banished us" (BGE 56).

To be the sort of philosopher Nietzsche has in mind, one must be able to close one's ears to "the siren songs of old metaphysical bird-catchers" which would flatter and delude one (BGE 23); and to resist the lure of "mystical explanations" which, while "considered deep," actually "are not even superficial" (GS 126). And one must possess and be capable of cultivating a variety of characteristics "that usually destroy a man," but without being destroyed by them. This, he suggests, is "why the philosopher rarely turns out well." For one "must be a brief abstract of man," incorporating "a tremendous multiplicity of qualities," although this carries with it a "danger from antitheses." One further "must be inquisitive in the most various directions: danger of going to pieces." Moreover, one "must be just and fair in the highest sense," but also "profound in love [and] hate" as well, one must be both "spectator" and "legislator." And one must be "supple" and "firm and hard" (WP 976).

Nor is this all: "The dangers for a philosopher's development," Nietzsche observes, are "manifold today":

The scope and the tower-building of the sciences has grown to be enormous, and with this also the probability that the philosopher grows weary while still learning or allows himself to be detained somewhere to become a "specialist" — so he never attains his proper level, the height for a comprehensive look... Or he attains it too late, when his best time and strength are spent... It may be precisely the sensitivity of his intellectual conscience that leads him to delay somewhere along the way and to be late: he is afraid of the seduction to become a dilettante... (BGE 205)

And to this he adds, "by way of once more doubling the difficulties for a philosopher," that one is ultimately required to come to terms with "life and the value of life" in a way for which there is no method, so that his very intellectual conscience may make him "reluctant to come to believe that he has a right, or even a duty," to do anything of the sort. What is demanded of him is "a Yes or No" with respect to them — a fundamental and general affirmation or denial, which in either case will color and profoundly influence all of his subsequent thinking, and in the absence of which his thought will lack true seriousness.

This decision, for Nietzsche, is one the philosopher does have a "right" as well as a "duty" to make; but he "must seek his way to this right and faith only from the most comprehensive — perhaps most disturbing and destructive — experiences," and thus cannot be expected to arrive at it easily. If he "frequently hesitates, doubts, and lapses into silence," this is not to be wondered at; nor should it be surprising that few will manage actually to attain this right, overcome their hesitation and doubts concerning it, and "risk themselves" by venturing to take such a stand (*ibid.*). It is with reference to this view of the basic challenge to which the philosopher must be equal that Nietzsche says of his own thought:

Such an experimental philosophy as I live anticipates experimentally even the possibilities of the most fundamental nihilism; but this does not mean that it must halt at a negation, a No, a will to negation. It wants rather to cross over to the opposite of this — to a Dionysian affirmation of the world as it is, without substraction, exception, or selection... The highest state a philosopher can attain: to stand in a Dionysian relationship to existence — my formula for this is *amor fati.* (WP 1041)

These demands are so many and so hard that they would seem to ensure that the "genuine philosopher" will always be "a rare plant," and that Nietzsche's "philosophers of the future" will never be more than exceptions to the rule in the philosophical community. His insistence that these "new philosophers" must also be "spirits strong and original enough to provide the stimuli for opposite valuations and to revalue and invert 'eternal values'" (BGE 203) has the consequence of limiting inclusion in their ranks still further. And even the basic intellectual standard he sets for the philosopher is very high indeed. It is deserving of further comment here, because it is no less important a part of the portrait Nietzsche sketches than the rest, but tends to be overlooked.

To begin with, one can hardly exaggerate the importance he attaches to "intellectual integrity." There is nothing he finds more objectionable in a philosopher than a lack of it, or the sacrifice of it for the sake of preserving some conviction. "Here, if anywhere, we too are still *men of conscience,*" he writes; "we do not wish to return again to anything we take to be outlived and decaying, to something 'unworthy of belief,'" however painful its repudiation might be. And "we will permit ourselves no bridges of lies to old ideals," however much might stand and fall with them (D P:4). A philosopher must have the liveliest intellectual conscience, and a steadfast determination to tolerate nothing which critical scrutiny reveals to be "unworthy of belief." Nietzsche thus endorses Stendhal's dictum: "To be a good philosopher, one must be dry, clear, without illusion" (BGE 39). He often puts this point in terms of "truthfulness" and "honesty"; and his repeated demand that the philosopher must be "hard" is meant to underscore it. Thus he writes:

Honesty, supposing that this is our virtue from which we cannot get away, we free spirits — well, let us work on it with all our malice and love and not weary of "perfecting" ourselves in *our* virtue, the only one left us... Let us remain hard, we last Stoics! And let us dispatch to her assistance whatever we have in us of devilry: our disgust with what is clumsy and approximate, our *"nimitur in vetitum"* ["we strive for the forbidden"], our adventurous courage, our seasoned and choosy curiosity, our subtlest, most disguised, most spiritual will to power and overcoming of the world... (BGE 227)

As he here indicates, Nietzsche is well aware that the intellectual honesty he prizes will not take the philosopher very far in the absence of a cluster of other qualities. Those he mentions here are only some of those he further takes to be essential to the making of the sort of philosopher he calls for and himself attempts to be. One crucial trait is the fortitude to dispense with comforting illusions and confront disagreeable truths, to which he refers in suggesting that "the strength of a spirit should be measured according to how much of the 'truth' one could still barely endure..." (BGE 39). And another is a determination to "drive one's will to knowledge" far beyond ordinary bounds, and the ability to "liberate oneself from many things that oppress, inhibit, hold down and make heavy" most thinkers at present (GS 380).

There is also a kind of "objectivity" Nietzsche supposes to be necessary in the philosopher differing from that which he takes to be characteristic of the scholarly and scientific type of thinker. "'Objectivity' in the philosopher," he writes, involves "moral indifference toward oneself, blindness toward good or ill consequences; lack of scruples about using dangerous means; perversity and multiplicity of character considered and exploited as an advantage" (WP 425). Balanced against these traits, on the other hand, is a sense of responsibility which, while not that of the merely "moral" man, is no less demanding and of much higher significance. It extends beyond an uncompromising "will to knowledge," to what Nietzsche terms the enhancement of life. Thus he characterizes "the philosopher as *we* understand him, we free spirits — as the man of the most comprehensive responsibility who has the conscience for the overall development of man..." (BGE 61).

He further attaches great importance to the qualities of subtlety and acuteness in the observation and analysis of many different sorts of phenomena, from the linguistic and historical to the social and psychological to the physiological and biological, and ranging over such diverse domains of human activity and experience as art, religion, science, and politics. The philosopher must "be able to see with many different eyes and consciences" (BGE 211). He must be adept at "taking things apart" and "know how to handle a knife surely and subtly" (BGE 210) — or how to "philosophize with a hammer" (in the language of the subtitle of *Twilight*), excelling in "the sounding out of idols" which betray their hollowness when "touched with a hammer as with a tuning fork" (TI P). And he must possess "the courage and hardness of analysis" (BGE 209), and the capacity for "piling stone upon stone, pebble upon pebble," without being "ashamed of such modest work..." (HH I:37).

Related to this is another point: while Nietzsche's "philosophers of the future" are to be more than astute critics, "critical discipline and every habit conducive to cleanliness and severity in matters of the spirit will be demanded by these philosophers, not only of themselves" (BGE 210). They are to exhibit that "genuinely philosophical combination...of a bold and exuberant spirituality that runs *presto* and a dialectical severity and necessity that takes no false step..." (BGE 213). They also "will be men of experiments," whose thinking is characterized by "attempts and delight in attempts" to devise novel hypotheses and interpretations and assessments (BGE 210), but who "certainly will not be dogmatists" (BGE 43). For a further trait of philosophers of the sort Nietzsche has in mind (however odd this may seem to some) is modesty with respect to the status of the issue of their efforts. The modest acknowledgment that no interpretation is unsupersedable, and that at least a "little question mark" is best placed after one's own "special words and favorite doctrines" (BGE 25), is held to be a fitting accompaniment and needed complement to the originality and boldness of mind which philosophical profundity and power presuppose.

Indeed, Nietzsche goes further, joining to this commendation an appeal to the philosopher to avoid the "stiff seriousness that inspires laughter," to which so many of "our philosophers" are disposed (BGE 186). Thus he would have philosophers resist the tendency to "solemnity in gesture, word, tone, eye, morality, and task" (GS 382), even though the stakes for humanity could not be higher than they are here. He does consider the emergence of his new type of philosopher to mark a fundamental turning point, and holds that "it is perhaps only with him that the *great seriousness* really begins, that the real question mark is posed for the first time, that the destiny of the soul changes, the hand moves forward, the tragedy *begins*" (*ibid.*). But he does not take this to mean that the philosophical enterprise ought therefore to be carried on in a spirit of deadly earnestness. Rather, he constantly stresses the importance of light-heartedness, gaiety, playfulness and irony. "I would not know what the spirit of a philosopher might wish more to be than a good dancer," he writes (GS 381), in a work whose title expresses his conception of what philosophy ought to be: *The Gay Science*. He associates both Zarathustra and his sort of philosophizing with the beginning of "the great seriousness," and with "tragedy" as well (GS 382); but they are balanced and leavened by the "cheerful and koboldish laughter" of "the spirits of my own book" and thought (GS 383).

To be sure, a task like the "revaluation of all values" cannot be accomplished by one minded only to jest. Nietzsche's point here, however, is that it also cannot be carried through at all well if one fails "to shake off a heavy, all-too-heavy seriousness" and to "maintain cheerfulness" as one proceeds with such "a gloomy affair, fraught with enormous responsibility." And besides, he adds, "nothing succeeds if prankishness has no part in it" (TI P). One may find it easier to deal with a philosopher whose thought is without such qualities as these; but that by itself is no real mark in his favor. And it is Nietzsche's contention that without them, in matters of real substance, philosophical inquiry will not get very far. "There is something about 'truth,' about the *search* for truth," he writes, such that "when a human being is too human about it," in motivation or in approach, "— I bet he finds nothing" (BGE 35).

His own philosophical practice may often fall short of or diverge from the standards and principles he advocates; and the picture of the genuine philosopher and philosophy he sets forth may strike many as uncongenial in various respects. But he would be neither surprised nor disconcerted in either event, and would take neither circumstance to count against the picture itself. And if he proposes a conception of the tasks and concerns of the philosopher that embraces certain things at which many philosophers will look askance (with or without good reason), it must be allowed that this conception incorporates the basic features of any model of the philosopher deserving to be taken seriously. The only real question pertains to the merit of including in it those further features he also stresses. This is a question it may not be possible to settle by argument, or even settle at all. To my way of thinking, however, Nietzsche's conception of philosophy has greater attractions and promise than any other I know. Its issue may not measure up to certain standards of knowledge reflecting the convictions or longings of some philosophers; but Nietzsche with good reason takes it to surpass anything that might otherwise be achieved in acuteness, penetration and profundity. And for him and others like him, there is more to be said for it as well. So he writes, of the knowledge which he takes it to make possible:

And knowledge itself: let it be something else for others... — for me it is a world of dangers and victories in which heroic feelings, too, find places to dance and play. *"Life as a means to knowledge"* — with this principle in one's heart one can live not only boldly but even gaily, and laugh gaily too. (GS 324)

IV

I readily admit that there may appear to be a serious difficulty confronting my construal of Nietzsche's thinking with respect to the nature of philosophy and its interpretive character, and of his meaning in speaking of "knowledge" in passages such as this. This apparent difficulty has to do with certain things he has to say about "truth" which would seem at least to place a large question mark beside the suggestion that he takes any sort of thinking to be capable of issuing in the attainment of anything deserving of this designation, unless its meaning is transformed beyond all recognition. If *all* truth is and can be nothing more than what he calls "the kind of error without which a certain species of life could not live" (WP 493), and if no truths can be anything more than the *"irrefutable errors"* he says "man's truths" ultimately merely are (GS 265), it would indeed seem that no sort of philosophy — including his own —

would have anything to do with "truth" in any epistemically privileged or even significant sense.

It is my conviction, however, that to take this to be the thrust and upshot of Nietzsche's reflections on truth is to misunderstand him very seriously, where both truth and philosophy are concerned. I elsewhere[1] have presented an extended analysis and interpretation of what he has to say along these lines, in the course of which it is argued and shown that the difficulty mentioned is only apparent, and that his treatment of truth actually accords rather than conflicts with my construal of his conception of philosophy and what may come of it. I shall not attempt to cover the same ground again here; but before I conclude I perhaps should at least indicate briefly the general outlines of my way of dealing with and understanding what he says about truth.

The first point to be made, and stressed, is that Nietzsche has a great many different sorts of things to say about and in terms of "truth" and "truths." The two passages cited above, and others like them, cannot be ignored; they clearly are intended to make important points, and to be taken seriously. But it should not be supposed to be obvious exactly what these points are, and what their scope is, and what their implications are if it is agreed to take them seriously. Moreover, the same Nietzsche also said many other things, which deserve to be accorded the same serious attention. For example, he lauds those strong and courageous enough "to sacrifice all desirability to truth, *every* truth, even plain, harsh, ugly, repellent, unchristian, immoral truth. — For such truths do exist" (GM I:1). And he likewise writes:

At every step one has to wrestle for truth; one has to surrender for it almost everything to which the heart, to which our love, our trust in life, cling otherwise. That requires greatness of soul; the service of truth is the hardest service. (A 50)

In addition, there are many other passages in which Nietzsche has things to say about truth differing significantly from what he says in passages of either of these sorts. Faced with this situation, one might conclude (as some have) that he meant some of the things he says but not others; or that he contradicted himself repeatedly, either out of confusion or by design; or that he was constantly changing his mind. The most reasonable conclusion, however, seems to me to be that he has a variety of different things in mind in the diverse multitude of passages in which the terms "truth" and "truths" appear, which need to be sorted out and explicated.

Elaborating upon this line of interpretive approach, I would further observe that good and interesting collective sense can be made of the many different things he says on these various occasions if one supposes them not to be meant to apply across the board, but rather to have application within a variety of contexts of restricted scope, and moreover to contribute to several distinct levels of analysis of what counts as "truth" and "truths" in these contexts. Clues to these scope restrictions and level distinctions, I suggest, are readily discernible through the juxtaposition of the various sorts of remarks Nietzsche makes and reflection upon the indications he often gives of their focus, referents or associations.

What emerges from this sort of consideration and interpretation, I have found, is a complex, subtle, and fundamentally coherent treatment of truth that has much to be said for it. In my view it both constitutes a significant contribution to the theory of truth and knowledge, and removes the apparent difficulty referred to above — even though it also makes clear that philosophical inquiry must proceed without benefit of any royal road to knowledge. It provides different accounts of a number of categories of "truths," and different assessments of their fundamental epistemic status and place in human life and thought. I cannot elaborate and discuss them here; but I would at least identify them.

The broadest of them, which Nietzsche sometimes characterizes as "man's truths," comprehends a wide range of things which have come to be considered "truths" in various commonplace domains of discourse; and these in turn are seen to admit of differing particular analyses, and also of analysis on several different levels. One of these levels of analysis consists in analyzing what might be termed the "surface conditions" or criteria employed within a particular domain of discourse, in virtue of the satisfaction of which a particular proposition may be considered "true." Another is also descriptive, or at any rate analytically interpretive, but on a deeper level. It consists in attempting to determine what is fundamentally involved — what is going on beneath the surface, conditioning the character of the surface — in the emergence of such forms of discourse and "truth."

The "truths" espoused by metaphysical and religious thinkers wedded to the idea of some sort of reality transcending the world in which we live, on the other hand, are accorded different treatment by Nietzsche and are suggested to have a different sort of status and significance. They thus constitute a category of "truths" importantly different from those he takes to be woven into the very fabric of human life as we do and apparently must live it, and to which he is quite differently disposed. And from both yet a third category is to be distinguished, exemplified at least in intention for Nietzsche by the insights into the character of our human existence and of life and the world he believes himself to have achieved and given expression. They too may be interpretive; but he supposes them to transcend both of the former sorts of "truths," and indeed to stand in marked contrast to them. Here one encounters what

Nietzsche takes to be at least the possibility of what might be called "truth and knowledge *with a difference*"; and, briefly put, he proposes that they be explicated and construed in terms of the notions of "aptness" and "justice."

If one avails oneself of these distinctions, one not only can make coherent and interesting sense of the many things Nietzsche has to say about "truth" and "truths," but also can see how it is that he is able to embrace the conception of the nature and potential issue of genuine philosophical thinking set forth above, even while saying the sorts of things he often does about "man's truths" generally and about ideas of the sort long passing as "truths" in philosophical and religious thought. To be sure, one may wonder whether his reasons for denying anything more than "merely human" or "all too human" significance to both of the latter kinds of "truths" do not apply with equal force to anything he or his new and genuine philosophers might ever come up with. It should count for something, however, especially among those who derive inspiration from him, that he clearly does not suppose his own interpretive efforts to be on a complete epistemic par with the interpretations and pragmatically conditioned modes of conceptualization upon which he brings his critical guns to bear. And while he might be mistaken about this in the cases of some of the particular conclusions he reaches and views he advances, it seems to me that he is entirely and crucially right to insist upon the possibility of a difference, upon its attainability, and upon its importance. For as he realized and stressed, more than the future of philosophy is at stake.

University of Illinois
at Urbana-Champaign

David Couzens Hoy

Nietzsche, Hume, and the Genealogical Method

Genealogy is for Nietzsche a way of doing philosophy that shows not only the inadequacy of traditional metaphysics or "first philosophy," but also the prospects for nonmetaphysical philosophy. In the preface to the *Genealogy of Morals* (§4) he says his own adaptation of the method of genealogy was motivated by his reaction to Paul Rée's *Origin of the Moral Sensations*. This "upside-down and perverse species of genealogical hypothesis, the genuinely *English* type" is criticized for being too unhistorical, haphazard, or random. What is perverse is Rée's social-Darwinian hypothesis that the most recent product of human evolution is, because of the survival of the fittest, also the highest product of human evolution. Nietzsche parodies Rée cruelly in laughing at the idea that the fittest and highest human type is the modern "moral milksop" (*Moral-Zärtling*, GM Preface 7) who thinks of morality as "selflessness, self-sacrifice, or sympathy and pity" (GS 345). Equally perverse and "English" is Rée's own "refined indolence," his inability to take the problems of morality seriously.

In a manner that English-speakers tend to find typically "German," Nietzsche insists on taking *extremely* seriously the problems of morality, or more accurately, morality itself as a problem. I will assume that when Nietzsche criticizes Rée for being too much like the English psychologists, Nietzsche has the doctrines of Englishmen like Herbert Spencer in mind.[1] But the method of inquiring into the "origins" of moral ideas is presumably a general one, and more notable British philosophers are also genealogists. To

---

[1] He mentions Spencer favorably a few pages later in the *Genealogy* (I:3), but for a typical tirade against Spencer for doctrines similar to Rée's see *The Gay Science* 373. Walter Kaufmann in a footnote to this paragraph, but also in his *Nietzsche: Philosopher, Psychologist, Antichrist* (Princeton University Press, 1974, 4th ed., p. 274) notes that William James in his 1884 essay, "The Dilemma of Determinism," caricatured Spencer much as Nietzsche did.

show this, I take David Hume as a prime example. Commentators like Arthur Danto and Mary Warnock have noted similarities between Nietzsche and Hume on epistemological topics, but there is a more general methodological kinship between the two, particularly when their views on morality are considered as well.[2]

Nietzschean genealogy is like British genealogy in being a form of what Hume called "experimental reasoning," formulating hypotheses about what causes could have led to given effects. The method for Hume provides a common basis for doing both epistemology and ethics, and the *Treatise on Human Nature* is subtitled *An attempt to introduce the experimental method of reasoning into moral subjects.*[3] Comparing not their moral theories so much as their applications of the method to particular examples, however, there is an obvious difference in that Nietzsche does not imitate Hume's detached, observational tone or the British pretension to neutral, value-free description. On the contrary, Nietzsche wants genealogy to be as value-laden as possible. Not only does he want genealogy to investigate the question of the value of morality, he also intends for it to come up with a definite valuation of the traditional moral virtues and principles. In particular, he plans it to be not simply a descriptive, but also a prescriptive (or at least critical) inversion of *both* the good-natured "English" pessimism of Rée and the world-weary German pessimism of Schopenhauer.[4]

Since Rée was already using the genealogical method, and since Nietzsche implies Rée was simply borrowing that method from the English, Nietzsche is not claiming to be the first to discover and use genealogy. Yet he does suggest in section four of the preface to the *Genealogy* that hitting on this method allowed him to bring together in a coherent framework points that were scattered in previous works. The method thus enables him to synthesize not

---

[2] See Arthur Danto, *Nietzsche as Philosopher* (New York: Macmillan, 1965), especially Chapter 3; Mary Warnock, "Nietzsche's Conception of Truth," in *Nietzsche: Imagery and Thought,* ed. W. Pasley (Berkeley: University of California Press, 1978).
[3] In *Hume's Moral Theory* (London: Routledge & Kegan Paul, 1980) J.L. Mackie suggests that the subtitle signifies that the *Treatise* "is an attempt to study and explain moral phenomena (as well as human knowledge and emotions) in the same sort of way in which Newton and his followers studied and explained the physical world" (p. 6).
[4] In the *Genealogy* Nietzsche does not seem to be aware of the methodological problem of the genetic fallacy, which he does mention in the *Gay Science* 345, where he sees clearly that the question of the *value* of morality is independent of morality's *origin*: "Even if a morality has grown out of an error, the realization of this fact would not as much as touch the problem of its value."

only his views about the nature of morality, as in this work, but also his other systematic views insofar as they were to be unified by the hypothesis of the will to power as the principle for the application of the genealogical method.

Since the validity of genealogy as a method does not necessarily depend on the soundness of the theory of the will to power, however, in this paper I discuss two features of the method which undermine any pretensions of the will to power to be a quasi-metaphysical doctrine. I maintain that genealogy need not be affirmative in the sense of asserting specific substantive doctrines but in the sense of being heuristically feasible. First, drawing on recent French poststructuralist readings of Nietzsche (but with critical reservations), I will be considering how genealogy is a philosophical tool that is at once anti-metaphysical and nonmetaphysical. Since the preface of the *Genealogy* singles out Schopenhauer as the crucial test of the method, the analyses of Schopenhauer's ascetic ideals in section 4-8 of the third essay are of particular importance. Nietzsche there uses the method wittily to bring out the extent to which Schopenhauer's metaphysical longings and ideals were a product of sexual desires, of what Schopenhauer called "the vile urgency of the will" (GM III:6). Without supplanting Schopenhauer's metaphysics of the will with yet another metaphysics, then, Nietzsche will use genealogy to destroy metaphysics altogether. Genealogy itself becomes a way to do nonmetaphysical philosophy.

Hume's own method of experimental reasoning is also intended to consign metaphysics to the flames, and to show reason to be the product of bodily instinct. The method allows him to inquire into the origin of morals without assuming as his contemporaries did that the virtuous dispositions were implanted in all of us by a divine creator. The degree of methodological similarity between Hume and Nietzsche is thus the second feature to be considered. In both cases the method is hypothetical, tracing ideas back to psychological impressions, and finding like causes for like effects. Perhaps an even better example of how close Nietzsche's use of the method comes to Hume's is the "genealogy" of religion offered by Hume's character Philo at the conclusion of the *Dialogues Concerning Natural Religion* (Part XII). There Philo traces the ideas and practices of religion back to the impression of terror, produced in states of illness and depression. Religion, suggests Philo, has little force and relevance in normal health and in the cheerful conduct of everyday affairs, Hume's insistence on which Nietzsche would again consider typically British. Of course, Nietzsche takes particular pains in the preface to distinguish his genealogies from those of the British, and he is especially right about Hume in remarking on the unhistorical character of their psychological studies. Nietzsche's own genealogies, however, do not provide the detailed historical studies the preface calls for, and I cannot see that they are less psychologically speculative than Hume's.[5]

Methodological Self-Justification

When Nietzsche attempts to justify his new method metaphilosophically, he sometimes claims that genealogy cuts through deceptive appearances until it sees the phenomena as they really are. This realist claim appears to fall back into metaphysics when the principle of will to power is posited as that which lies behind every phenomenon. Nietzsche sometimes makes this claim by drawing an analogy between genealogy and philology, where by philology he means close, accurate reading. In the preface to the *Genealogy* he states that the third essay is a paradigm of his own method of reading, and thus an example of how to read him. Presumably the readers of a genealogical analysis will themselves have to practice genealogy in the act of reading. Nietzsche may have developed his own aphoristic style because it requires readers to practice the genealogical method of reading:

> An aphorism...has not been "deciphered" when it has simply been read; rather, one has then to begin its *interpretation*,[6] for which is required an art of interpretation. I have offered in the third essay of the present book an example of what I regard as "interpretation" in such a case... To be sure, one thing is necessary above all if one is to practice reading as an *art* in this way,...something for which one has almost to be a cow and in any case *not* a "modern man": *rumination*. (GM Preface 8)

This passage shows the intimate connection for Nietzsche between genealogy and the process of reading and interpreting in general, a connection that is anticipated by sections 373 and 374 of Book Five of the *Gay Science*. Here he attacks both Spencer's moral philosophy and materialist, mechanistic philosophy of science. He thinks both divest existence of its "rich ambiguity" by trying to reduce it to frameworks that not only are simplistic and "meaningless," but also fail to recognize that "science" is only one possible *interpretation* of the world, and a "*most stupid*" one at that (GS 373).

What grounds does Nietzsche have, however, for preferring his own read-

---

[5] The contrast Nietzsche's preface wants is perhaps better illustrated by some recent *French* practitioners of genealogy. A book like Michel Foucault's *Discipline and Punish: The Birth of the Prison*, trans. Alan Sheridan (New York: Vintage Books, 1979), which reads like a historical case study of the theory of punishment in the second essay of the *Genealogy*, is perhaps a better example of historical genealogy than Nietzsche's own work.

[6] I have used "interpretation" for *Auslegung* instead of the translators' term "exegesis."

ings and interpretations to those of Spencer and the positivists? He wrestles with this question in section 374, "*Our new 'infinite.'*" Here he raises all the difficulties his genealogical theory of reading implies, but elusively and without taking the stand we would expect. After rejecting the reductionists who insist that "mechanics is the doctrine of the first and last laws on which all existence must be based as on a ground floor," he asks whether we need to think that there is any ground floor for our perspectives or interpretations. Since we could not get out of our own conceptual framework to ask how reality would be independent of that framework, he infers that whether reality exists independently of our interpretations, or even whether the very idea of uninterpretable reality makes sense "cannot be decided." That is, we cannot decide either that "existence without interpretation, without 'sense,'" is "'nonsense,'" or that all existence is interpretive in essence.

Why does he insist on this undecidability when he seems already to have decided? That there is no ground floor to interpretation, but only interpretation all the way down, should be a liberating thought. He knows, however, that to claim the essence of existence is such that there are only interpretations would be tantamount to saying paradoxically that the essence of things is not to have an essence. Moreover, if we cannot say anything about things as they are independently of our interpretations, then he recognizes that a Kantian would insist that we also cannot deny that the things might involve relations other than those we attribute to them. The next few lines give us a clue to why he lets himself get caught in the Kantian dilemma when he clearly believes in the richly interpretational character of our cognitive and moral capacities. Instead of speaking mainly about interpretations in these lines, he speaks about perspectives, thus suggesting (mistakenly, I will argue) that the terms perspective and interpretation are interchangeable with no significant differences. He says first that we are trapped in our own human perspectives: "the human intellect cannot avoid seeing itself in its own perspectives, and *only* in these." From the thought that we cannot get out of our own corner I would have expected him to narrow down the possibilities of interpretation to our best-confirmed hypotheses, and thus to avoid relativism. Instead he insists we shun the "ridiculous immodesty that would be involved in decreeing from our corner that perspectives are permitted only from this corner."

Why, however, should we *not* embrace this immodesty? Nietzsche is hardly a person to praise modesty. Is immodesty here really ridiculous? For some people to refuse to recognize the possibility of other people having some different perspectives could, of course, be narrow-minded and dogmatic. In this passage, however, the question is about perspectives other than those a *human* intellect could possibly have. Yet the idea of a conceptual scheme other than the human is difficult and perhaps impossible for us to render intelligible.[7] Nietzsche could have insisted more strongly that positing an uninterpretable reality independent of our sense-making faculties indeed cannot make sense, and that for something to count as making sense it must first be part of an interpretation.

Nietzsche seems to have been led by his notion of perspective into a logical corner. He expresses the dilemma characteristically well:

> Rather has the world become "infinite" for us all over again, inasmuch as we cannot reject the possibility that *it may include infinite interpretations.* Once more we are seized by a great shudder...

Interestingly enough, Nietzsche is himself sometimes interpreted today, especially in France, as the proponent of the possibility of infinite interpretations.[8] Yet here the thought leads to a shudder, and to the recognition that if the infinity of interpretation cannot be rejected, it also cannot be so easily accepted. Why is there a shudder? The passage suggests two reasons. First, there would be too many possibilities of interpretation, which is itself a nauseating possibility because it includes so many nauseating interpretations. Second, there would be no grounds for rejecting interpretations just because they were nauseating, since they could nevertheless be right.

The worry here is that the idea of an infinity of perspectives on reality makes reality not only unknowable but also unintelligible, because contradictory interpretations would be equally possible. This idea is itself indigestible, even after long rumination. Notice that Nietzsche speaks of "our *new* 'infinite,'" of the world becoming infinite for us "*all over again.*" He realizes that the thought of infinite interpretations could tempt us to "deify again after the old manner *this* monster of an unknown world" (Nietzsche's emphasis).

The problem of the unknowability of the world arises because a perspectival theory of knowledge usually involves thinking of the mind as representing reality. On this representational model the only way to question the accuracy

---

[7] See Donald Davidson, "On the Very Idea of a Conceptual Scheme" (1974), reprinted in his *Inquiries into Truth and Interpretation* (Oxford University Press, 1984); Richard Rorty, "The World Well Lost" (1972), reprinted in his *Consequences of Pragmatism (Essays: 1972-1980)* (Minneapolis: University of Minnesota Press, 1982); Alexander Nehamas, "Immanent and Transcendent Perspectivism in Nietzsche," *Nietzsche-Studien* 12 (1983):473-490; but contrast Ralph C. S. Walker, *Kant: The Arguments of the Philosophers* (London: Routledge & Kegan Paul, 1978), pp. 30-41.

[8] See Michel Foucault, "Nietzsche, Freud, Marx," in *Cahiers de Royaumont, Philosophie,* Numéro VI: *Nietzsche* (Paris: Les Éditions de Minuit, 1967); Maurice Blanchot, *L'Entretien infini* (Paris: Gallimard, 1969); Jacques Derrida, *Spurs: Nietzsche's Styles,* trans. B. Harlow (University of Chicago Press, 1979).

of representations is to represent the initial representation. This process of representing representations can go on without limit, and we would still not have proved the correspondence of our representations to reality as it is independently of our representations. The shudder is thus a logical one, and results from the threat posed by this infinite regress.

A possible psychological reaction to this logical difficulty is to resort to metaphysics and posit reality as a nonphenomenal domain that is unknowable but at least harmonious with our own purposes. Nietzsche thinks this Kantian tactic is now bankrupt, since metaphysics could not claim to know that the unknowable is unified, single, and harmonious rather than multiple, incoherent, and horrible. Probably reflecting on Schopenhauer's substitution of blind, chaotic will for Kant's rational, holy will, Nietzsche concludes that the unknown so construed could include infinite interpretation in the sense of "too many *ungodly* possibilities of interpretation," "too much devilry, stupidity, and foolishness of interpretation."

An alternative to the logical and metaphysical shudder is suggested by Nietzsche's own images, but in a way he does not exploit in paragraph 374. If we should conclude that we are necessarily confined to our own corner, then it ceases to be a corner. We can decide *both* that there is no uninterpretable reality and that there is no unintelligible infinity of interpretations. For if existence is not unknowable (or at least, not uninterpretable), but indeed exists only insofar as it is interpreted, then only an intelligibly finite and not an infinite range of interpretation is really possible for us.

Of course, narrowing down the range of possible interpretations from infinity would not help much if the range turned out to be finite, but indefinite. The insistence on infinity is one form of methodological, "Pyrrhonian" skepticism, since it says that the range of interpretations is unbounded in principle. That is, interpretations are not constrained in any identifiable respects by that which they interpret. On this view, our present interpretations could be succeeded by completely incommensurable ones. A more *modest* skepticism would recognize that future interpretations would not be total revisions of our current ones, but would incorporate much of what is taken as true in the current ones. However, these interpretations could themselves be succeeded by further ones that had only the vaguest family resemblance to present ones, until finally interpretations were produced that had little in common with present ones. Two arguments against skepticism are required: one that the range of interpretations is not infinite, and another that it is not indefinite. I think infinity of interpretation is in principle impossible, but I do not know of an *a priori* argument that indefiniteness is any more than improbable in practice. However, if indefinite proliferation is practically

Genealogy as Hermeneutics

While Nietzsche's rhetoric sometimes leads him into logical corners he knows he should avoid, his understanding of genealogy contains other ways of avoiding such corners. What I wish to argue is that if he had fully developed his account of the nature of interpretation, he would have come up with the notion of the hermeneutic circle. And since circles have no corners, he could not have backed into the logical difficulties he encounters when he tries to provide metaphilosophical justifications of his genealogical method.

Let me proceed by drawing a sharper contrast than Nietzsche does between the notions of perspective and interpretation. To someone trained in the "English" philosophical tradition with its empiricist background, the term perspective connotes a visual relation between a perceiver and a thing perceived. The thing perceived is itself usually thought of as a medium-sized physical object. Nietzsche's appeal to perspectivism then appears as an antidote to the rationalist tendency to project an aperspectival, godlike comprehension of the whole. In contrast to the metaphysical belief that there is only one correct description capturing reality in its own terms, perspectivism implies that there can be many different perspectives on the same thing. Since Nietzsche's perspectivism extends beyond simple epistemological cases to scientific theories and even to moral systems, however, the original connection between the point of view and the comprehended reality becomes metaphorical and tenuous. The reason that the perception of medium-sized physical objects under normal conditions seems unproblematic is that the verification procedures are reasonably well satisfied simultaneously with the act of perception. But Nietzsche's perspectivism does not imply that these verification procedures serve to validate all knowledge. On the contrary, verification procedures are both internal and relative to the particular kinds of perspectives. There is no general epistemology to specify a single verification procedure that any particular perspective would have to satisfy.

I think this account of what Nietzsche is saying is standard, and its obvious paradoxes are fully exploited by him. What is not so obvious is the sense in which perspectivism preserves what it appears to negate. Let me use a term of Hilary Putnam's and call the view that is usually contrasted with perspectivism "metaphysical realism."[9] This is the view that reality may be different

---
[9] Hilary Putnam, *Reason, Truth and History* (Cambridge University Press, 1981), see Chapter 3.

from the way it appears to us, and that our scientific terms refer only to these phenomena, not to the things as they are in themselves. A consequence of metaphysical realism is that our best-confirmed physical theories could be completely wrong, even in the long run. But perspectivism also leads to this skeptical conclusion. Perspectivism is often construed as implying that there is a thing that can be validly grasped from different perspectives, and is thus independent of any particular perspective. More problematically, the idea of different perspectives implies that *from within* a given perspective, especially a complex, long-standing, and heuristically successful one, there are respects in which the perspective would inevitably be inadequate, distorting, and even wrong. Furthermore, since verification procedures are internal to perspectives, there would be no way ever to rectify these deficiencies.

What I have just described is close to Hume's position that we will never get in touch with the "secret springs" of the world. How he even knew there were secret "springs" if causation is only a subjective and never an objective property is, of course, the question Kant raised. I think that genealogy ought not to be defended by appeal to perspectivism. Perspectivism is too weak a justification for genealogy, because the genealogist does claim to be capturing the phenomenon as it really is. Genealogy is *not* simply another perspective. How the genealogist could make this claim as a perspectivist is not clear. Why would the genealogist need to think of the genealogical discovery as another perspective? Only, I think, as the result of some metaphilosophical reflection whereby the genealogist is asked to justify the outcome of the analysis. A thoroughgoing genealogist could avoid metaphilosophy altogether by suggesting that the only way to challenge the results of one genealogical analysis would be to produce another genealogical analysis either of the original phenomenon or of the initial genealogical account itself. Genealogy is not easy to do successfully, and I see no *a priori* reason to believe there is an infinite regress here. The challenge is a practical one, and in practice there would have to be strong motivation to attempt a genealogy of a genealogy. Even with strong motivation, moreover, the second-order genealogy will not necessarily succeed. If it does succeed, then we will be concerned with the substance of its concrete findings, and metaphilosophical justification will be unnecessary.

As two French Nietzsche scholars, Jean Granier and Sarah Kofman, have both brought out, Nietzsche sometimes offers an alternative account of genealogy.[10] Instead of thinking of genealogy as a perspective, he often

---

[10] Jean Granier, *Le Problème de la vérité dans la philosophie de Nietzsche* (Paris: Seuil, 1966); Sarah Kofman, *Nietzsche et la métaphore* (Paris: Payot, 1972).

suggests that it is simply good, rigorous philology. The *Genealogy*'s third essay, the paradigm case of genealogy, is thus construed not as incorrigible perception, but as close reading. One advantage of this way of thinking of genealogy is that metaphilosophical justification is beside the point if the genealogical analysis appears compelling. Another advantage of this more hermeneutical and less epistemological understanding of the genealogical method is that Nietzsche thereby avoids the paradoxes of perspectivism and the metaphorics of vision by construing the phenomenon not as a physical object but as a text. Traditional problems about how the senses can be known to be in touch with the object, or how the mental hooks up with the physical, are now circumvented. A text is a physical object in some minimal sense (black marks on a page, for instance), but that is an uninteresting sense. We do not read black marks on a page, we read sentences. Texts come to be only in readings and have no existence independent of readings. Of course, the same text occurs in different readings, but there is no special problem as there was for the empiricists in explaining what "same" means. To know two interpreters are talking about the same text even though they read it somewhat differently is just to know that despite their differences, their readings agree for the most part on much of what is going on in the text. The text is the product of a reading, and in the hermeneutical process of reading, interpreting, and understanding there is no mental-physical dichotomy, as well as no problem about a gap between our knowledge and the given.

Genealogy as Critique

I think it is significant, then, that in the preface to the *Genealogy* Nietzsche avoids the earlier problems of the *Gay Science* and does not suggest that his genealogy of morals is just a perspective. Calling genealogy an art of reading and interpretation rather than a science does not mean that "anything goes." On the contrary, he says "no" to every aspect of Paul Rée's genealogy, thus implying he believes genealogies can be wrong, and that his own is better than any alternatives of which he knows. Of course, there are different ways for genealogies to be wrong. They may be wrong by not corresponding to the facts, but they may also be wrong by being shallow and leaving important questions unexplained. For instance, Rée and Spencer take for granted the value of altruism, without asking the question *why* altruism should be morally valued. Nietzsche's criticism of Rée is reminiscent of Kant's complaint that teleological, heteronomous moral theories (like Hume's, for instance) do not explain *why* helping others is moral. Hume's genealogy of morals traces our moral beliefs back to personal sentiments, such as sympathy for our fellows, and then argues that these sentiments are universal. Thus, Hume's genealogy of morals goes into great detail about how moral qualities are useful to ourselves and others. His genealogy itself will have some effect on our moral actions, since by having a clearer idea about the origin of our actions we may decide to cultivate certain qualities rather than others. For example, in describing virtue according to the degree of usefulness, Hume says we may be inclined to give money to beggars because of our desire to help them, but may cease giving money if we find out that we are not really helping but hurting them by encouraging habits not really useful to them.[11]

Although this example is not one of Hume's more felicitous ones, I cite it because it is especially susceptible to Nietzsche's criticisms of the utilitarians. In *Daybreak* (IV: 230) Nietzsche complains against the utilitarians that sentiments crisscross, and what seems useful to one person will seem wrong to another for that same reason. Genealogy thus cannot stop with identifying what is useful, but must identify that in terms of which we can say something is genuinely useful or not. Neither utility nor pleasure are stable and informative enough to provide a ground floor for a universal ethical theory.

While this objection to Hume echoes Kant, Nietzsche is equally critical of Kant's universalistic moral theory. Kant's conception of moral personality points beyond the phenomenal world to a noumenal or intelligible world we supposedly inhabit as well, and from which we give ourselves our moral laws. Nietzschean genealogy follows Hegel's and Schopenhauer's criticisms of this idea of reason as an autonomous law-giver. Genealogy undercuts the motive behind metaphysics by showing that Kant's projection of a two-world view as the presupposition of morality can itself be explained as an attempt to escape the recognition that the phenomenal world is for us the only intelligible world.

Although Nietzsche shares Kant's rejection of Hume's appeal to utility and pleasure, Nietzsche's "method of ethics" goes beyond both Hume's and Kant's. Kant's arguments are transcendental ones. That is, they start from some feature of experience we take as essential and then argue that if we are to speak, think, and act as we do, we must also believe certain other features also obtain. Thus, for the Kantian if we make moral judgments, we must believe we are free; and since as phenomenal beings we are not free, we must believe we are free in some other world than this one. While Nietzsche's critical arguments are sometimes transcendental in form, their *purpose* differs from that of these conceptual ones. Nietzsche's arguments do not simply

---

[11] David Hume, *An Inquiry Concerning the Principles of Morals* (New York: Bobbs-Merrill, 1957), Section II ("Of Benevolence"), Part II, p. 13.

confirm that our ways of speaking, thinking, and acting are intelligible in the same terms in which we describe them to ourselves. Genealogy tends to find an incoherence in our own self-understanding (for instance, between our various self-descriptions, or between the way we think and the way we act) and then to show how that incoherence is produced from within us. Rather than confirm the adequacy of our present self-descriptions and the coherence of our practices, genealogy makes us more intelligible to ourselves by showing us the *inadequacy* of our present self-understandings and practices, and then giving an interpretation of how such an inadequacy could have come about.

I stress that Nietzsche is giving an interpretation, not an explanation of the sort that would deduce a single necessary conclusion from universal principles and observable facts. Furthermore, there are counterfactual elements in the interpretation. To understand how something could have come about implies that a different outcome was also possible. But even Hume's genealogies do not result in interpretations in this sense. He calls his reasoning experimental, in that moral ideas can be traced back to moral sentiments we can identify in ourselves. He believes further that a sentiment such as sympathy is universal, and constant enough to constitute the basis for generalizable moral judgments. There is thus an important difference in both form and content between Hume's and Nietzsche's use of the hypothetical method. In content, placing *ressentiment* rather than Hume's universal sympathy at the origin of morality leads Nietzsche to reject the universal status of ethics. A distinction like that between the values of the noble and the values of the slavish calls into question Hume's claim that there are natural (psychologically universal) as well as artificial (socially useful) virtues. If the virtues of the nobles are more natural than those of the slaves, they are not invariable features of human nature since slave morality can corrupt and replace them.

The arguments against the utility of particular virtues will also be different in form. Nietzsche says, for instance, that asceticism is the result of willing nothingness rather than not willing (GM III:28). Such a claim is both weaker and stronger than Hume's. It is weaker in that it does not claim to be identifying psychological facts. We are not aware psychologically of willing nothingness, and Nietzsche's suggestion that we are willing nothingness although we are not aware of doing so is just an interpretation of what we are willing. The psychological fact is that we think we are willing something. The interpretation is that contrary to what we think, we are really willing nothingness.

But in another respect Nietzsche's claim is stronger than Hume's. As in Kant, there is some logical consideration involved, for supposedly we *must*, on reflection, come to accept Nietzsche's interpretation rather than our own of what we are doing. For instance, the claim is that we are willing nothingness rather than doing something else, namely, not willing. But of course it is impossible not to will. We could perhaps try not to will, knowing that trying is already willing, and therefore that in trying not to will, we fail in not willing. But Nietzsche follows Kant in believing that it is irrational to try to do the impossible. So the alternative of not willing is inevitably counterfactual. Willing nothingness turns out to be an alternative that is *forced* on the ascetic. But a lifetime of willing nothingness is impossible in practice, and would be self-defeating. Nietzsche thus derives what Kant called an *absurdum practicum* to show the incoherence of the attempt to put a certain theory into practice throughout a life.[12] While different in purpose from Kant's use of transcendental arguments in ethics, Nietzsche's arguments nevertheless share with them this kinship in structure.

The Feasibility of Genealogical Interpretations

Because Hume's genealogies, in contrast to Nietzsche's counterfactual ones, are factual and experimental, they are defeasible. The inductive generalizations can be falsified. Thus, if we found a tribe of human beings, for instance, the Ik, lacking the sentiments of humanity and sympathy, Hume's hypothesis of the universality of moral sentiment would have to be discarded (unless he is allowed to salvage his theory with the *ad hoc* stipulation that the repugnant mores of the Ik are caused only by extreme scarcity).[13] Nietzsche's genealogi-

---

[12] On the *absurdum practicum* see Kant, *Lectures on Philosophical Theology,* trans. Allen W. Wood and Gertrude M. Clark (Ithaca: Cornell University Press, 1978), pp. 122-123.

[13] On the African tribe of the Ik, who appear to take pleasure in the suffering of one another, see Colin Turnbull, *The Mountain People* (New York: Simon and Schuster, 1972); cited by Raymond Geuss, *The Idea of a Critical Theory: Habermas and the Frankfurt School* (Cambridge University Press, 1981), pp. 49-54. Geuss gives a succinct characterization of the criticism of Christianity in the *Genealogy* to show how it exemplifies critical theory:

This criticism...appeals to a purported fact about the 'origin' of Christianity — that Christianity arises from hatred, envy, resentment, and feelings of weakness and inadequacy.... How do we know that these motives are 'unacceptable'?... Since it is a central doctrine of Christianity that agents ought to be motivated by love, and not by hatred, resentment, envy, etc., Christianity itself gives the standard of 'acceptability' for motives in the light of which it is criticized. If Nietzsche's account of its 'origins' is correct, Christianity 'requires' of its adherents that they not recognize their own motives for adhering to it (p. 44).

Genealogy thus ought to be a form of immanent rather than external criticism, one that also explains the fact of the blindness of the agents to their own real motives and interests.

cal hypothesis that the will to power is at the basis of all formations of the will cannot be similarly falsified. For one thing, will to power is not equivalent to a psychological state. Even people who conceived of themselves as out for power could be mistaken. For another, showing people that their moral values really express, say, *ressentiment* rather than Humean sympathy, is not likely to be confirmed by their agreement. They are probably going to find the interpretation implausible, and even if they were to assent, that assent would itself have to be interpreted in turn to see if it was motivated by *ressentiment*. How a Nietzschean genealogy of a particular case could be confirmed or disconfirmed is not at all clear. If the confirmation is itself only a further interpretation, then there seems to be no end to the task. Nietzsche's shudder suggests he does not accept that result willingly, so we must look elsewhere for the answer.

One point to notice is that what is being interpreted is itself an interpretation. This is not to say there are not some facts. There are facts that any interpretation would have to take into account. These facts would be, for instance, the psychological ones about the self-descriptions of the agents. But those facts themselves are only part of an interpretation, namely, the agent's self-interpretation. The facts might be the sorts of sentences the agent utters about itself, and the self-interpretation would be the reconstructed account of how these utterances fit together systematically into a coherent self-understanding. Other facts might include the social actions of the agents of a particular society, and a social self-understanding could also be constructed. But the genealogist need not accept either the individual agent's or the group's self-interpretations as the last word. The genealogist can try to build an interpretation that will take account of the agents' self-interpretations and at the same time explain what the genealogist takes to be a further fact, namely, that there are basic incoherencies in these self-interpretations. The genealogist can even explain why these incoherencies were themselves not explicit for the agents. That is, the genealogist's interpretation makes plausible *both* why the agents did not understand themselves the way the genealogist does, and nevertheless why they *could* have understood themselves as the genealogist does.

For Nietzschean genealogy it is thus not entirely right to say there are no facts, only interpretations. There are facts, but only insofar as they inhere in interpretations. The interpretation will determine what counts as a fact. Thus, the ascetic moralist will believe certain things to be valuable, and will have an interpretation, whether implicit or explicit, of why these beliefs are reasonable. For the genealogist there is another interpretation of these beliefs that is more reasonable than the moralist's own interpretation and that explains both why the beliefs were believed at one time, and why they are no longer believed.

So interpretations are defeasible, although not because particular beliefs can be shown to be false in isolation from any interpretation. Interpretations can be shown to be superior to other interpretations if they explain features of these interpretations that could be perceived as problems for the interpretation from within, but for specifiable reasons are not so perceived. Hegel, of course, had used this strategy before Nietzsche, but Nietzsche demurs, as far as I can see, from any attempt to show a dialectical transition between the earlier and the later interpretations, such that the earlier necessarily evolves into the later. As detailed cultural analysis Nietzschean genealogy could establish empirical plausibility, but not logical or dialectical necessity. Genealogy is not dialectical, and does not assert a general teleology (even though there may be *internal* teleologies, as, for instance, in the devolution of Platonism first into Christianity and then into explicit nihilism).

What, however, is the test for the critical dimension of Nietzschean genealogy? Even though by avoiding an epistemological doctrine like perspectivism Nietzsche could avoid many familiar epistemological problems, there are other kinds of problems with a hermeneutical reformulation of the genealogical method. Most troublesome is how the genealogist is to justify the inference that some interpretations are better than others. The genealogist is forced to have preferences. For instance, genealogical philosophy is preferred to metaphysical, or "first," philosophy that seeks to ground certainty through presuppositionless foundations or incorrigible axioms. If every philosophical theory (counting *both* genealogy and metaphysics as philosophical theories) is an interpretation, what is the basis for preferring the hermeneutical view that there are no noninterpretive theories over the dogmatic view that there must be only one right theory? The attempt to construct a theory that is not just another interpretation is not obviously incoherent even if so far it has not been successful.

The genealogist has preferences for certain sorts of theories and values but ought not to smuggle these preferences into the genealogical analysis by presupposing *a priori* schemas or moral standards. Sarah Kofman accounts for the genealogist's preferences of some interpretations over others by distinguishing the conditions holding for first-order interpretations from those holding for second-order ones.[14] The first-order interpretations are the immediate result of the instinctual need to make life intelligible. The second-

---

[14] See in particular, Sarah Kofman (note 10 above), pp. 120-145, 173-206.

order interpretations of these first-order ones often mask the interpretive character of the first.

This suggestion is a fruitful one, and I would like to take it one step further by noting how Nietzsche's insistence on honesty can be converted into a methodological principle for rationally preferring some interpretations to others. A strict philology should be honest with itself, and this means two things. First, it should present its interpretation explicitly as an interpretation. This recognition might seem implicitly relativistic or even nihilistic insofar as it seems to be an admission of the arbitrariness of the genealogical account. However, the second feature of methodological honesty is that the relation between the interpretation and that which is interpreted should *not* be arbitrary, or at least it should be supportable by rational argument. What is being interpreted is itself a given interpretation, and the second-order interpretation is asserting itself to be a nonarbitrary and indeed valid account of the advantages and disadvantages of the first-order interpretation.

Kofman, however, takes her own interpretation yet another step further, and in so doing, I think, goes *beyond* Nietzsche. Kofman thinks a satisfactory middle ground between dogmatism and relativism is pluralism. What distinguishes healthful from sick (life-affirming from life-abnegating) interpretations on her account is that the former are deliberately an active "multiplying of perspectives" to enrich and embellish life.[15]

On *Nietzschean* grounds there are two difficulties with this pluralism. First, it obscures the basic difficulty about preferring an interpretation to another. For to say that the life-affirming interpretations are those that multiply rather than inhibit the formation of other interpretations is simply *to prefer* pluralistic interpretations of interpretation to nonpluralistic ones. Insofar as multiplying perspectives or interpretations is only a criterion for discriminating among *second-order* interpretations, it does not serve the genealogist in critically evaluating the *first-order* interpretations. So although I think Kofman is right to suggest that the will to power is not asserted by Nietzsche as a dogmatic "truth," but only as an interpretive hypothesis, I think something must also be said about how hypotheses are tested and how one determines their utility. She suggests that Nietzsche's hypothesis of the will to power has the advantage of "permitting an indefinite interrogation and an indefinite multiplicity" of further hypotheses (p. 380). I would agree that a good hypothesis will lead to the formulation of *some* other determinate hypotheses, but I think that a hypothesis that led to an *indefinite* (i.e., endless and

---

[15] Sarah Kofman, p. 378. For further discussion see my article, "Philosophy as Rigorous Philology? Nietzsche and Poststructuralism," *New York Literary Forum* 8-9 (1981).

boundless) multiplicity should be rejected *for that reason alone.*

Second, I think Kofman (like Derrida, Foucault, and Blanchot) does Nietzsche an injustice by suggesting that genealogy leads to an infinite proliferation of interpretations. This reading of Nietzsche loses an essential feature of Nietzsche's claim that genealogy reveals various forms of will to power. Although it is true for him that no one project is the best manifestation of will to power, and that will to power is "multiple," it does not follow that the point of genealogy is only to multiply interpretations. On the contrary, genealogy must criticize some interpretations, and it does so by discriminating between healthful and sick manifestations of the will to power. Nietzschean genealogy is thus *not* akin to recent methodologies maintaining either that anything goes (Feyerabend), or that interpretations are undecidable (Derrida). Nietzsche would see the defenses of sheer proliferation and of undecidability as hidden *ressentiment* of a sickly indecisiveness.

I think Nietzsche would insist that interpretations conflict and compete, and that some *must* be preferred to others. The principles of proliferation and undecidability are too thin to account for this feature. They cannot be used to decide which interpretations are better, but at most only to reject a specific second-order interpretation of interpretation, namely, the dogmatic theory requiring a single correct reading. The pluralists' principle of proliferation cannot even be used to reject dogmatic first-order interpretations asserting of any given text that it must be read in just this way. In fact, pluralism seems forced to controvert its intentions by saying, "the more of these dogmatic readings the better." The pluralists' principles of proliferation and undecidability thus lack survival value, and this in itself provides a Nietzschean reason for rejecting them.

Nietzsche as Affirmative Thinker?

A crucial question in thinking about the feasibility of Nietzschean genealogy today, then, is how the genealogist can argue for and against particular interpretations, both first-order and second-order. In Nietzsche's terms, how can the genealogist discriminate critically between healthful and sickly interpretations? I wish to draw a positive conclusion from my reflections on proliferation, pluralism, and undecidability. A minimal condition of such critical discrimination is that healthful interpretations be those that set out the conditions for finding their own inadequacies, and the strategies for revising themselves.

To put the point in this methodological way is not to go beyond Nietzsche's own metaphors of health and sickness, but simply to express them in another way. In aphorisms 120 and 382 of the *Gay Science,* for instance, Nietzsche makes clear that what counts as health is something that must continually be called into question and challenged. Health can be acquired only gradually, and only by risking it and even giving it up. Health and sickness are different not in kind, but merely in degree. Furthermore, there is no universal criterion for health. Health is instead relative to the individual's goals and make-up. These medical metaphors I interpret as implying that the standards for what makes an interpretation a live option are internal to the interpretation, and that a sickly interpretation would be one that refused to investigate itself and to raise the question of its own viability.

In the remarkable second paragraph of the preface to the second edition of the *Gay Science,* Nietzsche sketches a genealogy of the will to philosophize and traces that will back to a sickness of the body. This move back to the body is typical of both Hume's and Nietzsche's use of genealogy. Hume recognizes, for instance, that there are apparent counterexamples to his claim that the feelings of "humanity" and benevolence are universal. Characteristically he thus tries to explain away a misanthrope like Plutarch's Timon by asserting that Timon did not really lack the feeling of humanity, but was simply suffering from a bad spleen.[16] Nietzsche differs from Hume, however, in that Hume accepts most people's feelings at face value and has to explain away a few exceptional cases, whereas Nietzsche often seems to be making the exception the rule by explaining away entirely the generally-accepted explanations of behavior.

While neither Nietzsche nor Hume, as skeptics, assess constructive philosophy highly, Nietzsche goes beyond Hume in saying that any philosophy that is "affirmative" is probably the result of a sickly will: "Every philosophy that ranks peace above war, every ethic with a negative definition of happiness, every metaphysics and physics that knows some *finale,* some final state of some sort, every predominantly aesthetic or religious craving for some Apart, Beyond, Outside, Above, permits the question whether it was not sickness that inspired the philosopher" (GS Preface 2). Nietzsche does not *want* to be an affirmative thinker in this sense, but he also does not want to be simply a critic, as his tirades against critical (Kantian) philosophy make clear. This paragraph calls for a "philosophical *physician."* The goal of this physician cannot be simply to cure him- or herself, but "to pursue the problem of the total health of a people, time, race or of humanity." Hence, the physician will be offering an interpretation that will prove its use only insofar as it

---

[16] David Hume, *An Inquiry Concerning the Principles of Morals,* Section V, p. 53.

exposes what counts as both sickness and health, and shows the "patients" how to move away from sickness toward health. But the physician must be aware that the diagnosis could itself be motivated more by sickness than by health, and its prescriptions must be monitored continuously and changed when they appear to do more harm than good. The medicines themselves are poisons when used in extremes. In the second *Untimely Meditation,* for example, the sickness of too much history is said to be controllable with touches of the unhistorical and supra-historical, even though if these antidotes began to dominate they would themselves become the sickness.

Nietzsche's medical analogy shows, therefore, that to be healthful and feasible, an interpretation must be defeasible. Furthermore, since the conditions for an interpretation's defeasibility are internal, it will be "honest" about itself only if it makes these conditions explicit. If I am right in this rendering of the special Nietzschean virtue of honesty, then doubts arise about the honesty of applications of genealogy which find sickness everywhere, but never health. Nietzsche was wise not to publish his own thought that will to power could be found everywhere, not only in people, but in the world as such (WP 1067). The claim that everything is will to power explains nothing. To avoid the vacuity of this level of generality, commentators like Kofman stress that the concept of will to power is only a hypothesis and a diagnostic tool, not a metaphysical principle. What must also be recognized, however, is that Hume was right not to make the exception the rule. Genealogy would be methodologically defective if it always discovered only *degenerate* manifestations of will to power. Nietzsche's metaphor of the philosophical physician clearly implies that not everything is sickly, for even to make the diagnosis of sickness there must be a contrasting conception of health. Unlike traditional philosophical methods, genealogy is not aprioristic. Hence, the genealogical physician should not prescribe in advance the same diagnosis and fatal prognosis for every possible patient.

University of California
Santa Cruz

Bernd Magnus

Nietzsche and the Project of Bringing Philosophy to an End[1]

> "At the very moment when one begins to take philosophy seriously, the whole world believes the opposite is the case."
>
> *Human, All-too-Human* II: 380

Nietzsche commentators disagree about most aspects of his thinking — as one would expect — especially about what an *Übermensch* is supposed to be, what eternal recurrence asserts, whether he had developed or had intended to formulate a full-blown theory of the will to power, as well as what his perspectivism may be said to assert. These are disagreements concerning the substance, goal, and success of Nietzsche's attempted transvaluation of all values. On the other hand, there is considerably less disagreement about identifying the deconstructive aspect of his work, the sense in which he sought to disentangle Western metaphysics, Christianity, and morality in order to display what he took to be their reactive decadence. Put crudely and misleadingly, there is considerably less disagreement concerning the negative, deconstructive side of Nietzsche's thinking than there is about the positive, reconstructive side.

These, then, are the two faces of Nietzsche with which I shall be concerned; the one looks at our past and vivisects our common cultural heritage at its roots; the other seems to be turned toward the future, suggesting visions of possible new forms of Western life. In what follows I shall first sketch the negative, deconstructive, backward-glancing Nietzsche, the face which is more easily recognized by his commentators. I shall then try to depict Nietzsche's positive, reconstructive face, only to be beset by an immediate

---

[1] This paper was made possible through the generous assistance of the John Simon Guggenheim Memorial Foundation, the National Endowment for the Humanities, and the Riverside Division of the Academic Senate, University of California. I am indebted to all three. The paper first appeared in the *Journal of the British Society for Phenomenology* (Oct. 1983); it is reprinted here with their permission.

difficulty. For this other, future-directed face turns out to be not one portrait but two possible ones. One sketch portrays Nietzsche's remarks about truth, knowledge, superhumanity, eternal recurrence and will to power as his answers to perennial, textbook philosophical problems: his theory of knowledge, his moral philosophy, his ontology. On this reading of his reconstructive side Nietzsche seems to be shattering the foundations of past theories as one demolishes false idols, in order to erect his own, better phoenix from their ashes. The alternative rendering of this reconstructive side of Nietzsche rejects the positive/negative dichotomy itself and depicts him instead as attempting to liberate us precisely from the felt need to provide theories of knowledge, or moral theories, or ontologies. The first reconstructive portrait assimilates Nietzsche's project to the great tradition of "the metaphysics of presence" — to Plato, Descartes, and Kant. The alternative portrait sees the negative, deconstructive side of Nietzsche as already constructive, in the therapeutic manner of the later Wittgenstein, late Heidegger, Derrida, Rorty, and Foucault.

What is at the bottom of these conflicting portraits is an unarticulated difference scarcely recognized among Nietzsche commentators, not to say philosophers generally. It is the difference between those who believe that one is paying him a compliment by reading Nietzsche as "a philosopher" giving Kantian style answers to textbook questions, and those who view that characterization as denigrating his achievement.[2]

Deconstructing Traditions

One way of reading Nietzsche is to see him telling a story about how we in the West became who we are. It will have to be a sweeping tale, to be sure, centering on our philosophical, religious, and moral heritage. The use of the singular "heritage" already begs the question in Nietzsche's favor; for it suggests that, deep down, there is a family resemblance among the many things that have been called "philosophy" which is more interesting than their differences, that there has been a resemblance within the Judeo-Christian tradition as interesting as its internecine strife, that there are more and

---

[2] Although I allude to nameless "commentators" I take explicit issue with none in what follows, nor do I mention them explicitly. My colleagues will recognize their influence soon enough, it is hoped, and they are too numerous to acknowledge. Among the quick, I have profited most from my colleagues in the North American Nietzsche Society, especially from the work of its many officers; among the dead, I am here stalked primarily by ghosts of Heidegger, Jaspers, and Kaufmann.

different things to be said about moral philosophy than are captured in the utilitarian/deontological debate, for example. For Nietzsche's story to succeed two further assumptions must be added. The first is that there are important points of intersection between the history of "philosophy," "religion," and "morality," motivational intersections which make it possible to speak of all three simultaneously as expressing a single ascetic ideal motivated by the will to power; the second assumption is that of all the complex historical factors — social, economic, political, demographic, ethnocentric and so on — that have shaped Western civilization and character, none are as important as the first-mentioned trio — philosophy, religion, and morality — in telling us how we became who we are.

Nietzsche appears to have been persuaded from early on that what we today call essentialism and realism are false, so to speak, that there is no indwelling structure of the universe — no "natural kinds" — which it is reason's task to unveil. Even some of our most basic stock-in-trade distinctions — subject/object, mind/world, consciousness/reality, and their successors, such as transcendental unity of apperception/constituted object, language/referent, conceptual scheme/content of scheme, signifier/signified — would appear to be optional products of natural languages. This is because

> The singular family resemblance between all Indian, Greek and German philosophizing is easy enough to explain. Where there exists a language affinity it is quite impossible, thanks to the common philosophy of grammar — I mean thanks to unconscious domination and directing by similar grammatical functions — to avoid everything being prepared in advance for a similar evolution and succession of philosophical systems: just as the road seems to be barred to certain other possibilities of world interpretation. (BGE 3)

But the domination of thought by the tyranny of common grammatical functions is not some lamentable fact which is to be overcome. As a matter of fact, this way of putting the issue begs the question in favor of separating thought from language. And this, precisely, is dubious: "for we cease to think when we refuse to do so under the constraint of language" (WP 522). Nietzsche offers a thoroughly naturalistic and instrumentalist account of the origins of consciousness and language.

> *[C]onsciousness evolved at all only under the pressure of need for communication* — it was from the very first necessary and useful only between man and man...and also evolved only in proportion to the degree of this usefulness. Consciousness is really only a connecting network between man and man — only as such did it have to evolve... — My idea, as one can see, is that consciousness does not really belong to the existence of man as an individual but rather to that in him which is community and herd. (GS 354)

Rather than understanding languague and thought as communication instruments with which to cope, however, humanity's genius for self-deceptive self-descriptions did not take long to evolve either.

The significance of language for the evolution of culture lies in this, that mankind set up in language a separate world beside the other world, a place it took to be so firmly set that, standing upon it, it could lift the rest of the world off its hinges and make itself master of it. To the extent that man has for long ages believed in the concepts and names of things as in *aeternae veritates* he has appropriated to himself that pride by which he raised himself above the animal: he really thought that in language he possessed knowledge of the world. (HH 11)

So the significance of language for our history lies not only in the dichotomy of mind and world which it supplied for Indo-European vocabularies, but in presenting the dominating metaphor of the mind as the faculty for accurate representations of the world as it is in itself. This in turn helps to explain the later denigration of the apparent (phenomenal) world in favor of some other "true" world: "'Reason' is the cause of our falsification of the testimony of the senses... The 'apparent' world is the only one: the 'true world' is merely added by a lie" (TI "'Reason' in Philosophy" 2). And Nietzsche further suggests that because "the prejudice of reason forces us to posit unity, identity, permanence, substance, cause, thinghood, being, we see ourselves somehow caught in error, compelled into error" (*ibid.* 5). So Nietzsche suggests that there are no fixed standpoints, no common measure between representation and represented — no common measure between "language," "consciousness," "idea," "transcendental ego," "conceptual scheme," "signifier" on the one hand, and "world," "object," "thing," "phenomenon," "content," and "signified," on the other hand. But he also adds:

You will guess that it is not the opposition of subject and object that concerns me here: This distinction I leave to the epistemologists who have become entangled in the snares of grammar (the metaphysics of the people). It is even less the opposition of 'thing-in-itself' and appearance; for we do not 'know' nearly enough to be entitled to any such distinction. We simply lack any organ for knowledge, for 'truth': we 'know' (or believe or imagine) just as much as may be *useful* in the interests of the human herd, the species; and even what is here called 'utility' is ultimately also a mere belief, something imaginary, and perhaps precisely that most calamitous stupidity of which we shall perish some day. (GS 354)

And what follows from these considerations is that

Henceforth, my dear philosophers, let us be on guard against the dangerous old conceptual fiction that posited a "pure, will-less, painless, timeless knowing subject..." There is *only* a perspective "knowing"; and the *more* affects we allow to speak about one thing, the *more* eyes, different eyes, we can use to observe one thing, the more complete will our "concept" of this thing, our "objectivity," be. (GM III: 12)

The claim that there is only a "perspective 'knowing'" is formulated in various ways in Nietzsche's published and unpublished writings of his mature period. Sometimes he connects this thesis with phenomenalism and perspectivism and argues that our "animal consciousness" as such grasps the world only in terms of its lowest common denominator.

> This is the essence of phenomenalism and perspectivism as I understand them: Owing to the nature of *animal consciousness,* the world of which we can become conscious is only a surface- and sign-world, a world that is made common and meaner; whatever becomes conscious *becomes* by the same token shallow, thin, relatively stupid, general, sign, herd signal. (GS 354)

At other times he offers his perspectivism to counter prevailing philosophic orientations, positivism, for example.

> Against positivism, which halts at phenomena — "There are only *facts*" — I would say: No, facts is precisely what there is not, only interpretations.
> In so far as the word "knowledge" has any meaning, the world is knowable; but it is *interpretable* otherwise, it has no meaning behind it, but countless meanings. — "Perspectivism." (WP 481)

At still other times Nietzsche seems simply to believe that his perspectivism permits a collapse in distinctions between the definition of truth, criteria for truth claims, and the justification for truth claims, as when he suggests, boldly, "there is no truth" (WP 540), "truth is error" (WP 454), and "truth is the kind of error without which a certain species of life could not live. The value for *life* is ultimately decisive" (WP 493).

From considerations of this sort, and others I have not mentioned, it follows for Nietzsche that language systematically "falsifies" the world. Language interprets the world according to a scheme we cannot throw off. Categories ossify and congeal, but the imposition of language, of categories which congeal, is not a contingent fact about ourselves. Rather, language schemes seem to be based upon our psychological need to find meaning, order, and stability in the world. This also helps to account for other putative facts, for example that we tend to seek permanence where there is none; that we seek natural grounded starting points for inquiry where there are none, that we seek an order in everything. For, on this view, we *need* coherence, purpose, unity, and meaning.

Such views, of course, require enormous adjustments in our conception of the role of philosophy (*and* science), religion, and morality in our lives. Indeed they require an adjustment in our conception of culture itself, for it too must now appear as the imposition of form upon chaos. What holds for individuals is meant to hold for cultures as well. On this view, each culture copes with its world, imposes its order upon an indeterminate continuum.

As a result, says Nietzsche, "I learned to view the origins of moralizing and idealizing very differently from what might be desirable: the *hidden* history of philosophers, the psychology of their great names came to light for me" (EH Preface 3). And Nietzsche then announces a theme of his thinking for which, at first, he became notorious:

> Gradually it has become clear to me what every great philosophy so far has been: namely, the personal confession of its author and a kind of involuntary and unconscious memoir... Accordingly, I do not believe that a "drive to knowledge" is the father of philosophy; but rather that another drive has, here as elsewhere, employed understanding (and misunderstanding) as a mere instrument ... (BGE 6)

The drive which overpowers philosophy is the will to power self-deceptively exhibited as the will to truth: "Their 'knowing' is *creating,* is a lawgiving, their will to truth is — *will to power*" (BGE 211). And so the family resemblance of all philosophy hitherto is that it carves up world and discourse into two unequal chunks. There is the "true world," reality as it is in itself. Only philosophers have access to this domain, not the *hoi polloi*. This reality is captured in philosophic vocabularies which contrast with slippery, transitory, second-rate discourse directed at the merely "apparent" world. And so Nietzsche asks: "You ask me which of the philosophers' traits are really idiosyncrasies? For example, their lack of historical sense, their hatred of the very idea of becoming, their Egypticism." And he answers that

> They think that they show their *respect* for a subject when they de-historicize it, *sub specie aeterni* — when they turn it into a mummy... they threaten the life of everything they worship. Death, change, old age, as well as procreation and growth, are to their minds objections — even refutations... And above all, away with the body, this wretched *idée fixe* of the senses, disfigured by all the fallacies of logic, refuted, even impossible, although it is impudent enough to behave as if it were real! (TI "The Problem of Socrates" 2)

And he adds, in an unpublished 1888 note which bears the title "Why philosophers are slanderers,"

> The history of philosophy is a secret raging against the preconditions of life, against the value feelings of life, against partisanship in favor of life. Philosophers have never hesitated to affirm a world provided it contradicted this world and furnished them with a pretext for speaking ill of this world. It has been hitherto the grand school of slander. (WP 461)

This is scarcely a flattering picture of the role of philosophy and philosophers in culture, but it follows from Nietzsche's allegation that

> Judgments, judgments of value, concerning life, for it or against it, can, in the end, never be true: they have value only as symptoms, they are worthy of consideration

only as symptoms; in themselves such judgments are stupidities. One must by all means stretch out one's fingers and make the attempt to grasp this amazing finesse, *that the value of life cannot be estimated.* (TI "The Problem of Socrates" 2)

If the value of life cannot be estimated, then the world-denigrating pronouncements of traditional philosophers, their preference for dualisms of all sorts, must be viewed in a self-referring light. If "the wisest men of all ages have judged alike" concerning life that "*it is no good*" (*ibid.*), then such views must be read as symptoms of the persons who offer such decadent appraisals.

If the history of metaphysics is at bottom a disguised power game, for Nietzsche, then morality and religion are easier to construe as parallel developments. On this view, religion, like philosophy, is ultimately a power game, even if the power is directed at oneself — and morality is the favored means for both.

Life itself is to my mind the instinct for growth, for durability, for an accumulation of forces, for *power:* where the will to power is lacking there is decline. It is my contention that all the supreme values of mankind *lack* this will — that the values which are symptomatic of decline, *nihilistic* values, are lording it under the holiest names. (A 6)

Nietzsche identifies corruption with decadence, and identifies both with humankind's highest, supreme values; the sustaining and informing values of humankind have all been decadence-values, Nietzsche asserts here. The history of our highest aspirations is the history of nihilism. And one should not take lightly Nietzsche's identification of nihilism with a sublimated instinct of self-destruction, as well as his conclusion that the loss of an instinctual vitality reappears as a counterfeit "under the holiest names." On this view, the highest values hitherto — identified by Nietzsche as "the ascetic ideal" — have been thanatological values dressed up in life-affirming disguise.

Even Jesus of Nazareth, often depicted by Nietzsche as an apostolic anticleric, had to be transvaluated if "Christianity would become master over *beasts of prey:* its method is to make them *sick;* enfeeblement is the Christian recipe for *taming,* for 'civilizing'" (A 15). And in a clever series of steps Nietzsche argues that the notion of a "moral world order" had to be invented to reinstate priestly authority:

From now on all things in life are so ordered that the priest is indispensable everywhere; at all natural occurrences in life, at birth, marriage, sickness, death, not to speak of "sacrifices" (meals), the holy parasite appears in order to denature them — in his language: to "consecrate." (A 26)

And the most powerful instruments for the reascendancy of the priest are the notions of sin and guilt: "the priest rules through the invention of sin" (A 49).

Psychologically considered, "sins" become indispensable in any society organized by priests: they are the real handles of power. The priest *lives* on sins, it is essential for him that people "sin." Supreme principle: "God forgives those who repent" — in plain language: those who submit to the priest. (A 26)

As Nietzsche reads post-Nazarene Christianity, the entire scaffolding of its ideology, the entire redemptive drama is designed to retain the power of the priestly class, born of *ressentiment:* "'Last Judgment,' 'immortality of the soul,' and 'soul' itself are instruments of torture, systems of cruelties by virtue of which the priest became master, remained master" (A 38). So the history of Christianity, Nietzsche seems to argue, is the history of an error, a misunderstanding in which the original symbolism of Jesus becomes transvaluated into a crass ecclesiastical tale, a tale which becomes as vulgar as the slave's mentality which seeks power and revenge in and through it.

The destiny of Christianity lies in the necessity that its faith had to become as diseased, as base and vulgar, as the needs it was meant to satisfy were diseased, base, and vulgar. In the church, finally, *diseased barbarism* itself gains power. (A 20)

The figure most responsible for the emergence and triumph of Christianity as "diseased barbarism" is Paul, of course; and "Paul was the greatest of all apostles of vengeance" (A 45), says Nietzsche.

In Paul the priest wanted power once again — he could use only concepts, doctrines, symbols with which one tyrannizes masses and forms herds. What was the one thing that Mohammed later borrowed from Christianity? Paul's invention, his means to priestly tyranny, to herd formation: the faith in immortality — *that is, the doctrine of the judgment."* (A 42)

Jesus, as Nietzsche deconstructs him, had set aside notions of guilt, sin, and atonement; but the ludicrous image of Jesus crucified required, step by step, notions of sin and atonement once again, of the doctrine of resurrection, above all. And Paul seizes precisely on this resurrection requirement:

Paul, with that rabbinical impudence which distinguishes him in all things, logicalized this conception, this *obscenity* of a conception, in this way: "*If* Christ was not resurrected from the dead, then our faith is vain." And all at once the evangel became the most contemptible of all unfulfillable promises, the *impertinent* doctrine of personal immortality. Paul himself still taught it as a *reward.* (A 41)

Thus, through Paul, Jesus the evangel is transvaluated, becoming the Redeemer, the dysangel.

Nothing remained untouched, nothing remained even similar to the reality. Paul simply transposed the center of gravity of that whole existence *after* this existence — in the *lie* of the "resurrected" Jesus. At bottom, he had no use at all for the life of the Redeemer — he needed the death on the cross *and* a little more. (A 43)

The "little more" Paul needs to gain supremacy is the notion of the potential immortality of each and every soul, ultimate democratization of and through the spiritual realm.

> That everyone as an "immortal soul" has equal rank with everyone else, that in the totality of living beings the "salvation" of *every* single individual may claim eternal significance...cannot be branded with too much contempt. And yet Christianity owes its triumph to this miserable flattery of personal vanity: it was precisely all the failures, all the rebellious-minded, all the less favored, the whole scum and refuse of humanity who were thus won over to it. The "salvation of the soul" — in plain language: "the world revolves around *me*." (*ibid.*)

Many commentators have observed, quite rightly, that for Nietzsche democracy and socialism — as well as nationalism and world wars — would have a different etiology without the triumph of Christianity as a Pauline invention, had they indeed been possible at all. And throughout *The Antichrist* Nietzsche remarks repeatedly on the political consequences of the triumphal slave's morality, as for example,

> The aristocratic outlook was undermined from the deepest underworld through the lie of the equality of souls; and if faith in the "prerogative of the majority" makes and *will make* revolutions — it is Christianity, beyond a doubt, it is *Christian* value judgments, that every revolution simply translates into blood and crime. (*ibid.*)

Further, Christianity ultimately undermines any distinction in rank, merit, through a "tarantula" morality in which the base inveigh against nobility. "Christianity is a rebellion of everything that crawls on the ground against that which has *height:* the evangel of the 'lowly' *makes* low" (*ibid.*). And,

> out of the *ressentiment* of the masses it forged its chief weapon against *us,* against all that is noble, gay, high-minded on earth, against our happiness on earth. "Immortality" conceded to every Peter and Paul has so far been the greatest, the most malignant, attempt to assassinate *noble* humanity. (*ibid.*)

On this view, flattered, self-congratulatory conceit, borne in and nurtured by resentment, which finds expression in Pauline Christianity, mocks noble values and converts the "noble" into the "evil" ones. But this self-congratulatory conceit veils itself as modesty, as humility, argues Nietzsche.

> What really happens here is that the most conscious *conceit of being chosen* plays modesty: once and for all one has placed *oneself,* the "community," the "good and the just," on one side, on the side of "truth" — and the rest, "the world," on the other. (A 44)

In *The Antichrist* the distinction between life-affirming, noble, nondecadent values, on the one hand, and life-denying, base, decadent values, on the other, is couched in the language of a contrast between aristocratic and chandala moralities. This contrast, in substance and form, parallels Nietzsche's earlier contrast between "base" and "noble" moralities. Mention of the two primary types of morality which he had identified was first made explicit by Nietzsche in *Beyond Good and Evil*. He had called them "master morality and slave morality" (BGE 260). Nietzsche's characterization is not intended to denigrate. The characterization, rather, is connected to Nietzsche's genealogical method. A certain moral outlook originates with slaves, he suggests, another presumably originates with their masters. Echoes of their respective conditions can be heard as sublimated in their respective moral perspectives. Yet Nietzsche suggests that all advanced civilizations display a mixture of both moral outlooks — those of slave morality as well as master morality — and elements of each moral scheme are generally simultaneously present in every person. Nietzsche's distinction between master and slave morality is therefore neither primarily historical nor etiological. It appears to be primarily typological. From this perspective, the morality of the aristocrat, master morality, initially identifies "good" and "bad" as expressions ascriptive of persons rather than actions. To say that X is "good" is to say that X is "noble." To say that Y is "bad" is much the same as to say that Y is "base," "despicable." And again, it is presumably masters who judge the baseness of persons, not their actions.

Those who are base are slaves and are essentially weak and powerless. Nietzsche maintains, therefore, that among the powerless the moral standard naturally championed is that which is useful or beneficial to the community *simpliciter*. Predictably, therefore, slave morality extols qualities such as sympathy, kindness, and humility, all of which have high utility for the community. In contrast, independent, strong individuals come to be regarded with suspicion. They are perceived as threatening and, accordingly, are judged "evil." Thus we have come full circle. The person judged "good" (i.e., "noble") by the standards of master morality is judged "evil" precisely for those traits by the standards of slave morality. The "good" man becomes "evil" in this story. This schema is of course symmetrical. The "good" man in slave morality terms is "base" when couched in terms of master morality.

Nietzsche characterized slave morality, generally in strident tones, as herd morality, chandala morality, or worse. On this view, the moral valuations and standards of "slave morality" are to be read as expressions of the needs of the herd (i.e., the community).

Nietzsche later gives the notion of resentment, *ressentiment*, prominent display, for it functions just precisely as the sort of explanatory tool which is needed to account for some moral attitudes and beliefs. The concept of resentment is then also used to explain why Christianity is slave morality sanctioned and incarnate.

Nietzsche's account began with two types, the aristocratic master, the servile slave. The master is, and his morality extols, health, competition, beauty, independence, power, self-control, pride, spontaneity, and passion. The self-directed master derives his values not from the community, not from "the herd," but presumably from the abundance of his own life and strength. The slave, however, fears the strength and power of the master; and he despises him. He is dependent, powerless, without self-direction, discipline or self-control. To seize control over his own psychic destiny, the slave must curb and tame his master. He must displace him in a sense. And the method of "overcoming" the master and his morality, the means to his displacement, is to render the values of the herd absolute and universal. This revolt of the slaves in moral matters is both creative and resentful. Powerless to effect a fundamental change in his condition, he wreaks vengeance against the master by converting the master's attributes into vices. And while master morality sanctions coexistence with "inferior" types and morals, the resentment of the slave yearns for universality. Nothing is to escape its moral clutches alive. Nietzsche does not mean to suggest that the slave's resentment of and revenge against the master is either direct or conscious.

It is in this context, the context of moral-psychological imperialism, that the slave's resentment is to be understood. Since the slave cannot displace the master in reality, he avenges himself symbolically, mythically. Hence the triumph of the religion of the slave — Christianity (and Judaism). Christianity is first of all the ideology of slave morality for Nietzsche. It expresses the slave's resentment against the attributes of master morality by vilifying them. The virtues of the master become "sin." In place of power, it is said that the meek shall inherit the earth. Pride is sin. Humility is virtue. Charity, chastity, and obedience replace competition, sensuality, and autonomy.

Finally, the innocence of existence, its topic neutrality, too, is abolished in the triumph of slave morality *qua* Christianity. On this view, Christianity is the fruit of resentment. As a product of weakness it represents the decline of life, decadence, degeneracy, in contrast to the exuberant ascent of life which seeks expression in master morality. And so it also follows for Nietzsche that Christianity, like Platonic philosophy, severs body and soul, that it deprecates the human body, impulse, instinct, passion, beauty, the intellect, as well as aesthetic values generally.

Nietzsche goes so far as to see even in the rise of democratic and socialist movements the vestiges of Christianity, vestiges of the slave morality I have been mentioning:

"We shall wreak vengeance and abuse upon all whose equals we are not" — thus do the tarantula-hearts vow.

"And 'will to equality' shall henceforth be the name for virtue; and against all that has power we want to raise our clamor!"

You preachers of equality, the tyrannomania of impotence clamors thus out of you for equality: your most secret ambitions to be tyrants thus shroud themselves in words of virtue!

Aggrieved conceit, repressed envy — perhaps the conceit and envy of your fathers — erupt from you as a flame and as the frenzy of revenge. (Z "On the Tarantulas")

Note that the will to equality is here characterized by Nietzsche as a disguised lust for power. The objective, as in all slave morality, is to slake the thirst to be tyrants. "Tyrannomania" is possible only for those who feel and indeed are unequal, for those who must legislate to others in order to feel equal, for those who must dominate. For those who are genuinely superior, domination is cultural. It is self-directed. It needs no "other." For Nietzsche this struggle between spirit and power is always and everywhere in evidence.

In the end, no one can spend more than he has: that is true of the individual, it is true of a people... Culture and the state — one should not deceive oneself about this — are antagonists... One lives off the other, one thrives at the expense of the other. (TI "What the Germans Lack" 4)

We may now be in a better position to appreciate the force of Nietzsche's claim that democracy and socialism are to be understood as growing on the soil of Christianity; for we now need to see the state as the supplanting deity in the lives of Europeans. The state is a surrogate god. Even Hegel's philosophizing is sometimes understood by Nietzsche in the coarse sense in which it was later to be assimilated by other authors, as providing nurture for authoritarian-totalitarian readings of history and destiny. For example,

Hegel: ...Right is with the victorious: they represent the progress of mankind. Attempt to prove the dominion of morality by means of history. (WP 415)

The significance of German philosophy (Hegel): to evolve a pantheism through which evil, error, and suffering are not felt as arguments against divinity. This grandiose project has been misused by the existing powers (state, etc.), as if it sanctioned the rationality of whoever happened to be ruling. (WP 416)

The nation-state retains a transcendent value and mission, a providential role, which history expresses and seeks to realize. "Bismarckophobia" and virulent "nationalism" may generally be read as interchangeable expressions in Nietzsche's litany without much loss of sense. And again it is the herd instinct, the morality of the slavish, which seeks expression here. Dreams of universality now attach to the nation and its state with missionary fervor and zeal. The slaughter of rivals and the conquest of the earth proceed under the banner of universal brotherhood. But that is merely symptomatic of "the tyrannomania of impotence." Again, the herd instinct, the need to be in it *together,* collective revenge, is what runs rampant in nationalism. And just as the God of Christianity represented life at ebb tide, at bottom, just as God represented a force essentially hostile to life, so the nation-state, too, represents the aspirations of the "base," the "despicable," the "slave," on this view.

If Western man has been dominated by and has come to depend upon moral values which have been associated with Platonism and Christianity, it will be difficult to wean him from those values without a cultural transvaluation of staggering proportions. When the death of God informs our lives, when the "true world" has been abolished with it, loss of faith in values *per se* accompanies loss of faith in those values specifically nurtured by Christianity. With the collapse of the Platonic and theological foundations and sanctions for "morality," only a pervasive sense of ultimate purposelessness, meaninglessness, remains. And the triumph of meaninglessness, of the Absurd, is at the same time the triumph of nihilism. When the highest values become devalued nihilism is a danger not because there are no other possible values, but because most of Western humanity knows no other values than those associated with a dualistic ascetic ideal.

Reconstructing Traditions

The deconstructive side of Nietzsche sketched above begged a lot of questions and lacked subtlety, shading, nuance: it was flat; it was sloganeering. Nevertheless, its broad strokes are not likely to provoke much criticism from commentators. That is because there exists some measure of agreement about what Nietzsche's diagnosis of the West consists in, what it was that he wished to set aside or would have us set aside. No such general agreement is near, however, concerning what he would put in its place, or indeed whether he thought there was even a point in putting anything in its place.

One way to bring out this difference in points of view is to contrast approaches to several planks in Nietzsche's reconstructive platform — his perspectivism, eternal recurrence, and *Übermensch* — in an equally sloganeering style.[3] I shall devote most of the remaining space to this task, before offering brief concluding remarks on some wider implications of the contrasts I sketch.

---

[3] The will to power will not be discussed, in part because of the sheer enormity of the textual questions it poses. But it is interesting to note in passing how much energy has been expended on will to power, as if having or failing to have produced an "ontology" puts Nietzsche's philosophic pedigree in question.

Here is one way to construe Nietzsche's perspectivist remarks: Nietzsche's perspectivism is, roughly, his theory of knowledge. It wants to assert four distinguishable claims: (1) no accurate representation of the world as it is in itself is possible; (2) there is nothing to which our theories stand in the required correspondence relation to enable us to say that they are true or false; (3) no method of understanding our world — the sciences, logic, or moral theory — enjoys a privileged epistemic status; (4) human needs always help to "constitute" the world for us. Nietzsche tends to run (1)-(4) together; often he confuses them. But the most serious difficulty for Nietzsche's perspectivism lies elsewhere: the self-reference problem. Are we to understand his many naturalistic theses as accurate representations of the world as it is in itself, as corresponding to any facts of the matter, as privileged perspectives, ones which are conditioned by no need whatsoever? If we are, then Nietzsche's perspectivism is self-contradictory in all four versions mentioned. But that is just to say that the theories Nietzsche offered either are not to be taken perspectivally — in which case his perspectivism must be abandoned — or they are only perspectives — in which case they may not be true and may be superseded. But to say that they may not be "true" is just to say that what he maintains may be "false"; but then how can he assert thesis (2) above? How can he maintain that there is nothing to which our theories stand in the required correspondence relation to enable us to determine whether they are true or false? Nietzsche's remarks about truth, interpretation, and perspective seem to suffer from the liar's paradox disease. For example, in saying that there is no truth, did Nietzsche mean to say something true? If he told the truth, then what he said is false, for there had to be a truth to be told for him to say, truly, that there is no truth. If what he said is false, on the other hand, then it is false to assert that there is no truth. But then at least *something* is true. And similarly, if every great philosophy is really only "the personal confession of its author and a kind of involuntary and unconscious memoir" (BGE 6), then what is Nietzsche confessing? What is his involuntary and unconscious memoir *really* about? Perhaps the best way to understand his perspectivism, then, is to construe it in a neo-Kantian way, as providing a transcendental standpoint in which putative "facts" about human needs and human neurophysiology play a role not unlike that of Kant's categories and forms of intuition. Think of it as the empirical turn gone transcendental.

Here is another way to construe Nietzsche's perspectivist remarks: Nietzsche's "perspectivism" is not a *theory of* anything, and it is certainly not a *theory* of knowledge. To say that there are only interpretations (or perspectives) is just to rename all the old facts "interpretations" (or "perspectives"). Similarly, to say that "truth" is "error" is not to offer a theory of truth so much as it is to rename it. The point of the renaming is to help us set aside the vocabulary of accurate representation which still holds us in its Platonic thrall. So Nietzsche's tropes concerning "truth" and "error," "fact" and "interpretation" are best understood as rhetorical devices to help us confront our preconception ("intuition") that there must be something like a final truth about the world as such which it is the goal of some discipline or other to disclose. A theory of knowledge is not something Nietzsche has, it is what he parodies. Knowledge is the sort of thing about which one ought to have a theory only when the Platonic picture has seduced us, only when we construe "knowledge" in terms of visual metaphors — of the mind's eye seeing the way things are — only if we see philosophy as culture's referee, as allowing or barring moves made elsewhere in culture which claim to be items of knowledge. Yet precisely this picture of philosophy is what Nietzsche urges ought to be set aside. "Knowledge" and "truth" are simply compliments paid to successful discourse. To give an account of such success is always to say why this *specific* item — e.g., the superiority of the heliocentric over the geocentric account of planetary motion — is "true" or "known." There can be explanations and illustrations of successful discourse on a case by case basis; but there can only be a misconceived "theory of" successful discourse.

Here is one way to construe Nietzsche's remarks about eternal recurrence: To overcome the dominance of dualism, Nietzsche proposed a theory which says, roughly, that the number of possible states of the universe is a finite number, and that time is infinite. Given this conjunction it follows that every possible state of the universe must recur an infinite number of times; hence, the eternal recurrence of the same. Such a theory rules out any possible dualism or otherworldliness and places upon each moment the weight of its eternal repetition.

Here is another way to construe Nietzsche's remarks about eternal recurrence: The doctrine of eternal recurrence admonishes us to behave *as if* it were true; it does not assert the truth of recurrence. Nietzsche's emphasis is on the putative psychological consequences which the teaching of eternal recurrence is to have upon our actions if we believe it to be true — if we behave *as if* recurrence were true. The point is that if we act as if recurrence is true the psychological effect is believed to be considerable, because it is as if we were choosing our eternally recurring future selves at every moment of our present lives. Behave as if each moment were immortal, forever to be relived, the doctrine tells us.

Here is yet another way to construe Nietzsche's remarks about eternal recurrence: Recurrence is a diagnostic tool. When the real or possible truth of recurrence is called upon to play a role at all, that role is primarily diagnostic.

Recurrence (and its real or possible truth) is a representation of a particular attitude toward life. The attitude toward life Nietzsche wishes to portray is the opposite of decadence, decline of life, world-weariness. The attitude he wishes to portray is the attitude of affirmation, of overfulness; the attitude which expresses ascending life, life as celebration, life in celebration. Eternal recurrence asks the question, how well disposed would we have to become, have to *be,* toward life, toward our lives and the world, in order to affirm eternal recurrence? And how life affirming would one have to be to crave *nothing* more fervently than eternal recurrence? Eternal recurrence, in its principal sense, is offered by Nietzsche as an illustration of the attitude of *Übermenschlichkeit,* of what it is like to be a superman. It illustrates the being-in-the-world — the basic attunement — of the *Übermensch.* It is not merely one possible attitude among many possible ones. It is *the* attitude *simpliciter* which Nietzsche wishes to portray if passive and active nihilism are to be overcome.

Here is one way to construe Nietzsche's remarks about the *Übermensch:* The *Übermensch* represents Nietzsche's nondualistic vision of human perfectibility. Like Goethe, the *Übermensch* is the Dionysian who has overcome his animal nature, has sublimated his impulses, organized the chaos of his passions, lived authentically, and has given style to his character. He is a free human being, joyous, without guilt, the master of instinctual drives which do not overpower him. He represents ascending life, self-overcoming, and self-possession. In him intelligence, strength of character and will, autonomy, passion, and taste are fully integrated. Think of him as Christ's soul in Caesar's body, or as instinct spiritualized.

Here is another way to construe Nietzsche's remarks about the *Übermensch:* The *Übermensch* is not yet another link in a long chain which attempts to articulate the human ideal, an ideal which can be realized if only we were to do something or other — sublimate our impulses, consecrate our passions, spiritualize our instincts, give style to our character, live authentically — assuming all the while, or course, that we would know how to begin to *do* any of these things. Rather, the *Übermensch* is the *nonspecific* representation — the undetermined embodiment — of a certain attitude toward life and world — the attitude which finds them worthy of *infinite* repetition. An *Übermensch,* and only an *Übermensch,* would be so well disposed to himself and the world that he would crave *nothing* more fervently than the eternal repetition of his life, not even the life of God or the gods.

The Hidden Agenda

It would be a great comfort to suppose that one could decide on textual grounds which of the competing versions of Nietzsche's perspectivism, eternal recurrence, and *Übermensch* is the correct one or is more nearly correct. No such comfort is available, however. That is because textual evidence can be found to support any of the rival interpretations, and because the attempt to establish authorial intention is if not futile then certainly defeasible in principle; but it seems to me that mostly it is because Nietzsche wanted to have it both ways and that this was not always clear to him.[4]

Consider a single telling illustration. Reflecting on his work Nietzsche says in *Ecce Homo:*

> The last thing I should promise would be to "improve" mankind. No new idols are erected by me; let the old ones learn what feet of clay mean. *Overthrowing idols* (my word for "ideals") — that comes closer to being part of my craft ... (EH Preface 2)

Remarks such as these could be taken to support, for example, the diagnostic construal of *Übermenschlichkeit* against the ideal-type reading; and similar remarks can also be found to support the last among the rival interpretations of eternal recurrence and perspectivism which were sketched in the previous section. Then, however, having just written the sentences above — that he is a shatterer of ideals not an "improver" of humankind — Nietzsche goes on to say almost immediately,

> The *lie* of the ideal has so far been the curse on reality; on account of it, mankind itself has become mendacious and false down to its most fundamental instincts — *to the point of worshipping the opposite values of those which alone would guarantee its health, its future, the lofty right to its future.* (ibid., my italics)

I do not see how this long final sentence can be read as consistent with the earlier sentence. Here he is not merely practicing his deconstructive craft, one which exposes feet of clay; here the shrill voice tells us that only "ideals" which are the opposite of those which have sustained our common heritage "would guarantee" humankind's "health, its future, the lofty *right* to its future." Contrast that last remark with "no new idols are created by me." Don't "the opposite" ideals, the opposite values of those which have sustained us heretofore still count as "ideals"? Are they not therefore the proposed "new idols" Nietzsche eschews offering?

There is another, perhaps more interesting reason for our inability to

---

[4] That *I* want to have it both ways *is* clear to me; for having acknowledged the difficulty of establishing an author's intention I immediately ascribe one to Nietzsche.

decide among certain competing versions of the reconstructive side of Nietzsche than conflicting textual evidence or Nietzsche's own ambivalence. This has to do with our preconceptions about the nature and role of philosophy itself; for just as Nietzsche has taught us that there are no immaculate perceptions of the world, there can be no immaculate perceptions of a text either. And if Nietzsche was right in asserting that we remain in the thrall of an essentially Platonic picture of the relation between representation and represented, then we should not be surprised to find ourselves "making sense" of Nietzsche in terms of an essentially Platonic picture of what it means to make philosophic sense.

Many commentators will be attracted to different versions of the *first* construals of perspectivism, eternal recurrence, and the *Übermensch* which were outlined in the previous section, because they regard offering theories of knowledge, theories about the nature of the universe, and theories of the ideal life as philosophical tasks proper, tasks it is our duty to undertake. From this perspective one has difficulty grasping how anyone would or should *care* about Nietzsche's remarks concerning perspective, eternal recurrence, and the *Übermensch* unless these remarks are recast either as proposing a theory — in some sense — or as contributions to a theory of perspectivism, the universe, and the ideal life. A more charitable version, on this view, is to say that one may *care* about Nietzsche's remarks on philosophical matters but the concern must remain a literary or historical one unless these remarks can be read as attempts to handle philosophic questions proper, unless they are construed as the doing of original philosophy.

Some commentators will be attracted to different versions of the *last* construals of perspectivism, eternal recurrence, and the *Übermensch* which were sketched in the previous section. Such readers will regard as quaint, or worse, attempts to interpret Nietzsche as a philosopher who proposes new answers to (putative) standard philosophic questions. They will have concluded previously that what are called the "perennial problems of philosophy" are just each generation's revisionist reading of the great monuments of the past, to make them conform to the current generation's interests by reading their predecessors' works as addressed to the very same matters which engage their current attention; but that is always a self-deceptive revisionist metahistory. Such commentators will conclude that those who read Nietzsche as a philosopher addressing textbook questions are really only trying to make Nietzsche's concerns and insights conform to their own foundationalist conception of philosophy as a Platonic-Cartesian-Kantian undertaking. And they will see this as pointless and naive, since Nietzsche attempted to liberate us precisely from the notion that the Platonic-Cartesian-Kantian enterprise is worth undertaking, that it still has any point, that there *are* problems of knowledge, or morals, or ontology which are left over after the present state of "knowledge," social practices, have been subtracted from our common vocabulary. They will read Nietzsche as having performed the therapeutic function of showing us that only on a certain optional conception of "philosophy" are there any metahistorical "perennial problems" at all; and they will regard him as among the first in a line of liberating voices — along with Kierkegaard's and James', Dewey's and Heidegger's, Wittgenstein's and Derrida's, Rorty's and Foucault's — which tried to tell us that we can abandon without loss the need to satisfy our Platonic yearning, our felt need to see philosophy as the mirror of nature.

Which commentators are right? Can one decide such a question? Is it a good question?

There is no fact of the matter which will tell us who is right here. If the foundationalists continue to prevail over the therapists then it will be business as usual. If the therapeutic lineage prevails that will simply mean that Kierkegaard and James will be read more earnestly than (the *begeisterte* side of) Hegel and (the dialectical side of) Marx, Dewey and Heidegger more earnestly than Russell and Husserl, that the later Wittgenstein will be read as defeating his own *Tractatus,* that Derrida, Rorty, and Foucault will be read with as much seriousness by students of philosophy as is now expended on Quine, Kripke, and Rawls. We shall then come to see the Platonic picture as something which held us captive for two thousand years but which no longer seduces us; and "if that day comes, it will seem as quaint to treat a man's knowledge as a special relation between his mind and its object as it now does to treat his goodness as a special relation between his soul and God."[5]

If that day ever comes, we shall be writing our revisionist history of our discipline, one in which Nietzsche will have been the first to try to show the fly the way out of the fly-bottle.

University of California
Riverside

---

[5] R. Rorty, *Consequences of Pragmatism* (University of Minnesota Press, 1982), p.33.

Gianni Vattimo

Nietzsche and Contemporary Hermeneutics

1. There are many good reasons to support not only the thesis that Nietzsche has contributed decisively to the rise and development of contemporary hermeneutic ontology but, more radically, that the very sense of the Nietzsche-Renaissance which has taken place in these last decades is the full inclusion of Nietzsche within this philosophical trend. I am perfectly aware that the very meaning of the expression "hermeneutic ontology" would require clearer and more precise explanations; in fact it is difficult to see whether or not this "school" of contemporary thought is unified by a basic set of assumptions. I propose to leave unsolved this problem, for the excellent "hermeneutic" reason that we know approximately what we mean when speaking of hermeneutics and hermeneutic ontology — this last term is better suited to indicate not only a technical discipline related to the exegesis and interpretation of texts, but a specific philosophical orientation. In this wide sense, hermeneutics includes Heidegger and Gadamer, Paul Ricoeur or the Italian Luigi Pareyson, and, going backwards, Schleiermacher and Dilthey; and even, in more recent times, Hans Robert Jauss, Apel, Habermas and Richard Rorty; in an even wider sense we can also include Foucault and Derrida.

If this is our *Vor-verständnis,* that is, our pre-comprehension of what hermeneutics means, the effort to show how and why Nietzsche is to be included in it will help pinpoint and qualify in a more articulate way the contents of this pre-comprehension; and it will also help to clarify the very meaning of Nietzsche's thought, as I will try to show. We can start agreeing that what we call hermeneutic ontology in contemporary philosophy is the philosophical trend which takes as its central theme the phenomenon of interpretation, considered as the essential trait of human existence and as the very basis for the critique and "destruction" of traditional metaphysics (in the sense in which Heidegger, in *Sein und Zeit,* speaks of a destruction of the history of ontology). This provisional definition is wide enough to include, with all their distinctions, the philosophers I mentioned above, and it also fits Nietzsche. It is obvious that many of the most characteristic theses of Nietzsche, above all the statement "there are no facts, only interpretations," can be quoted as evident examples of a hermeneutic philosophy. The same is true of other theses and themes in the work of the young Nietzsche, and in those of the period between *Human, All-Too-Human* (1) and *The Gay Science* (54).[1] This does not mean, merely, that we can show many hermeneutic themes in Nietzsche's works; my point is more radical, and in this form, as far as I know, it has not yet been proposed — even if we could maintain that it is implicitly accepted by many Nietzsche interpreters. What I mean is that the only possible way to place Nietzsche in the history of modern philosophy is to consider him as belonging to the "school" of hermeneutic ontology.

It could be objected that problems of historiographical collocation are not essential to the understanding of a philosopher, because they serve only the purposes of teaching philosophy. I would answer that precisely the development of a hermeneutic self-consciousness in philosophy has shown that the historiographical work expended on the materials of the past is a cognitive activity of great relevance. This can also be seen specifically in the case of Nietzsche. The current popularity of Nietzsche's philosophy is full of ambiguities. Of course, this proves that his thought is still very much alive and open to multiple "uses," suitable to our present situation. But these ambiguities — which allow to quote Nietzsche in support of and against almost every philosophical thesis — show that there is also a need for clarification. Thus the difficulties of placing Nietzsche in a clear position within a handbook of contemporary philosophy is not only a practical problem for philosophy historians, but it reflects the present situation of the *Nietzsche-Forschung* and its earlier development as well.

In its first stage, the reception of Nietzsche's thought has not been a specifically philosophical phenomenon, but rather a predominantly literary or generally "cultural" one. In his essay on *The Essence of Philosophy* (1907) Dilthey places Nietzsche in a list alongside of Carlyle, Emerson, Ruskin, Tolstoy, and Maeterlinck, considering them "philosophical writers" or a mixture of philosophers and poets. This literary "reception" of Nietzsche's thought was widespread in the ealy decades of this century (D'Annunzio and Papini in Italy, the *George Kreis* in Germany, etc.). This stage was followed by the nazi interpretation of Nietzsche — led by Alfred Baeumler — which

---

[1] Nietzsche's works will be quoted by title and number of section or aphorism; the posthumous notes will be quoted on the basis of the edition published by K. Schlechta, *Werke* (München: Hanser, 1969).

gained a wide popularity; even György Lukács can be considered, paradoxically, as one of its supporters, at least in the sense that, although evaluating Nietzsche differently, he considers the Nietzsche of Baeumler as the true Nietzsche. A large part of the post-war *Nietzsche-Forschung* is dominated by the problem of freeing his image from the nazi masks, also on the basis of a renewed contact with the original texts of the posthumous works. The current debate on Nietzsche refers to this rediscovery (largely influenced by some anti-nazi Nietzsche interpretations of the 1930s and 1940s, such as those of Jaspers, Löwith, Heidegger, Bataille), and shows that Nietzsche has not yet been framed within a definite historiographical scheme. The thesis I propose here is that the problem of Nietzsche's historiographical collocation can be solved by regarding him as belonging to the development of hermeneutic ontology.

This thesis has to confront the current ways of interpreting Nietzsche, which, apart from the idea of a "hermeneutic" Nietzsche, are essentially two: an interpretation (we could call it the "French Nietzsche," mainly represented by Deleuze, but also including Foucault, Klossowski, and influenced by Bergson and Bataille) which tends to regard Nietzsche within the framework of an "energetic" or "vitalistic" ontology (to this view are also related interpreters such as Pautrat, Rey, S. Kofman); the other one, which accepts and develops the Heideggerian interpretation of Nietzsche, presents him as the philosopher of technique, of the will to power considered as the will to organize and dominate the whole world, in a totally arbitrary way. In Heidegger's terms, Nietzsche is the accomplisher of Western metaphysics *because* he regards the modern technique as unconditioned will to power.

This subdivision seems to leave aside some very important interpretations of Nietzsche's thought, such as those of Löwith and Jaspers, or all the interpretations (including, I think, those of Kaufmann) which regard Nietzsche as a psychologist, a "master of suspicion." I maintain that the main contents of these interpretations, too, can be included in what I call the "hermeneutic Nietzsche": thus, not only psychology and suspicion (which represent the unmasking aspect of Nietzsche's hermeneutics), but also many of the still valid contents of Löwith's and Jasper's views; for instance the idea of eternal recurrence, which is a dominant theme in Löwith, is clearly involved with the problem of the overcoming of metaphysics, which is central in the hermeneutic view of Nietzsche's philosophy.

But, even if we assume that it is possible to summarize the current interpretations of Nietzsche within the scheme I propose (vitalistic-technological-hermeneutic), nonetheless a question remains: why should we prefer the "hermeneutic Nietzsche"? Very generally speaking, it seems to me that the interpretation centered on hermeneutics comprehends (includes and understands) more aspects of Nietzsche's philosophy than any other, and avoids contradictions and ambiguities which inhere in the others. So the vitalistic interpretation developed by the French authors has the disadvantage to take the most "metaphysical" aspect of Nietzsche's philosophy, the idea of eternal recurrence, too seriously; it is not obvious at all that Nietzsche intended this doctrine to be read as a "description" of the true reality of being. The thesis that there are no facts, only interpretations, is probably only an interpretation itself, "and so much the better" (BGE 22). Can we really think that Nietzsche's polemic against all kinds of metaphysics (all kinds of "true" essence of reality) resolves itself into a theory stating that the true reality of all being is *fluxus* and will to power? As to the "technological Nietzsche," its limit is that it involves a still strongly subjectivistic notion of the will: the subject of the will to power, who wants to take possession of the whole world by means of technology, is still "human all too human," is the *bisherige Mensch* which Nietzsche planned to overcome. If we read the notes which Nietzsche wrote, in the last period, on "Der Wille zur Macht als Kunst," we see that the will to power, being regarded as art, is to be understood as an experience in which the subject itself undergoes a process of deconstruction (and, maybe, of liberation), which has nothing, or very little, to do with the strong will to plan and organize the world by means of technology.

There is, nevertheless, some other objection which can be raised against the "hermeneutic Nietzsche": namely, and above all, the fact that neither Gadamer in *Wahrheit und Methode* (where he retraces the forerunners of contemporary hermeneutic ontology, such as Dilthey or Husserl), nor Heidegger himself in his courses on Nietzsche seem to consider Nietzsche as a "hermeneutic" thinker. This fact, which, at least in the case of Heidegger, should be discussed in more detail (Heidegger's position towards Nietzsche as the last thinker of metaphysics is full of ambiguities), is ultimately related to another important aspect of the question of what Nietzsche means to today's hermeneutics: namely the fact that, neither Gadamer, nor, in a more subtle way, Heidegger seem to be aware of the nihilistic implications of hermeneutic ontology. When for instance Heidegger speaks of the necessity of *"das Sein als den Grund des Seienden fahren zu lassen"* — "forgetting Being as Foundation,"[2] he clearly grazes the borders of nihilism: if we do not want to run the risk of remaining within metaphysics which identifies Being with beings, Being has to be thought of only in terms of rememoration: Being is something which always is (already) gone, and therefore, in fact, *is* not (longer with us).

---

[2] M. Heidegger, *Zur Sache des Denkens* (Tübingen: Niemeyer, 1969) p. 6.

Is this not nihilism? The connection of hermeneutics and nihilism should be discussed in much more detail; but I wanted to point out that the problem of whether or not Nietzsche is a hermeneutic thinker involves this question, i.e. is there a deep connection between nihilism and hermeneutics, a connection which has not been recognized by Heidegger and Gadamer themselves, and which, in case there is, can affect the sense of hermeneutics as a philosophy?

In short, the title "Nietzsche and contemporary hermeneutics" alludes to a twofold possible development: first of all it suggests a way of giving Nietzsche a more precise collocation within the history of contemporary thought, provoking at the same time a reorganization of the current interpretations of Nietzsche's philosophy; secondly, the inclusion of Nietzsche in hermeneutic ontology gives rise to a whole host of effects within this field; more specifically, it can determine the development of hermeneutics towards the nihilistic issues which are involved in its essence but are not yet expliticly recognized.

2. Obviously I do not venture to develop here all the themes sketched above. In a much less pretentious way, I will try to adduce some arguments in order to show, first, the contents of what can be called Nietzsche's hermeneutic philosophy and, secondly, the reasons for its actuality in connection with hermeneutical problems today.

For the sake of brevity, I propose to define Nietzsche's hermeneutics through some major "contradictions" peculiar to it. The term "contradictions" is perhaps excessive; they can be considered polar tensions, as it were, which express contrasting exigencies that Nietzsche recognized and maintained in spite of the logical need for unity and coherence. I will try to show that these "contradictions" are also crucial for contemporary hermeneutic ontology, although in a different sense.

(a) The first "contradiction" opposes the ideal of historical knowledge sketched in the second *Unzeitgemässe Betrachtung* to what one could call "the philosophy of masks" which Nietzsche develops starting from *Über Wahrheit und Lüge im aussermoralischen Sinn* onwards. In the second *Unzeitgemässe Betrachtung,* Nietzsche's contribution to the maturation of hermeneutic philosophy consists in the discovery of the historical essence (Nietzsche would say: *vital* essence) of historiography. To know history is a historical act, which does not simply mirror the events of the past, but creates historical innovation as well. This "discovery," as it were, has many implications. One of them is that, when historiography forgets its vital character, and more generally speaking, culture and education become pure reconstructions of the past, society and individuals fall into *décadence*. The excess of historiographical knowledge without an adequate capacity of original creation is like the excess of undigested food in the stomach; in Hegelian terms we could say, that there is no adequation between content and form, or between the inner and the external aspects of personality. The conclusion of the essay is that the past has to be interpreted from a point of view capable of forgetting in order to create. The ideal of historical knowledge which is the result of the second *Unzeitgemässe Betrachtung,* is definable in terms of *strong stylistic unity:* "Only from the point of view of the highest force of the present you can interpret the past" (*Nur aus der höchsten Kraft der Gegenwart dürft ihr das Vergangene deuten*).[3] The extreme opposite of this view can be seen in one of the letters Nietzsche wrote from Turin to Jakob Burckhardt when madness has already overrun his mind, in the days in which he used to sign his letters with names such as Dionysos, the Crucified, Caesar. In that letter Nietzsche says explicitly that he is "all the names in history" (*Werke* III:1351). Of course, as the rest of this letter shows clear symptoms of madness, it would be too great a risk to consider it as a document of Nietzsche's authentic thought. Nevertheless, I think we should do so because, during the period which separates the second *Unzeitgemässe Betrachtung* from the letter of 1889, Nietzsche had developed a philosophy which made it possible for him to say that he was "all the names in history." This is what I propose to call the philosophy of the mask, whose premises are to be found first of all in the revaluation of historicism which is one of the meanings of *Human, All-Too-Human.*

In the second *Unzeitgemässe Betrachtung* Nietzsche has described the decadent character of modern personality through the metaphor of the man who considers history as a storehouse of theatrical costumes which can be worn and taken off arbitrarily, because they are considered as pure masks, with no deep relation to the inner content of the person. In *Human, All-Too-Human* and in the following works, it seems to me that Nietzsche discovers the legitimacy of this attitude of free identification with the forms of historical past, an identification which reverses the ideal of a strong stylistic unity he had adopted in the second *Unzeitgemässe Betrachtung*. It is true that, in *Human, All-Too-Human* (one of the main texts we have to refer to in order to appreciate Nietzsche's "historicism"), he speaks of the construction of personality in terms of "seeing oneself as a necessary chain of rings" (HH I: 292); this seems to recall the "highest force of the present" quoted above. But, in the same page of *Human, All-Too-Human,* Nietzsche's attitude is rather that of a genealogical tolerance for the *whole* past of mankind. This impression is confirmed by the aphorism (HH II: 223) which refers, with a diametrically

---

[3] *Unzeitgemässe Betrachtungen* II: *Vom Nutzen und Nachteil der Historie für das Leben,* ch. 6.

opposite sense, to the same image of Heraclitus' river which Nietzsche had recalled in the second *Unzeitgemässe Betrachtung*; while there Nietzsche used the image of the river, where *panta rei,* in order to show the paralyzing effect of the excess of historical knowledge upon man's creativity, here he says that, because of the essentially historical constitution of our being, if we want to plunge into its most peculiar and personal essence, we have to accept that we can never plunge twice into the same river. To know ourselves does not mean to grasp our interiority in an act of introspection, but to become conscious of the potentially infinite past which constitutes our individuality.

Both the doctrine of the metaphorical origin of truth (in the essay *Über Wahrheit und Lüge im aussermoralischen Sinn*) and the idea of art elaborated in works like *Human, All-Too-Human, The Gay Science,* not only confirm the view that Nietzsche corrected his view of historicism as expressed in the second *Unzeitgemässe Betrachtung,* but also suggest that he is inclined to view the relation to the past in almost the same terms he had violently criticized in that early text. The "good will of appearance," of which *The Gay Science* speaks in aphorism 107, expresses this same attitude: history is the storehouse of masks and appearances which, far from violating the "authentic" essence of individuality, constitute it and are its only richness. Of course Nietzsche's substantial anti-historicism remains: he refuses to accept the idea that history is a providential and necessary series of events, whose result and culmination would be our civilization. We are not the *telos* of history, but its casual production, which means that in order to know ourselves we have to plunge into the past, but without *strong* criteria of order or choice. This fact intensifies the impression that one of the constitutive traits of the *Freigeist* (which is an earlier form of the later *Übermensch*) is the very capacity of playing with historical forms taken as *masks,* at least in the sense that they do not have any internal order and necessity.

In parallel with this rediscovery of historicism (in the limited sense I mentioned), Nietzsche develops, from *Human, All-Too-Human* onwards, his critique of the pretended unity and ultimacy of the subject and of self-consciousness. The extreme radicalization of this critique is to be found in the posthumous notes of *The Will to Power,* where Nietzsche describes the subject as the mobile play of conflicting forces (*Werke* III:537). Nietzsche maintains that it is problematic to speak of a subject at all: maybe we could do without this *abkürzende Formel* which is the little word *ich* (III:480). For the late Nietzsche, the subject is nothing more than a "surface effect" whose very necessity for the ends of life is doubtful. Besides, there are no facts, only interpretations, but interpretation is not to be thought of as an action of a subject; subject is itself something *Hinzu-Erdichtetes,* added poetically by interpretation or invention (III:903).Nietzsche thus reaches a view which is diametrically opposed to the second *Unzeitgemässe Betrachtung:* the relation to the past is no longer conceived in terms of the strong constitution of a closed horizon, but as the act of playing with historical forms, considered, more or less explicitly, as masks.

Nevertheless, the need for a "center" of interpretation is still very deeply felt by Nietzsche. The world of the interplay of forces, of the continually readjusted perspectives, can also be described as the *Machinerie* of the industrial world, dominated by a "more and more economic exploitation of man and mankind" (III:628). According to Nietzsche this world needs a counter-movement, which is the ideal of *Übermensch.* The main characteristic of *Übermensch* recalls very clearly the ideal of the closed and strong horizon described in the second *Unzeitgemässe Betrachtung.* This means that, together with the development of his radical critique of subjectivity, Nietzsche still holds the opposite exigence, that is, the need of a strong center of the interpretive activity in order to give sense to the world of the will to power, considered as the interplay of conflicting perspectives.

(b) The second "contradiction" in Nietzsche's hermeneutics opposes the so-called *Schule des Verdachts* (school of suspicion) to the unmasking of the very notion of truth. The school of suspicion is summarized in the title of the first aphorism of *Human, All-Too-Human:* "chemistry of ideas and feelings," but also of values, taboos, metaphysical structures and so on. All these systems of values and structures are, in Nietzsche's view, effects of the processes of sublimation which we can unmask, now that God is dead. The contradiction arises because the value of truth, too, undergoes a process of unmasking, so that the end of the process can be thought of neither in terms of the critique of ideology, nor in terms of the Freudian "*wo es war soll ich werden*" (at least in its pre-Lacanian interpretation). The unmasking activity of the thought cannot lead us to any *Grund,* to any truth beyond ideologies and psychological sublimations, because the very idea of truth is among the values which we unmask as "human, all too human." Even the idea that, at the end of the process of unmasking, we could find that "life," or the self-preservation impulse, or something similar, has to be abandoned: there is no "subject" which could have the will to self-preservation; nor is there something like "life," but only historically determined forms of life, themselves "produced," not "primitive."

In this case too, as in the first contradiction, one could get the impression that we are not facing an authentic contradiction, but only an evolution in Nietzsche's thought from the idea of chemistry, in *Human, All-Too-Human,* to the loss of the very idea of *Begründung,* in the last works. (This could be confirmed by a reference to the *Twilight of Idols,* in which Nietzsche explicitly says that the true world in the end has become a fable.) But to the last, Nietzsche's unmasking (or demythologizing) attitude remains an essential trait of his thought, justifying Nietzsche's image as *Kulturkritiker* which has been most popular among his readers. Therefore, we are likely to accept — and this could be corroborated by a more extended quotation of texts — that Nietzsche has maintained, until the end, that there is no fundamental truth and, at the same time, that the task of thought is unmasking and demythologizing.

(c) The last "contradiction" or polar tension I want to point out is related in the deepest sense to the very core of Nietzsche's thought; it is the contradiction between the thesis that there are no facts, only interpretations, and the metaphysics of the will to power and of eternal recurrence. This contradiction repeats, in a slightly different form, the other two, but also leads them to their extreme consequences. In fact, both the idea of subjectivity Nietzsche seems to maintain in spite of his critique of it, and the need for an unmasking thought despite his denial of any fundamental truth, can be brought back to the substantial tendency of conceiving the interpretive character of all reality in a metaphysical sense. Will to power and eternal recurrence appear as a *metaphysical* description of the *true reality* of a world in which there are no facts, only interpretations; but, taken in a metaphysical sense, they are *not* only interpretations. This is probably one of the reasons why Heidegger considered Nietzsche as a thinker still belonging to the history of metaphysics. Even the "nazi" mis-interpretation of Nietzsche's philosophy could be brought back to this contradiction: if one assumes the universality of interpretation as a metaphysical description of an ontological structure, the result cannot be but a view of reality as a permanent conflict of forces, in which only the strongest is right.

3. If we agree, at least hypothetically, that Nietzsche's hermeneutics is characterized by these main contradictions, the last point we have to discuss is: are these contradictions — and with them the entire hermeneutics of Nietzsche — relevant for the hermeneutic ontology of today? I will develop this point in an extremely summary way, by indicating some problems which, at least in my view, are decisive for contemporary hermeneutics. As to the contradiction (a), which can be summarized as the opposition between *Übermensch* and the twilight (or decline) of subjectivity, I propose to recognize its actuality in the fact that contemporary hermeneutics, e.g. the theory of Hans Georg Gadamer, runs the risk of considering all possible experience of truth as the simple articulation and development of the pre-comprehension (or prejudices), given

to each individual with the language he speaks, this language being the only possible reality of what the tradition has called *logos*. The notion of *logos* identified with the actual life of the historical language of a community has been developed by Gadamer in the essays written after *Wahrheit und Methode*;[4] *logos* conceived in this sense involves the characteristics of both Heidegger's *Geschick* and Hegel's objective spirit, as well as the everyday language of analytic philosophy. But this thesis of Gadamer seems to forget (as Habermas remarked) that this conception of *logos* has not the ideal unity it should have if it had to function as a *normative* horizon. This means that individuals within a linguistic community are faced again and again with the problem (very clearly pointed out by Heidegger in *Sein und Zeit*) of "deciding" about the truth. Therefore, hermeneutics cannot simply identify the *logos* with the historical language of a community; truth and *logos* need a reference to the inner evidence of consciousness as well. This polarity has many analogies with the other one I pointed out in Nietzsche, between the universalization of the pure interplay of forces (i.e., the social rules of true and false) and the "transcending" power of *Übermensch*.

As to the second "contradiction" (unmasking vs. elimination of the very notion of truth), its analogies in contemporary hermeneutics seem to be recognizable in the recurrent tendencies to associate hermeneutics with the critique of ideology, for instance the work of Karl Otto Apel.[5] Insofar as the critique of ideology involves the ideal of the complete self-transparency of the subject, it is totally opposed to hermeneutics. Nevertheless, as in the case of the analogous "contradiction" in Nietzsche, it is difficult to decide whether we are faced here with a pure misunderstanding of hermeneutics or with a more general problem involved in every theory of interpretation.

Finally, the third "contradiction" I pointed out, i.e. that between universality of interpretation and the metaphysical sense of notions like eternal recurrence and will to power, has possible analogies in contemporary hermeneutics when the question arises as to the nihilistic implications of a hermeneutic ontology. It seems to me that the very "resistance" I mentioned above, to include Nietzsche among the precursors of hermeneutic ontology, reveals the persisting tendency to interpret this ontology (and its basis in Heidegger's thought) in a metaphysical sense which refuses all possible nihilistic implica-

---

[4] See, for instance, the essays included in *Vernunft im Zeitalter der Wissenschaft* (Frankfurt: Suhrkamp, 1976).

[5] I refer especially to the essays included in *Transformation der Philosophie* (Frankfurt: Suhrkamp, 1973). For a more extended discussion of Apel's theses, see G. Vattimo, *Al di là del soggetto* (Milan: Feltrinelli, 1984²), ch. 4.

tions. Hermeneutic ontology appears to be exposed to the same risks Nietzsche ran when, although having theorized that there are no facts, only interpretations, he strove to demonstrate, even on the basis of the physical sciences, the "reality" of eternal recurrence.

Maybe the fact of retracing these analogies in Nietzsche does not help us to solve the problems of contemporary hermeneutics; but it can help us to get a clearer awareness of them and realize in a more radical way the possible implications of what can be called the "hermeneutic turn" in modern philosophy.

University of Torino

Robert C. Solomon

A More Severe Morality: Nietzsche's Affirmative Ethics

> She told me herself that she had no morality, — and I thought she had, like myself, a more severe morality than anyone.
> Nietzsche, in a letter to Paul Rée, 1882.

A mad dog, foaming at the moustache and snarling at the world; that is how the American artist David Levine portrays Friedrich Nietzsche in his well-known caricature in *The New York Review of Books*. It is not so different in its malicious intent, nor further wrong in its interpretation of Nietzsche, than a good number of scholarly works. This is indeed the traditional portrait — the unconsummated consummate immoralist, the personally gentle even timid arch-destroyer. Of course, Nietzsche himself made adolescent comments about his own destructiveness not infrequently — throughout the whole of *Ecce Homo*, for example. Nevertheless, these give a false impression of his intentions as well as of the good philosophical sense to be made of his works.

In recent years, we have been treated to a rather systematic white-washing of Nietzsche. Gone is the foam and the snarl; indeed, what has come to replace the "revaluation of all values" has become so tame that, a certain impatience for scholarship aside, one of these new Nietzsches (perhaps not the French one) would find himself very much at home on most university campuses. This new Nietzsche, founded by Walter Kaufmann and now promoted by Richard Schacht, is the champion of honesty against the forces of hypocrisy.[1] Or, more recently, he is Harold Alderman's benign Californish guru, urging us simply to "be ourselves," preferably by reading Heidegger.[2] This picture is no less false than the first, but it has the undeniable virtue of welcoming

---

[1] Walter Kaufmann, *Nietzsche: Philosopher, Psychologist, Antichrist*, 4th ed. (Princeton: Princeton University Press, 1974); Richard Schacht, *Nietzsche* (London: Routledge & Kegan Paul, 1983).
[2] Harold Alderman, *Nietzsche's Gift* (Columbus: Ohio University Press, 1977).

Nietzsche, belatedly, back to the fold of professional philosophers. Better respectable than rabid, one might suppose, though I would guess Nietzsche himself would opt for the latter.

The new French Nietzsche, on the other hand, enjoys the *philosophe* at the extremes, almost beyond the limits of the imaginable, an adolescent implosion of forces dancing on the edge of nothingness. He is, accordingly, a thoroughly playful Nietzsche. He is the "anti-Oedipe" as well as the "antichrist," a deconstructionist, a Derridaidian, a Dada-idian, before his time. He does not destroy but rather revels in the destruction we have already inflicted upon ourselves. He is a burst of energy rather than a philosopher, an explosion instead of a visionary. Most of all, he plays, and he reminds us of the importance of dancing and the unimportance of serious scholarship and Truth. And, we are assured (for example, by David Allison in his introduction to "The New Nietzsche"), he is wholly outside of that somber and intellectually fraudulent onto-theological tradition that he so playfully attacks, but in which we less imaginative and playless scholarly souls are still enmired.[3]

Perhaps. But of all the authors in German history, Nietzsche must surely be the most historical and even "timely," as well as one of the most solemn (as opposed to bourgeois "serious"). He was, from all evidence, incapable of even the uptight version of dancing propounded by his Zarathustra. His playfulness seemed largely limited to the scholarly joke. Lou Andreas Salomé once described him:

...a light laugh, a quiet way of speaking, and a cautious, pensive way of walking... He took pleasure in the refined forms of social intercourse... But in it all lay a penchant for disguise... I recall that when I first spoke with him his formal manner shocked and deceived me. But I was not deceived for long by this lonesome man who only wore his mask as unalterably as someone coming from the desert and mountains wears the cloak of the worldly-wise...[4]

Playful, indeed. And as for "the tradition," as it has come to be called, Nietzsche as philosopher can be understood only within it, despite his unselfcritical megalomania about his own "untimely" and wholly novel importance.

It is decidedly *within* that somber philosophical tradition, typically traced in misleading linear fashion back to Socrates, that I want to try to understand Nietzsche's ethics. His reputation as arch-destroyer and philosophical outlaw

---

[3] David Allison (ed.), *The New Nietzsche* (New York: Dell, 1977).
[4] Lou Salomé (1882) quoted in Karl Jaspers, *Nietzsche* (Tucson: University of Arizona Press, 1965), pp. 37-38 and in R.C. Solomon (ed.), *Nietzsche* (New York: Doubleday, 1963), p.8

has so enveloped Nietzsche's notorious "reputation," largely at his own bidding, that the kernel of his moral philosophy — and I do insist on calling it that — has been lost. There is in Nietzsche, unmistakably, an ethics that is considerably more than nihilism or academic good fellowship or playfulness, an ethics that is very much part of "the tradition." It is, however, a brand of ethics that had and has been all but abandoned in the wake of Kant and the anal compulsiveness of what is now called "rationality" in ethics. It is this other brand of ethics, for which Nietzsche quite properly failed to find a name, that I would like to indicate in this essay.

Nietzsche's Nihilism and Morality

Nietzsche's novelty is to be found, in part, in his energetic descriptions of what he calls "nihilism." It is, first of all, a cultural experience, a profound sense of disappointment not only, as some ethicists would have it, in the failure of philosophy to justify moral principles, but in the fabric of life as such, the "widespread sensibility of our age" more sympathetically described by Camus half a century later. It is also, Nietzsche keeps reminding us, a stance to be taken up as well as a phenomenon to be described. Zarathustra, in one of his more belligerent moments, urges us to "push what is falling" and, in his notes, Nietzsche urges us to promote "a complete nihilism," in place of the incomplete nihilism in which we now live (WP 28). Here again we note Nietzsche's self-conscious "timeliness," and his devotion to a tradition dedicated to completeness in ethics.

"Nihilism," obvious etymology aside, does not mean "accepting nothing." Like most philosophical terms, subsequently raised to an isolated and artificial level of abstraction, this one does its work in particular contexts, in specific perspectives, often as a kind of accusation. Some traditional but much-in-the-news Christians use the term as a more or less crude synonym for "secular humanism," on the (false) assumption that a man without God must be a man without Christian values as well. (The dubious argument by Ivan Karamazov: "if there is no God, then everything is permitted.") But note that I say "Christian" values, for the accuser might well allow, indeed insist, that the nihilist does have values — subjective, self-serving and secularly narrow-minded though they be. (Brother Mitya, perhaps: hardly a paragon of virtue.) Similarly, an orthodox Jewish friend of mine refers as "nihilists" to any people without a self-conscious if not obsessive sense of tradition, assuming that others must lack in their experience what he finds so essential in his own. Marxists use the term (sometimes but not always along with "bourgeois individualism") to indict those who do not share their class-conscious values. Aesthetes use it to knock the Philistines, and my academic colleagues use it to chastize anyone with looser standards and higher grade averages than themselves. Stanley Rosen attacks it at book length without ever saying exactly what's wrong with it, except that it falls far short of his own rather pretentious search for Hegelian absolute truth.[5]

If Nietzsche made us aware of anything in ethics, it is the importance of *perspectives,* the need to see all concepts and values *in context.* How odd, then, that the key concepts of Nietzsche's own ethics have been so routinely blown up to absolute — that is non perspectival — proportions. Nihilism is an accusation, in context. Outside of all contexts, it is nothing (which, of course, leads to some quaint and cute Parmenidean word-play.) As Blanchot has written, nihilism is a particular achievement of a particular sort of society.[6] It becomes a world-hypothesis only at the expense of losing what is most urgent and cleansing in Nietzsche, the attack on the transcendental pretension of understanding the world "in itself" on the basis of our own limited and limiting moral experience.

Nietzsche's nihilism is an accusation *within* the context of traditional ethics. (What other kind of ethics could there be?) It points to a tragic or at any rate damnable hollowness in "the moral point of view," which we might anticipate by asking why moral philosophers ever became compelled to talk in such a peculiar fashion. Indeed, it is part and parcel of the whole history of ethics that morality is emphatically *not* just "a point of view"; it is necessary and obligatory. Such talk already betrays a fatal compromise; "perspectivism" and Morality are warring enemies, not complementary theses. What is morality, that it has been forced and has been able to hide behind a veneer of pluralism, to search for "reasons" for its own necessity which — successful or not — leave the acceptance of morality unchallenged?

What is morality? This, perhaps more than any other question, guided Nietzsche's ethics. It is the concept of morals that intrigues Nietzsche: how morals ever became reduced to Morality, how the virtues ever got melted together into the shapeless form of Virtue. But, as I shall argue shortly, there are many meanings of "morality" just as there are many different sorts of morals. It is the terms themselves — but not just the terms — that is most in

---

[5] Stanley Rosen, *Nihilism* (New Haven: Yale University Press, 1969); cf. his more recent *G.W.F. Hegel: An Introduction to his Science of Wisdom* (New Haven: Yale University Press, 1974).
[6] Maurice Blanchot, "The Limits of Experience: Nihilism," in his *L'Entretien Infini,* repr. in Allison, pp. 121-128.

question here. The definition of "morality" that preoccupies Nietzsche, and which I shall be employing here, is the definition provided by Kant — of morality as a set of universal, categorical principles of practical reason. "Morals," on the other hand, is a term much less precise, and I shall be using that term much as Hume used it in his *Enquiry*: morals are those generally agreeable or acceptable traits that characterize a good person — leaving quite open the all-important non-conceptual question what is to count (in what context) as a good person. Ethics, finally, I take to be the overall arena in which morality and morals and other questions concerning the good life and how to live it are debated. Morality in its Kantian guise may not be at all essential to ethics; indeed, one might formulate Nietzsche's concern by asking how the subject of ethics has so easily been converted into Moral Philosophy, that is, the Kantian analysis of Morality rather than Hume's somewhat pagan celebration of the virtues, which is not to say that Nietzsche would have felt very much at home with the Scotsman either, whatever their philosophical affinities.

In his recent book, *After Virtue*,[7] Alasdair MacIntyre has attacked Nietzsche and nihilism together, as symptoms of our general decay ("decadence" would be too fashionable and thus too positive a term for our moral wretchedness). But in doing so, he has also rendered Nietzsche's own thesis in admirably contemporary form; morality is undone, hollow, an empty sham for which philosophers busily manufacture "reasons" and tinker with grand principles if only to convince themselves that something might still be there. What philosophers defensively call "the moral point of view," is a camouflaged retreat. It serves only to hide the vacuousness of the moral prejudices they serve. Morality is no longer a "tablet of virtues" but a *tabula rasa*, for which we are poorly compensated by the insistence that it is itself necessary. Or, in Hume's terms, morality is the repository of those "monkish" virtues, whose degrading, humiliating effects are disguised by the defenses of reason.[8] For Hume as for Nietzsche, "some passions are merely stupid, dragging us down with them." And this will be the area where an adequate understanding of morals will emerge, in the realm of passion rather than reason. The good person will emphatically not be the one who is expertly consistent in universalizing maxims according to the principles of practical reason.

---

[7] Alasdair MacIntyre, *After Virtue* (Notre Dame, IN.: University of Notre Dame Press, 1981).
[8] David Hume, *A Treatise of Human Nature* (Oxford: Oxford University Press, 1978), Book II, esp. pp. 297ff.

Nietzsche, Kant and Aristotle

Nihilism is not a thesis; it is a reaction. It is not a romantic "Nay-saying" so much as it is a feature of good old enlightenment criticism in the form of a critical phenomenology or a diagnostic hermeneutics. Indeed, in Germany romanticism and *Aufklärung* were never very clearly distinguished, except in rhetoric, and so too, beneath the bluster of nihilism a much more profound and, dare I say, reasonable Nietzsche can be discerned. In fact, I want to argue that Nietzsche might best be understood, perhaps ironically, in the company of that more optimistic decadent of ancient times — Aristotle, and in close contrast to the most powerful moral philosopher of modern times — Immanuel Kant. They were hardly nihilists; indeed they remain even today the two paradigms of morality, the two great proponents of all-encompassing ethical world views. Next to them, the contemporary fiddling with so-called "utilitarianism" seems, as Hegel complained in the *Phenomenology,* rather petty and devoid of anything deserving the honorific name "moral philosophy."[9]

It has always seemed to me perverse to read Aristotle and Kant as engaged in the same intellectual exercise, that is, to present and promote a *theory* of morality. They were, without question, both moralists; that is, they had the "moral prejudices" that Nietzsche discovers beneath every philosophical theory. This, of course, would not bother them (except perhaps the word "prejudices"). They were both also, Nietzsche would be the first to argue, *reactionaries,* trying to prop up with an ethics an *ethos* — an established way of life — that was already collapsing. To do so, both ethicists appealed to an overriding (if not absolute) *telos* of reason and rationality, the suspicious status of which Nietzsche deftly displays vis-à-vis Socrates in *Twilight of the Idols.* Both philosophers too saw themselves as defenders of "civilized" virtues in the face of the nihilists of their time, though Aristotle displays ample affinity with Protagoras and Kant had no hesitation about supporting Robespierre. But, nevertheless, there is a profound difference between these two great thinkers that too easily gets lost in the need to sustain the linear tradition that supposedly begins with Socrates, ignoring the dialectical conflict that is to be found even within Socrates himself. Aristotle and Kant represent not just two opposed ethical theories, "teleological" and "deontological" respectively, synthesized by the *telos* of rationality. They represent two opposed ways of life.

---

[9] G.W.F. Hegel, *The Phenomenology of Spirit,* trans. A.W. Miller (Oxford: Oxford University Press, 1977), see esp. pars. 559-562 and Hegel's attack on the Enlightenment emphasis on "the Useful" ("an abomination" and "utterly detestable").

Aristotle may be a long way from the Greece described by Homer, but the form of his ethics is still very much involved with the Homeric warrior tradition. The virtue of courage still deserves first mention in the list of excellences, and pride is still a virtue rather than a vice. It is an ethics for the privileged few, though Aristotle, unlike Nietzsche, had no need to announce this in a preface. But most important of all, it is an ethics that is not primarily concerned with rules and principles, much less *universal* rules and principles, categorical imperatives. Indeed, Aristotle's much-heralded discussion of the so-called "practical syllogism" in Book VI of the *Nicomachean Ethics* — in which something akin to principles universal in form (and as ethically invigorating as "eating dry foods is healthy") — is quite modest, hardly the cornerstone of his ethics, as some recent scholars have made it out to be.[10] Aristotle's ethics is not an ethics of principles, categorical or otherwise. It is an ethics of *practice,* a description of an actual *ethos* rather than an abstract attempt to define or create one. Ethos is by its very nature bound to a culture; Kantian ethics, by its pure rational nature but much to its peril, seems not to be. Of course, any philosopher can show how a practice is *really* a rule-governed activity, and then proceed to formulate, examine and criticize the rules.[11] Indeed, one might even show that children playing with their food follow certain rules, but to do so clearly is to misdescribe if not also misunderstand their activity.[12] But what is critical to an ethics of practice is not the absence of rules; it is rather the overriding importance of the concept of *excellence* or virtue (*aretē*). What Aristotle describes is the ideal citizen, the excellent individual who is already (before he studies ethics and learns to articulate principles of any kind) proud of himself and the pride of his family and community. He is surrounded by friends; he is the model of strength, if not only the physical prowess that was singularly important to Achilles (who was far from ideal in other virtues). He may have been a bit too "civilized" already for Nietzsche's Homeric fantasies, but he represents a moral type distinctively different from that described by Kant, two thousands years later. His ethics are his virtues; his excellence is his pride.

---

[10] See, for example, G.E.M. Anscombe in *Intention* (Oxford: Oxford University Press, 1957), esp. pp. 58-66, and John Cooper's rebuttal in his *Reason and Human Good in Aristotle* (Cambridge, Ma.: Harvard University Press, 1975).

[11] E.g. William Frankena, *Ethics,* 2nd ed. (Englewood Cliffs, N.J.: Prentice-Hall, 1973), pp. 62-67.

[12] The delightful use of this example is in MacIntyre, contrasting descriptive reports of practices with prescriptive rules.

Kant, on the other hand, is the outstanding moralist in a very different tradition. The warrior plays no role and presents us with no ideal; individual talents and the good fortune of having been "brought up well," which Aristotle simply presupposes, are ruled out of the moral realm from page one.[13] Kant's ethics is the ethics of the categorical imperative, the ethics of universal rational principles, the ethics of obedient virtue instead of the cultivation of the virtues. It is an ethics that minimizes differences and begins by assuming that we all share a common category of "humanity" and a common moral faculty of reason. The good man is the man who resists his "inclinations" and acts for the sake of duty and duty alone. This extreme criterion is qualified in a number of entertaining ways, for example, by suggesting that the rule that one should cultivate one's talents is itself an example of the categorical imperative and that one has a peculiar duty to pursue one's own happiness, if only so that one is thereby better disposed to fulfill one's duties to others.[14]

What I want to argue here should be, in part at least, transparent. Nietzsche may talk about "creating new values," but, as he himself often says, it is something of a return to an old and neglected set of values — the values of masterly virtue — that most concerns him. There are complications. We do not have the *ethos* of the *Iliad,* nor even the tamer *ethē* of Homer or Aristotle, nor for that matter even the bourgeois complacency of Kantian Königsberg with its definitive set of practices in which the very idea of an unconditional imperative is alone plausible. There is no context, in other words, within which the new virtues we are to "create" are to be virtues, for a virtue without a practice is of no more value than a word without a language, a gesture without a context. When Nietzsche insists on "creating new values," in other words, he is urging us on in a desperate state of affairs. He is rejecting the mediocre banality of an abstract ethics of principles, but he has no practice upon which to depend in advancing his renewed ethics of virtue. No practice, that is, except for the somewhat pretentious and sometimes absurd self-glorification of nineteenth century German romanticism, which Nietzsche rebukes even as he adopts it as his only available context.[15] This is no small

---

[13] Immanuel Kant, *Grounding for the Metaphysics of Morals,* trans. J.W. Ellington (Indianapolis: Hackett, 1981), part 1, p. 7.
[14] Ibid., p.12.
[15] E.g. "At first, I approached the modern world...*hopefully*. I understood...the philosophical pessimism of the nineteenth century as if it were the symptom of a

point: Nietzsche is not nearly so isolated nor so unique as he needs to think of himself. Dionysus, like "the Crucified," is an ideal only within a context, even if, in *Der Fall Nietzsche*, it seems to be a context defined primarily by rejection.

Nietzsche's nihilism is a reaction against a quite particular *conception* of morality, summarized in modern times in the ethics of Kant. Quite predictably, much of Judeo-Christian morality — or what is often called "Judeo-Christian morality" — shares this conception. It too is for the many, not just the few. It too treats all souls as the same, whether rational or not. It too dwells on abstractions, whether such categorical imperatives as "the Golden Rule" or the universal love called *agapē*, which applies to everyone and therefore to no one in particular. Hegel was not entirely wrong when, in an early essay, he had Jesus on the Mount deliver a sermon taken straight from *The Critique of Practical Reason*.[16] Nor was Kant deceiving himself when he looked with pride on his moral philosophy as the heart of Christian ethics, interpreting the commandment to love as well as the desire to be happy as nothing more nor less than instantiations of the categorical imperative, functions of practical reason rather than expressions of individual virtues and exuberance for life.[17]

Aristotle and Achilles versus Kant and Christianity. It is not a perfect match, but it allows us to explain Nietzsche's aims and Nietzsche's problems far better than the over-reaching nonsense about "the transvaluation of *all* values" and "Dionysus versus the Crucified." On the other hand, it is not as if Kant and Nietzsche are completely opposed. It is Kant who sets up the philosophical conditions for the Nietzschean reaction, not only by so clearly codifying the central theses to be attacked but also by conceptually undermin-

---

greater strength of thought, of more daring courage, and of a more triumphant *fullness of life*... What is romanticism? Every art and every philosophy may be considered a remedy and aid in the service of growing and struggling life, but there are two kinds of sufferers: first those who suffer from an *overfullness of life*... and then there are those who suffer from the *impoverishment of life*... To this dual need of the *latter* corresponds all romanticism...

The will to *eternalize* also requires a dual interpretation. First, it can come from gratitude and love ... But it can also be that tyrannic will [i.e. *ressentiment*] of one who is seriously ailing, struggling, and tortured..." (GS 370).

Cf. Novalis: "The world must be made more romantic. Then once more we shall discover its original meaning. To make something romantic... the lower self becomes identified with the higher self" (from *Fragments,* 1798).

[16] G.W.F. Hegel, "The Life of Jesus" (1795), trans. Peter Fuss (Notre Dame: University of Notre Dame Press, 1984).

[17] Kant, p.12.

ing the traditional supports of morality. The (*Aufklärung*) attack on authority ("heteronomy") and the emphasis on "autonomy" by Kant is a necessary precondition for Nietzsche's moral moves, however much the latter presents himself as providing a conception of morality which precedes, rather than presupposes, this Kantian move. It is Kant, of course, who so stresses the importance of the Will, which is further dramatized (to put it mildly) by Schopenhauer and which, again, Nietzsche attacks only by way of taking for granted its primary features. (Nietzsche's attacks on "the Will," especially "free will," deserve some special attention in this regard. "Character" and "will to power" are not the same as "will power.") It is Kant who rejects the support of morality by appeal to religion, arguing instead a dependency of the inverse kind, and though Nietzsche's now-tiresome "God is dead" hypothesis may be aimed primarily at the traditional thesis, the bulk of his moral arguments rather presuppose the Kantian inversion: religion as a rationalization, not the precondition, of moral thinking.

Meanings of Morality

It was Kant too, perhaps, who best exemplified the philosophical temptation to suppose that "morality" refers to a single, specific, unified phenomenon. Indeed, whether or not it even makes sense to speak of "moral*ties*," as Nietzsche often does, it is too easily assumed that "morality" refers to a single phenomenon, faculty, or feature of certain, if not all, societies. Moral theories and some specific rules may vary, according to this monolithic position, but Morality is that one single set of basic moral rules which all theories of morality must accept as a given. This is stated outright by Kant, at the beginning of his second *Critique* and his *Grounding for the Metaphysics of Morals*. Every society, one might reasonably suppose, has some "trump" set of rules and regulations which prohibit certain kinds of actions and are considered to be absolute, "categorical." Philosophers might argue whether there is a single rationale behind the variety of rules (a "utility principle" or some principle of authority). Others might challenge the alleged universality and disinterestedness of such principles, but morality everywhere is assumed to be the same, in form if not in content, or in at least intent, nevertheless. Indeed even Nietzsche, in his later works, is tempted by the monolithic image; his pluralistic view of a "tablet of virtues hanging over every people" is explained by his familiar exuberant account: "it is the expression of their Will to Power!" In his repeated "campaign against morality," he too makes it seem too much as if morality is a monolith rather than a complex set of phenomena whose differences may be as striking as their similarities.

What is in question and what ethics is about, according to moral philosophers since Kant, is the *justification* of moral principles, and along with this quest for justification comes the search for a single *ultimate* principle, a *summum bonum,* through which all disagreements and conflicts can be resolved. The question "what is morality?" gets solved in a few opening pages; the search for an adequate answer to the more troublesome challenge, "why be moral?" becomes the main order of business. The question, however, is not entirely serious. "But there is no reason for worry," Nietzsche assures us (BGE 228); "Things still stand today as they have always stood: I see nobody in Europe who has (let alone *promotes*) any awareness that thinking about morality could become dangerous, captious, seductive — that there might be any *calamity* involved" (*ibid.*). Thus today we find a nearly total moral skepticism (nihilism?) defended in such centers of Moral Standards as Oxford and Yale, under such non-provocative titles as "prescriptivism" and "emotivism." But, whatever the analysis, these folks still keep their promises and restrain themselves to their fair share of the High Table pie. The quest for justification is not a challenge to the monolith; it is only an exercise.

In fact, it is the phenomenon of morality itself that is in question. More than half a century before Nietzsche issued his challenge to Kant, a more sympathetic post-Kantian, Hegel, attacked the Kantian conception of "morality" in terms that would have been agreeable to Nietzsche, had he been a bit more receptive to the German *Geist.* Hegel too treated the Kantian conception of morality as a monolith, but he also saw that it was surrounded by other conceptions that might also be called "moral" which were, in the *telos* of human development, both superior and more "primitive." One of these was *Sittlichkeit,* or the morality of customs (*Sitte*).[18] It is what we earlier called a morality of *practice,* as opposed to a morality of principles. Hegel proposed not just a different way of interpreting and justifying moral rules (though this would be entailed as well); he rather defended a conception of morals that did not depend upon rules at all, in which the activity of justification, in fact, became something of a philosophical irrelevancy, at best. The need to justify moral rules betrays an emptiness in those rules themselves, a lack of conviction, a lack of support. Since then, Hegel has mistakenly been viewed as lacking in his concern for the basic ethical question, leading several noted

---

[18] Hegel, *System der Sittlichkeit* (1802) and *The Phenomenology,* Part C (AA), Chapter VI ("Spirit"), esp. pars. 439-450.

ethical commentators (Popper, Walsh)[19] to accuse him of a gross amorality, conducive to if not openly inviting authoritarianism. It is as if rejecting the Kantian conception of morality and refusing to indulge in the academic justification game were tantamount to abandoning ethics — both the practice and the theory — altogether.

If we are to understand Nietzsche's attack on Morality, we must appreciate not so much the breadth of his attack and the all-out nihilism celebrated by some of his more enthusiastic defenders but rather the more limited and precise conception of Morality that falls under his hollow-seeking Hammer. We can then appreciate what some have called the "affirmative" side of Nietzsche's moral thinking, the sense in which he sees himself as having "a more severe morality than anybody." In *Beyond Good and Evil* he boasts, "*We immoralists!* — ... We have been spun into a severe yarn and shirt of duties and *cannot* get out of that — and in this we are 'men of duty,' we too... the dolts and appearances speak against us, saying, 'These are men *without* duty.' We always have the dolts and appearances against us" (BGE 226). To write about Nietzsche as a literal "immoralist" and the destroyer of morality is to read him badly, or it is to confuse the appearance with the personality. Or, he would say, it is to be a "dolt."

For Nietzsche as for Hegel and as for Aristotle, morality does not consist of principles but of practices. It is *doing* not willing that is of moral significance, an expression of character rather than a display of practical reason. A practice has local significance; it requires — and sets up — a context; it is not a matter of universal rule, in fact, universality is sometimes argued to show that something is *not* a practice. (For example, sociobiologists have argued that incest and certain other sexual preferences are not sex practices because — on the basis of their alleged universality — they can be shown to be genetically inherited traits.[20]) Some practices are based upon principles, of course, but not all are; and principles help define a practice, though they rarely if ever do so alone. Hegel and Aristotle, of course, emphasize *collective* social practices, in which laws may be much in evidence. Nietzsche is particularly interested in the "genealogy" of social practices in which principles play a central if also devious role, but he too quickly concludes that there is but one such "moral type" and one alternative "type," which he designates "slave" ("herd") and

---

[19] Karl Popper, *The Open Society and Its Enemies* (London: Routledge & Kegan Paul, 1954); W.H. Walsh, *Hegel's Ethics* (New York: St. Martin's, 1969).

[20] Edward O. Wilson toys with this argument, for example, in the infamous 27th chapter of his *Sociobiology* (Cambridge: Harvard University Press, 1978).

"master" moralities, respectively. In fact, there are as many moral "types" as one is willing to distinguish, and to designate as "master morality" the entire historical and anthropological gamut of relatively law-less (as opposed to lawless) societies is most unhistorical as well as confusing philosophically.

The monolithic image of morality, divorced from particular peoples and practices, gives rise to the disastrous disjunction — common to Kant and Nietzsche at least — it is either Morality or *nothing*. If Nietzsche often seems to come up empty-handed and obscurely calls for "the creation of new values," it is because he finds himself rejecting principles without a set of practices to fall back on. If only he had his own non-nihilistic world — something more than his friends and his study and his images of nobility — where he could say, "here is where we can prove ourselves!" But what he finds instead is the hardly heroic world of 19th century democratic socialism. In reaction, he celebrates self-assertion and "life." This is poor stuff from which to reconstruct Nietzsche's "affirmative philosophy." Add a synthetic notion, "the will to power," and Nietzsche's ethics is reduced to a combination of aggressive banality and energetic self-indulgence (would it be unfair to mention Leopold and Loeb here? They were not the least literate of Nietzsche's students). What we find in appearances, accordingly, is not an "affirmative" philosophy at all. Having given us his polemical typology of morals, the rejection of Morality — misinterpreted as a broad-based rejection of *all* morality (for example, by Philippa Foot, who is one of Nietzsche's more sensitive Anglo-American readers)[21] — seems to lead us to nothing substantial at all. The banality of Zarathustra.

"What is morality?" The very question invites a simple if not simple-minded answer. But "morality" is itself a morally loaded term which can be used to designate and applaud any number of different ethē and their justificatory contexts. Nietzsche famously insisted that "there are no moral phenomena, only moral interpretations of phenomena." I would add that there are only moral interpretations of "morality" too. Indeed, I would even suggest that Nietzsche might mean the very opposite of what his aphorism says, that there are *only* moral phenomena, in precisely the sense that Kant denied, especially regarding the supposedly neutral word "Morality" itself.

---

[21] Philippa Foot, "Nietzsche: The Revaluation of Values", in Solomon (ed.), pp. 156-168.

Areteic Ethics: Nietzsche and Aristotle

In *After Virtue,* Alasdair MacIntyre gives us a choice, *enter-eller*: Nietzsche *or* Aristotle.[22] There is, he explicitly warns us, no third alternative. MacIntyre sees Nietzsche's philosophy as purely destructive, despite the fact that he praises the arch-destroyer for his insight into the collapse of morals that had been increasingly evident since the Enlightenment. MacIntyre chooses Aristotle as the positive alternative. Aristotle had an *ethos*; Nietzsche leaves us with nothing. But Nietzsche is nevertheless the culmination of that whole tradition — which we still refer to as "moral philosophy" or "ethics" — which is based on a tragic and possibly irreversible error in both theory and practice. The error is the rejection of ethos as the foundation of morality with a compensating insistence on the rational justification of morality. Without a presupposed ethos, no justification is possible. Within an ethos, none is necessary (Nietzsche: "not to *need* to impose values..."). And so after centuries of degeneration, internal inconsistencies and failures in the Enlightenment project of transcending mere custom and justifying moral rules once and for all, the structures of morality have collapsed, leaving only incoherent fragments. "Ethics" is the futile effort to make sense of the fragments and "justify" them, from the Scots' appeal to the sentiments and Kant's appeal to practical reason to the contemporary vacuity of "meta-ethical" theory. Here is the rubble that Nietzsche's Zarathustra urges us to clear away. Here is the vacuum in which Nietzsche urges us to become "legislators" and "create new values." But out of what are we to do this? What would it be, "to create a new value"?

MacIntyre, by opposing Nietzsche and Aristotle, closes off to us the basis upon which we could best reconceive of morality: a reconsideration of Aristotle through Nietzschean eyes. Nietzsche, of course, encourages the antagonistic interpretation. But the opposition is ill-conceived, and the interpretation is misleading. MacIntyre, like Philippa Foot, takes Nietzsche too literally to be attacking *all* morality. But quite the contrary of rejecting the ethics of Aristotle, I see Nietzsche as harking back to Aristotle and the still warrior-bound aristocratic tradition he was (retrospectively) cataloging in his *Nicomachean Ethics*. Whatever the differences between Greece of the *Iliad* and Aristotle's Athens, there was a far vaster gulf — and not only in centuries — between the elitist ethics of Aristotle and the egalitarian, bourgeois, Pietist ethics of Kant. Nietzsche may have envisioned himself as Dionysus versus the

---

[22] MacIntyre, pp. 103ff.

Crucified; he is better understood as a modern-day Sophist versus Kant, a defender of the virtues against the categorical imperative.

When I was in graduate school my professor Julius Moravcsik began his lectures on Aristotle with a comparison with Nietzsche. They were two of a kind, he said, both functionalists, naturalists, "teleologists," standing very much opposed to the utilitarian and Kantian temperaments. Moravcsik never followed this through, to my knowledge, but his casual seminar remark has stuck with me for all of these years, and the more I read and lecture on both authors, so different in times and tempers, the more I find the comparison illuminating. Nietzsche was indeed, like Aristotle, a self-proclaimed functionalist, naturalist, teleologist, and, I would add, an elitist, though on both men's views this would follow from the rest. Nietzsche's functionalism is most evident in his constant insistence that we *evaluate* values, see what they are *for*, what role they play in the survival and life of a people. He never tires of telling us about his "naturalism," of course, from this flatly false declaration that he is the first philosopher who was also a psychologist (MacIntyre here substitutes sociology) to his refreshing emphasis on psychological explanation in place of rationalizing justification. Nietzsche often states this in terms of "this-worldly" as opposed to the "other-wordly" visions of Christianity, but I think that this is not the contrast of importance. Indeed, today it is the very "this-worldly" activity of some Christian power blocks that is a major ethical concern, and there is much more to naturalism (as opposed, for example, to Kant's rationalism) than the rejection of Heaven and Hell as the end of ethics. (Kant, of course, would agree with that too.)

Nietzsche's teleology is at times as cosmic as Aristotle's, especially where the grand *telos* becomes "the will to power." But on the strictly human (if not all-too-human) level, Nietzsche's ethics like Aristotle's can best be classified in introductory ethics readers as an ethics of "self-realization." "Become who you are" is the slogan in the middle writings; the *telos* of the *Übermensch* serves from *Thus Spoke Zarathustra* on. Indeed, who is the *Übermensch* if not Aristotle's *megalopsychos*, "the great-souled man" from whom Nietzsche even borrows much of his "master-type" terminology. He is the ideal who "deserves and claims great things." He is the man driven by what Goethe (the most frequent candidate for *Übermensch* status) called his "daemon" (the association with Aristotle's "eu-daimonia" is not incidental).

Aristotle's teleology begins modestly, with the *telos* of the craftsman, the physician, the farmer. Each has his purpose, his own criteria for excellence, his own "good." But such modest goods and goals are hardly the stuff of ethics, and Aristotle quickly turns to "the good for man," by which he means the ideal man, and the "function of man," by which he means man at his best.²³ There is no point to discussing what we banally call today "the good person," who breaks no rules or laws, offends no one and interests no one except certain moral philosophers. There is no reason to discuss *hoi poloi,* who serve their city-state well and honor their superiors appropriately. It is the superiors themselves who deserve description, for they are the models from whom the vision of humanity is conceived. What sort of insanity, we hear Aristotle and Nietzsche asking in unison, can explain the idea that all people are of equal value, that everyone and anyone can serve as an ideal, as a model for what is best in us? With leaders like Pericles, who needs the categorical imperative? ("What are morals to us sons of God?") With leaders like our own, no wonder we are suffocating with laws.

To reject egalitarian ethics and dismiss the banal notion of "the good person" as of no ethical interest is not to become an "immoralist." It does not mean breaking all the rules. It does not result in such inability as suffered by Richard Hare, a temporary incapacity to morally censure Hitler for any rational reasons.²⁴Or, if we want an "immoralist," he might be at worst the sort of person that André Gide created in his short novel of that name, a man who senses his own mortality and luxuriates in his own bodily sensations, amused and fascinated by the foibles of people around him. This is not, of course, the man whom Aristotle has in mind. The Stagirite was concerned with statesmen, philosopher-kings, the flesh and blood *Übermenschen* who actually exist, not just in novels and philosophical fantasies and Zarathustra's pronouncements. But Nietzsche too, when it comes down to cases, is concerned not with a phantom but with real life heroes, the "great men" who justify (I use the word advisedly) the existence of the society that created them — and which they in turn created. But though he may shock us with his military language, the Über*menschen* more near to his heart are for the most part his artistic comrades, "philosophers, saints and artists."²⁵ The rejection of bourgeois morality does not dictate cruelty but rather an emphasis on excellence. The will to power is not *Reich* but *Macht* and not supremacy but superiority. Nietzsche urges us to create values, but I believe that it is the value of creating as such — and having the strength and the *telos* to do so — that he most valued. The unspoken but always present thesis is this: It is only in the

---

²³ Aristotle, *Nicomachean Ethics,* trans. H. Rackham (Cambridge, Ma.: Harvard University Press, 1946), Bk. I, Ch. ii.
²⁴ Richard Hare, *Freedom and Reason* (Oxford: Clarendon, 1963), e.g., p.172.
²⁵ Alexander Nehamas has completed one long-needed bit of empirical research in this regard: in *Beyond Good and Evil,* he has found that better than three quarters of the candidates for *Übermensch* are writers. See his forthcoming *Nietzsche: Life as Literature* (Cambridge, Harvard University Press).

romantic practice of artistic creativity that modern excellence can be achieved.

Elitism is not itself an ethics. Indeed, I think both Aristotle and Nietzsche might well object to it as such. It is rather the presupposition of an ethics, the presupposition that people's talents and abilities differ. It is beginning with what is the case.[26] The purpose of an ethics is to maximize people's potential, to encourage the most and the best from all of them, but more by far from the best of them. It is also the recognition that any universal rule — however ingeniously formulated and equally applied — will be disadvantageous to someone, coupled with the insistence that it is an enormous waste as well as unfair (both authors worry more about the former than the latter) for the strong to be limited by the weak, the productive limited by the unproductive, the creative limited by the uncreative. It will not do to mask the point by saying that elitism does not treat people unequally, only differently. It presumes inequality from the outset, and defends it by appeal to the larger picture, Aristotle by appeal to the well-being of the city-state and the natural order of things, Nietzsche by a more abstract but very modern romantic appeal to human creativity. Of course, Nietzsche refuses to be so Kantian as to appeal to "humanity" as such, and so he appeals to a step beyond humanity — über-humanity. But what is the *Übermensch* but a projection of what is best in us, what Kant called "dignity" but Nietzsche insists is "nobility." The difference, of course, is that Kant thought that dignity was inherent in every one of us; Nietzsche recognizes nobility in only the very few.

What is essential to this view of ethics — let us not call it elitist ethics but rather an ethics of virtue, *areteic* ethics — is that the emphasis is wholly on excellence, a teleological conception. What counts for much less is obedience of rules, laws and principles, for one can be wholly obedient and also dull, unproductive and useless. This does not mean that the "immoralist" — as Nietzsche misleadingly calls him — will kill innocents, steal from the elderly and betray the community, nor even, indeed, run a car or a chariot through a red light. The *Übermensch* is perfectly willing to act "in accordance with morality," even, in a qualified way, "for the sake of duty," that is, if it is a duty that fits his character and his telos. In a much-debated passage, Nietzsche even insists that the strong have a "duty" to help the weak, a statement that is utterly confusing on the nihilist interpretation of Nietzsche's ethics.[27] What

---

[26] Cf. "It is upon a correct choice of a basic structure of society...that justice...depends" (John Rawls, *A Theory of Justice,* Cambridge: Harvard University Press, 1971).

[27] "When the exceptional human being treats the mediocre more tenderly than himself and his peers, this is not mere courtesy of the heart — it is simply his duty " (A 57).

the *Übermensch*-aspirant does not recognize are *categorical* imperatives, commands made impersonally and universally, without respect for rank or abilities. As a system of hypothetical imperatives useful to his purposes, however, the *Übermensch* might be as moral as anyone else.

MacIntyre's diagnosis of our tragic fate turns on his recognition that the singular ethos upon which a unified and coherent ethics might be based has fragmented. We no longer have a culture with customs and an agreed upon system of morals; we instead have pluralism. Our insistence on tolerance and our emphasis on rules and laws are a poor substitute, more symptoms of our *malaise* rather than possible cures. But Nietzsche is something more than the pathologist of a dead or dying morality. He is also the champion of that sense of integrity that MacIntyre claims we have lost. The question is, how is integrity possible in a society without an ethos or, in more positive terms, in a "pluralist" society with many *ethē,* some of them admittedly dubious? Does it make sense in such a society to still speak of "excellence," or should we just award "achievement" and recognize limited accomplishments in cautiously defined sub-groups and professions? Or should we rather express the atavistic urge to excellence with an intentionally obscure phrase — "will to power"?

Nietzsche's Problem

In Aristotle, two convening ideals made possible his powerful teleological vision: the unity of his community and the projected vision of the *telos* of man, which not incidentally coincided with the best images of his community. We no longer have that unified community — although those are not the grounds on which Nietzsche rejects bourgeois morality. (Indeed, sometimes it is the small-mindedness of small communities that he most violently reacts against.) It is not difficult to see Nietzsche's provocative ethics as precisely the expression of a rather distinctive if ill-circumscribed community, namely the community of disaffected academics and intellectuals, but this is not an ethos that Nietzsche could recognize as the basis for his rather extravagant claims for a new ethics. Nevertheless Nietzsche like Aristotle held onto the vision of an over-riding human *telos,* an enormous sense of human *potential,* a hunger for excellence that is ill-expressed by his monolithic expression, "will to power."

Depending on one's views of Aristotle (some rather priggish Oxford ethicists have called him a "prig"), this view of Nietzsche may or may not be considered another case of Anglo-American whitewash. After all, Aristotle may have retained some of the warrior virtues, but most of his virtues are distinctively those of the good citizen, concerned with justice and friendship and getting along together. There is little of the fire and ice that Nietzsche talks about, certainly no emphasis on cruelty and suffering. Aristotle was hardly the lonely wanderer in the mountains and desert whom Nietzsche sometimes resembled and celebrated in *Zarathustra*. However aristocratic they may be, Aristotle's virtues seem too genteel, too much in the spirit of party life to be comparable to Nietzsche's severe moral strictures (cf. Zarathustra's "party" in Part IV). It would be an unforgivable historical mistake to call Aristotle's virtues "bourgeois," but, nevertheless, they surely lack the cutting edge of Nietzsche's pronouncements.

The problem, however, is that Nietzsche's affirmative instructions are often without substantial content. It is all well and good to talk about the glories of solitude, but Nietzsche's own letters and friendships show us that he himself lived by his friends, defined himself in terms of them. Zarathustra, Biblical bluster aside, spends most of his time looking for friends. "Who would want to live without them?" asked Aristotle rhetorically in his *Ethics*. Surely not Nietzsche. And he was, by all accounts, a good friend, an enthusiastic friend. And if he remained lonely, that is a matter for psychiatric, not ontological diagnosis. As for the warrior spirit, the cutting edge of cruelty, the fire and ice, there is little evidence that Nietzsche either displayed or admired them, Lou Salomé's description of the glint in his eyes notwithstanding. His own list of virtues included such Aristotelian traits as honesty, courage, generosity and courtesy (*Dawn* 556). And, at the end, didn't he collapse while saving a horse from a beating?

One need not ask whether Aristotle lived up to his own virtues. But Nietzsche leaves so much unsaid, and gives us so much hyperbolically, that an *ad hominem* hint is not beside the point. One can grasp the struggle with morality that is going on in the man, so readily expressed in the murderous language of adolescence, without confusing the rhetoric with the ideals. There are different warriors for different times. Achilles suited the *Iliad*. Our warrior today is Gandhi.

Nietzsche's problem is that he sees himself as a destroyer, not a reformer or a revisionist ("On the Improvers of Mankind" in *Twilight of the Idols,* for example). He sees the Judeo-Christian tradition and the Morality that goes with it as a single historical entity, against which there is no clearly conceived alternative. Consequently, he gives us two very different prescriptions for our fate, which includes the moral collapse that has been so systematically described by MacIntyre. First, he urges us to recapture a sense of "master" morality — which I take to mean a morality of nobility, insofar as this is possible, given two thousand intervening years of Christianity (which

Nietzsche by no means sees as wholly a debilitating influence). But as Rousseau also insisted, "we can't go back." The *polis* Nietzsche so much admired — indeed, the war-torn pre-*polis* of the *Iliad* — is gone and, in the world of modern nation states, inconceivable. Democracy and socialism have rendered the aristocratic virtues unacceptable — even where these coincide exactly with the good bourgeois virtues (courtesy, for instance). The foundation is gone; human equality has become an *a priori* (i.e. unchallengeable) truth. If "Christianity is Platonism for the masses," then democratic socialism is Christianity for the middle class.

That is on the one side — an impossible nostalgia, not unlike the American (and European) fantasy about the American West, "where men were men" (but in fact unwashed and hungry refugees eking out a difficult living). But if there is no warrior ethos to which we can return, then what? "The creation of values!" Nietzsche says. But what is it to "create a value!" Not even Nietzsche suggests one — not even *one*! What he does is to remind us, again and again, of old and established values which can be used as an ethical Archimedean point, to topple the professions of a too abstract, too banal, morality that fails to promote the virtues of character. He appeals to weakness of will (not by that name) and resentment — what could be more Christian vices? He charges us with hypocrisy — the tribute that even "immoralists" pay to virtue. He points out the cruelty of Tertullian and other Christian moralists. He chastizes the Stoics for emulating wasteful nature. He attacks Spinoza for being too in love with "his own wisdom." He attacks Christianity as a whole as a "slave" morality, a "herd instinct" detrimental to the progress of the species as a whole. New values?

Ethics is an expression of an ethos. There is no such thing as "creating new values" in Nietzsche's sense. It is not like declaring clam shells as currency and it is not, as in MacIntyre's good example, Kamehamnha II of Hawaii declaring invalid "taboos" whose function had long ago been forgotten. Nietzsche does not reject morals, only one version of Morality, which has as its instrument the universalizable principles formalized by Kant whose ancestry goes all the way back to the Bible. But, as Scheler says in defense of Christianity, the diagnosis is not complete. Indeed, it would not be wrong (as Lou Salomé observed) to see Nietzsche as an old-fashioned moralist, disgusted with the world around him but unable to provide a satisfactory account of an alternative and unable to find a context in which an alternative could be properly cultivated.

None of this is to deny that Nietzsche is, as Kaufmann calls him, a moral revolutionary, or that he has an affirmative ethics. He is indeed after something new and important, even if it is also very old and something less than the creation of new values. He is, as MacIntyre puns, after virtues, even if he would prefer to think of them in Homeric rather than Aristotelian form. And in his writings and his letters, the focus of that alternative is as discernible as the larger concept of Morality he attacks. It is Aristotle's ethics of virtue, an ethics of practice instead of an ethics of principles, an ethics in which *character,* not duty or abstract poses of universal love, plays the primary role. "To give style to one's character. A rare art" (GS 290). In that one sentence, Nietzsche sums up his own ethics far better than in whole books of abuse.

One more word against Kant as a *moralist.* A virtue must be *our own* invention, *our* most necessary self-expression and self-defense; any other kind of virtue is a danger... "Virtue," "duty," the "good in itself," the good which is impersonal and universally valid — chimeras and expressions of decline, of the final exhaustion of life, of the Chinese phase of Königsberg. The fundamental laws of self-preservation and growth demand the opposite — that everyone invent *his own* virtue, his *own* categorical imperative. A people perishes when it confuses *its* duty with duty in general...*anti*-Nature as instinct, German decadence as philosophy — *that is Kant.* (A 11)

University of Texas at Austin

Alexander Nehamas

Will to Knowledge, Will to Ignorance and Will to Power in *Beyond Good and Evil*

> Error...is more intimately connected with animal existence and the soul continues longer in the state of error than in that of truth.
> Aristotle, *De Anima* III 3 427b 1-2

The question that opens and insistently runs through *Beyond Good and Evil* is posed for us by what Nietzsche calls "the will to truth," the drive, need, tendency and desire to know the world for what it is and not be deceived about it.[1] Forced by the will to truth to ask questions endlessly, we even question this will itself. "Indeed," Nietzsche writes,

we came to a long halt at the question about the cause of this will—until we finally came to a complete stop before a still more basic question. We asked about the *value* of this will. Suppose we want truth: *why not rather* untruth? and uncertainty? even ignorance? (5:15, BGE 1)

To put the value of the will to truth into question is still an effort to determine the truth about this matter. As such, in the paradoxical manner characteristic of Nietzsche's later writing, the question is itself prompted by the will to truth, which, in the very process of casting suspicion upon itself, secures its own perpetuation.

Self-perpetuating as it may be, the will to truth nevertheless questions its origins and aims, and its questions must be answered. Nietzsche hints at his own reply at the beginning of the second part of *Beyond Good and Evil*, where he writes that

from the beginning we have contrived to retain our ignorance in order to enjoy an almost inconceivable freedom, lack of scruple and caution, heartiness and gaiety of life

---

[1] I shall refer to Nietzsche's original text by citing the appropriate volume and page number of Friedrich Nietzsche, *Sämtliche Werke, Kritische Studienausgabe* (Berlin & New York: Walter de Gruyter, 1980). For the English translation I shall cite the acronym of the work and the appropriate section.

— in order to enjoy life! And only on this solid, granite foundation of ignorance could knowledge rise so far — the will to knowledge on the foundation of a far more powerful will: the will to ignorance, to the uncertain, to the untrue! Not as its opposite, but — as its refinement! (5:41, BGE 24)

Nietzsche is quite aware that such a view is, at the very least, peculiar. And, early on in the book, he has an imaginary interlocutor object immediately to the theme of the opening section:

How *could* anything originate out of its opposite? for example, truth out of error? or the will to truth out of the will to deception?... (5:16, BGE 2)

But the main purpose of *Beyond Good and Evil* is to insist that this "fundamental faith of the metaphysicians... the faith in the opposition of values"[2] is an assumption from which, as its very title suggests, we must move away. The origins and value of "the true, the truthful, the selfless," Nietzsche continues, may lie precisely in "deception, selfishness, and lust":

It might even be possible that what constitutes the value of these good and revered things is precisely that they are insidiously related, tied to, and involved with these wicked, seemingly opposite things — maybe even one with them in essence. (5:17, BGE 2)

The sweeping monism of Nietzsche's later thought, though neither always acceptable nor indeed often obvious, is well known. It is, of course, impossible to discuss here even in the broadest terms his view that the dualist "metaphysical" distinctions above are projections onto the world of our own moral valuations (12: 352-353, WP 507), which are themselves "merely foreground estimates, only provisional perspectives" (5:16, BGE 2). This is precisely why, he writes in *Ecce Homo*, he chose Zarathustra as his hero:

Zarathustra was the first to consider the fight of good and evil the very wheel in the machinery of things: the transposition of morality into the metaphysical realm, as a force, cause, and end in itself, is *his* work... Zarathustra created this most calamitous error, morality; consequently, he must also be the first to recognize it. (6:367, EH "Why I am a Destiny" 3)

In what follows I shall unavoidably not discuss the broad and complicated issues involved in Nietzsche's general attitude toward "metaphysics." I will simply concentrate on his view that truth and error, knowledge and ignorance, must not be construed as essentially opposed to one another, but rather as points along a single continuum — there are questions enough here. The view is already foreshadowed in the opening sections of Book III of *The Gay Science,* in which Nietzsche discusses knowledge, truth and morality and

---

[2] Ibid., translation slightly modified.

where he writes in relation to the concepts of cause and effect:

> we have uncovered a manifold one-after-another where the naive man and inquirer of older cultures saw only two separate things... It will do to consider science as an attempt to humanize things as faithfully as possible; as we describe things and their one-after-another, we learn how to describe ourselves more and more precisely. (3: 472-473, GS 112)

What is it then that Nietzsche is after? What does he have in mind when he writes that there are "only degrees and many subtleties of gradation," and not an opposition between truth and falsehood, knowledge and ignorance? What is it that causes him to doubt this opposition and to want to

> laugh at the way in which precisely science at its best seeks most to keep us in this *simplified,* thoroughly artificial world, suitably constructed and suitably falsified world — at the way in which, willy-nilly, it loves error, because, being alive, it loves life? (5:41-42, BGE 24)

What sort of error is it that, according to Nietzsche, science, "being alive," loves? The simplest construal of what he has in mind would be to say that he believes that the world *is not* as our most sweeping, most fundamental assumptions hold it to be, but that it *is something else* instead. On such a view, Nietzsche would be claiming that, in itself, the world is characterized by a set of features which all our sciences, at their very best, necessarily cannot reflect. The world is therefore falsified by every description. But I think that it is rather clear that this cannot be Nietzsche's view. His "perspectivism," so central to his later writings, is precisely an effort to move away from the idea that the world possesses any features, whether they can or cannot be ever captured, that are in principle prior to and independent of all interpretation. He writes that he is not concerned with "the opposition of 'thing-in-itself' and appearance," to which this idea is according to him committed, "for we do not 'know' nearly enough to be entitled to any such distinction. We simply lack any organ for knowledge, for 'truth'..." (3:593, GS 354). Or, as he puts it in his notes, "science has today resigned itself to the apparent world; a real world — whatever it may be like — we certainly have no organ for knowing it. At this point we may ask: by means of what organ of knowledge can we posit even this antithesis?" (13:280, WP 583).

Nietzsche seems to think that even to form the idea of a world in principle distinct from the world of appearance, within which we live and which we try to come to know, we must have some sort of cognitive relation to it. And if this is so, he asks, why can we not come to know that world as it is — and as he himself thought possible, after a fashion, at the time of the composition of *The Birth of Tragedy*? But, he now argues, we cannot know such a world in any way, and we are in no manner related to it. The idea that such a world exists behind appearance is a fiction. Consequently, so is the idea that the world in which we do live and which we do come to know is "merely" apparent: "No shadow of a right remains to speak here of appearance" (13:371, WP 567).

Perhaps, then, Nietzsche has a gentler view in mind when he writes that science inherently falsifies the world, and that the will to knowledge is a refinement of the will to ignorance. Some readers might find such a view in section 11 of *Beyond Good and Evil,* where we read that synthetic *a priori* judgements

> must be *believed* to be true, for the sake of the preservation of creatures like ourselves; though they might of course be *false* judgements for all that! Or to speak more clearly and coarsely: synthetic judgements a priori should not "be possible" at all; we have no right to them; in our mouths they are nothing but false judgements. Only, of course, the belief in their truth is necessary... (5:25-26)

Such an idea can be occasionally found in Nietzsche's writings.[3] We could take it to show that we simply don't have sufficient grounds for knowing that our most basic and general beliefs are true, however necessary our faith in and reliance upon them is for our self-preservation. After all, a careful reader may remark, all that Nietzsche has written in the passage we are considering is that synthetic *a priori* judgements "might" be false (*sie natürlich noch falsche Urtheile sein könnten*) and that they are false "in our mouth" (*in userm Munde*). Nietzsche may thus think that such judgements may after all, for all that we know, be true; all he is claiming is simply that we have no reasonable grounds for thinking that they are.

This interpretation is not, I think, impossible; but it is not true. It conflicts with a large number of statements on Nietzsche's part where the falsehood of such judgements is categorically asserted. But, more importantly for our present concerns, such a construal of his position is much too weak to account for the view that we are trying to understand: that the will to knowledge is not related to the will to ignorance as its opposite but as its refinement; that there even is such a thing as a will to ignorance. For even if we have no grounds for holding that such judgements are true, the possibility that they may be should have been sufficient to prevent Nietzsche from considering the tendency to hold them true a "will to ignorance." Unless we can show that such judgements are in some serious sense false, believing that they are true cannot be adequately described as a will to ignorance and deception. And we cannot show them to be false without having some notion of what is true instead. But if we have some notion of what the truth is like and if that truth is in principle

---

[3] Cf., for example, 3: 469-471, 518; 11: 477, 506; GS 110, 265; WP 493.

accessible to us, then Nietzsche's attempt to correlate the will to knowledge with the will to ignorance, and even perhaps to derive the former from the latter, loses not only its significance but also its sensibility. We need, that is, a very different approach to our problem.

By itself, of course, the claim that Nietzsche's attempt does not appear sensible is not an argument against the interpretation that we have been discussing. But it can become part of such an argument if we can construct an alternative interpretation which at least shows how Nietzsche's view is motivated and which may ideally even give this view some plausibility. In order to offer such an interpretation we shall have to take, as is often necessary with efforts to understand Nietzsche, a somewhat long and elaborate route. We shall have, for example, to bring to bear to our immediate concern a number of apparently irrelevant, unrelated passages. One such passage occurs in section 188 of *Beyond Good and Evil*. Here Nietzsche is arguing that every morality necessarily imposes extremely strict constraints upon those who practice it. The assumption that human nature is best expressed in perfect freedom, he very correctly insists, is unjustified; subjection to rules is in no way unnatural. On the contrary, it is generally true that

> all there is or has been on earth of freedom, subtlety, boldness, dance and masterly sureness, whether *in thought itself* or in government, or in rhetoric and persuasion, in the arts just as in ethics, has developed only owing to "the tyranny of such capricious laws"; and in all seriousness, the probability is by no means small that precisely this is "nature" and "natural"... (5:108)

For any sort of creative activity to be possible, he continues,

> what is essential...seems to be...that there should be *obedience* over a long period of time and in a *single* direction: given that, something always develops, and has developed, for whose sake it is worthwhile to live on earth; for example, virtue, art, music, dance, reason, spirituality... (5:108-109)

Nietzsche is here expressing the view, which we also find in section 353 of *The Gay Science* (3:589-590), as well as in *The Genealogy of Morals* (5:313-316, GM II:12), that an organized and organizing system of behavior can exist before a particular interpretation, used to guide people's lives in a new and different direction, is put upon it. This is exactly what Christianity, through a very long effort, succeeded in doing. What Nietzsche objects to in Christianity is not the fact that it has "tyrannized" its adherents or that it has led them toward a single, overarching direction; what he cannot in any way accept is the particular direction toward which Christianity has led.[4] On the contrary,

---

[4] This theme is the subject of the third essay of the *Genealogy*. I have discussed some aspects of Nietzsche's equivocal attitude toward discipline and unity in "How One Becomes What One Is," *Philosophical Review* (July 1983).

its being "tyrannical" was "essential and inestimable" in it, a feature for which we must be truly grateful, because

this tyranny, this caprice, this rigorous and grandiose stupidity has *educated* the spirit. Slavery is, as it seems, both in the crude and in the more subtle sense, the indispensable means of spiritual discipline and cultivation, too. Consider any morality with this in mind: what there is in it of "nature" teaches hatred of the *laisser aller,* of any all-too-great freedom, and implants the need for limited horizons and the nearest tasks — teaching *the narrowing of our perspective,* and thus in a certain sense stupidity, as a condition of life and growth. (5:109-110)

I would now like to return to the discussion of synthetic *a priori* judgements in light of these passages, especially in light of the end of the very last one. In particular, I want to exploit them in reading the final sentence of the passage from section 11, which I omitted from my previous quotation:

...in our mouths they are nothing but false judgements. Only, of course, the belief in their truth is necessary as a foreground belief and visual evidence belonging to the perspective optics of life. (5:26)

Consider now the following as a first approximation to Nietzsche's view that the will to knowledge and the will to ignorance are essentially related, and that falsification is essential to life. To engage in any activity and, in particular, in any inquiry, one must necessarily be selective. One must bring some things into the foreground and distance others into the background. Some things must be assigned relatively greater importance than others, still others must be completely ignored. We do not and can not begin with all the data: such an idea constitutes an impossibility. In every inquiry there are many, indefinitely many, perhaps infinitely many things about the world (all of them, of course, of the same order as those which we in every case foreground) that we must, that we must in some sense want to, push aside and ignore if we are even to begin inquiring and to begin to know anything.

The metaphor of perspective, as well as the whole family of visual metaphors to which it belongs, fits well in this context. Every inquiry presupposes the adoption of a particular point of view, and thus it excludes an indefinitely large number of other vantage-points. This is not to say that inquiry cannot reach correct results or that it is not "objective," since it is not possible to understand anything if one is trying to understand everything. It is to say, however, that no legitimate inquiry has more of a claim to representing the world as it really is than any other, that no particular point of view is privileged. Yet the traditional idea of knowledge, according to Nietzsche, is intimately tied to the assumption that we can, at least in principle, know everything that there is, that we can ultimately dispense with every point of view or that we can combine all our different points of view into a single overarching perspective. It is just for this reason that, though he is perfectly willing to use cognitive terms in describing many of our activities, he is also at times eager to deny that we can in fact know anything: "Our apparatus for acquiring knowledge," he writes, "is not *designed* for 'knowledge'" (11:183-184, WP 496).

Knowledge, in contrast to "knowledge," involves for Nietzsche an inherently conditional relation to its object, a relation that presupposes or manifests specific values, interests and goals. There is no reason to suppose that these can ever be eliminated or that they are ultimately commensurable. Objectivity, he insists, is not "contemplation without interest":

There is *only* a perspective seeing, only a perspective "knowing"; and the *more* affects we allow to speak about one thing, the *more* eyes, different eyes, we can use to observe one thing, the more complete will our "concept" of this thing, our "objectivity" be. (5:365, GM III:12)

These different eyes need not ever yield a single unified picture. Though Nietzsche writes, "They say: the world is only thought, or will, or war, or love, or hate...separately, all this is false: added up it is *true,*" the addition need not produce a unique stereoscopic image.

We must therefore try to connect the falsification of which Nietzsche so often writes with the simplification which almost as often accompanies it in his texts (5:41-42, 165-167, BGE 24, 229). Perspectivism implies that in order to engage in any activity we must necessarily occupy ourselves with a selection of material and exclude much from our consideration. It does not imply that we see or know an appearance of the world *instead of* that world itself. The perspective is not the object seen, a self-contained thing which is independent of and incomparable to every other. What is seen is simply the world itself *from* that perspective.

To pursue this visual metaphor (though we could make the same point through literature), we may consider the case of painting. There is no sense in which painters, even if we limit our examples to realistic depictions of one's visual field, can ever paint "everything" that they see. What they "leave out" is in itself quite indeterminate, and can be specified, if at all, only through other paintings, each one of which will be similarly "partial". Analogously, Nietzsche believes, there can be no total or final theory or understanding of the world. On his artistic model, the understanding of everything would be like a painting that incorporated all styles or that was painted in no style at all — a true chimera, both impossible and monstrous.

Perspectival approaches to the world are therefore not, as Nietzsche himself may have sometimes believed, disjoint from one another. Each approach is capable of correcting itself, and many can incorporate new material and even combine with others to form broader systems of practices and inquiries. What is not possible is that at some point we can incorporate "all" the material there is into a single approach or that we can occupy "every" possible point of view.

The will to knowledge, then, is dependent on the will to ignorance in that every effort to come to know something is at the same time an effort not to know something else. Sometimes, indeed, it may be necessary to ignore something about the very object of our inquiry in order to understand something else about it. We must constantly make decisions about what is and what is not relevant to our concerns. Nothing, of course, is wrong with such decisions in themselves; as Nietzsche insists again and again, they are essential for life. But they must be made, and in being made they abolish the possibility of seeing things in themselves, leaving us only with perspectival representations.

When Nietzsche opens *Beyond Good and Evil* with the question why we value truth and "why not rather untruth? and uncertainty? even ignorance?" we must therefore be very careful. We must try to take what he says seriously, but we must also be guided by the intuition governing this work. Nietzsche is not saying that falsehood is better and more valuable than truth or that we should abandon truth and search for what we take to be error instead. He is not saying that it is better to believe that some patently obvious fact is not the case. And he is not even saying that we could change our mind about such a fact if only we wanted to, if only we adopted a "different" perspective. Perspectives, as a large number of passages in this work suggest, cannot be adopted at will; interpretations can be reached only with great effort and only for what at least seems like good reason at the time (5:74, 108-110, BGE 55,188).

Nietzsche's point seems to be that just as the same character trait may have a different value in different contexts, just as "the virtues of the common man might perhaps signify vices and weaknesses in a philosopher" (5:48, BGE 30), so it may be wrong to think that the truth is always beneficial or valuable and that falsehood is always harmful:

Something might be true while being harmful and dangerous in the highest degree. Indeed, it may be a basic characteristic of existence that those who would know it completely would perish, in which case the strength of a spirit should be measured according to how much of the "truth" one could still barely endure — or to put it more clearly, to what degree one would *require* it to be thinned down, shrouded, sweetened, blunted, falsified. (5: 56-57, BGE 39; cf. BT 7)

The common pragmatist interpretation of Nietzsche, according to which he offers the idea of usefulness as an *analysis* of the concept of truth, becomes difficult to maintain in light of this statement.[5] And the case against this interpretation becomes stronger if we bring into our account the following passage:

> ...we "know" (or believe or imagine) just as much as may be useful in the interests of the human herd, the species: and even what is here called "utility" is ultimately also a mere belief, something imaginary, and precisely that most calamitous stupidity of which we shall perish some day. (3:593, GS 354)

As this statement shows, Nietzsche is not identifying truth with utility. Rather, he claims that we *take* as true that which we *think* is useful, and that we can be quite wrong about what we think is useful. This, it seems to me, is not a theory about what truth is, but, if anything, an implicit refusal to offer such a theory. A related point, I think, is made in section 121 of *The Gay Science*:

> *Life no argument.* — We have arranged for ourselves a world in which we can live — by positing bodies, lines, planes, causes and effects, motion and rest, form and content; without these articles of faith nobody could now endure life. But that does not prove them. Life is no argument. The conditions of life might include error. (3:477-478)

This seems to me sufficient to show that we should not take Nietzsche to have a theory to the effect that "*p* is true and *q* is false if *p* works and *q* does not."[6] But be that as it may, the more cautious "might" of the *The Gay Science* is changed into a strong indicative in *Beyond Good and Evil*. And Nietzsche's point appears to be not a theory of what constitutes truth and falsehood, but rather a caution against assuming that truth and knowledge are always beneficial and opposed in value to falsehood and ignorance. He wants to argue that ultimately the will to knowledge and the will to ignorance are not opposed in essence any more than they are opposed in value: every effort to understand something is, for him, a refusal to understand something else. Therefore, not everything can be known.

Earlier, I offered this reconstruction as a first approximation to Nietzsche's view. In offering it, I appealed, as is often useful with Nietzsche, to the situation of the artist, from which he often generalizes to other domains. In one sense, a novelist narrates everything that is there to be narrated in a novel

---

[5] The first clear statement of this view among English-speaking philosophers is to be found in Arthur Danto's important book, *Nietzsche as Philosopher* (New York: Columbia University Press, 1965), chap. 3. It has since been adopted by many other writers.

[6] Danto, p. 72.

just as a painter represents everything that is to be represented in a painting. In another sense, however, every such narration and representation leaves out an indefinitely large amount of information. A painter may paint exactly what he sees, but what he sees is necessarily a highly idiosyncratic "part" of the landscape, and sometimes not a part of the landscape at all. As Ernst Gombrich has demonstrated in *Art and Illusion,* even the most faithful representation of the most elementary subject-matter is not simple representation.[7] A painter must necessarily work with a style and, within that style, must make a large number of further more specific decisions. Every such decision, from the most general to the most specific, is a decision to foreground some set of elements from one's subject-matter at the expense of some other and it is thus responsible for the very creation of that subject-matter. The ambiguity, in the artistic context, between the notions of describing an antecedent subject-matter and of creating it as one goes along is important and will occupy us again. Impressionism cannot represent or even countenance the outlines of objects that characterize neoclassical works; but the interaction of colored shadows was, by the same token, beyond both the means and the imagination of neoclassical artists.

All this, I think, is part of what Nietzsche has in mind when he writes of the "simplification and falsification" in which we live. But it cannot be all of it, and that is why I have characterized my reconstruction as a first approximation. The reason is simple. Choosing, selecting and simplifying do not amount to falsifying what is before us unless we are convinced that a representation that depended on no selection and represented its subject completely is possible and that it constitutes what is true. But Nietzsche denies that such non-perspectival representation is possible. He is therefore not entitled to infer that in simplifying the world we also at the same time falsify it.

Consider again our analogy with painting. A painting may be said to falsify its subject if it flouts, without reason, the dictates of the style to which it belongs. A photorealist work, for example, would falsify its subject if it contained, without reason, a face colored in royal purple or drawn in the vocabulary of analytical cubism. If a reason why that feature is as it is can be found, it will no longer be obvious that the work does in fact belong to the style to which we took it to belong at the beginning: successful flouting is innovation, and the question of falsification remains open in that case. Falsification that consists in the groundless flouting of established rules, and which can be explained by appealing to the notion of coherence, is a phenomenon that Nietzsche is, naturally, perfectly willing to countenance. But it

---

[7] Ernst Gombrich, *Art and Illusion* (New York: Pantheon, 1961), p. 63.

cannot be what he is thinking of in the passages with which we are concerned, for it remains totally unclear how falsification of this sort is "a condition of life." And it is this latter view of his that we are trying to understand.

Simplification, we just saw, is not sufficient for falsification. What is it then that prompts Nietzsche to write of the two together? To answer this question we must, once again, take a longer route, and consider another apparently unrelated passage, this time from section 202 of *Beyond Good and Evil*:

> Morality in Europe today is herd animal morality — in other words, as we understand it, merely *one* type of human morality besides which, before which, and after which many other types, above all *higher* moralities, are, or ought to be, possible. But this morality resists such a "possibility," such an "ought" with all its power: it says stubbornly and inexorably, "I am morality itself, and nothing besides is morality." (5:124)

What is important for our purposes is not the specific set of moral views this passage involves, but the idea that a particular system of thought and action includes within itself, as it were, the premise that it is the only possible system of thought and action. Its claim to truth and correctness, to its being binding, consists precisely in that premise, and stands or falls with it. And though the point is made here specifically in connection with Christian morality, it is, as we shall see, much more general. Nietzsche believes that all human enterprises, moral, artistic or cognitive, involve the selection and simplification that we have been discussing; there can therefore always be alternatives to them, dependent on different bases of selection. But he also seems to believe that though we necessarily simplify the world in order to deal with it in any context, it also is the case that we think that we don't. It is here that falsification enters the picture. For it consists in the belief that the particular enterprise in which we happen to be involved or which we value most highly is exempt from such simplification.

Once again, however, it is not obvious that this interpretation accounts for Nietzsche's view that "untruth is a condition of life." Once we realize that "realism" is only one among many possible genres of painting, we can give up the belief that realistic paintings represent the visual world as it really is. Similarly, it might be argued, with whatever enterprise we happen to be involved in. At most, this interpretation implies that we should become more self-conscious and less arrogant about our enterprises, that we should be aware of their contingent basis, and that, perhaps, we should abandon the idea of finally representing the world as it really is, nonperspectivally. In doing so we would also do away with the element that introduces falsification into our life. And if we can accomplish this, then Nietzsche's view of the necessity of falsification appears to be little more than willful exaggeration.

Yet I would like to suggest that Nietzsche is offering us more than just that. Consider section 57 of *Beyond Good and Evil*:

> With the strength of his spiritual eye and insight grows distance and, as it were, the space around man: his world becomes more profound; ever new stars, ever new riddles and images become visible for him. Perhaps everything on which the spirit's eye has exercised its acuteness and truthfulness was nothing but an occasion for this exercise, something for children and those who are childish. Perhaps the day will come when the most solemn concepts which have caused the most fights and suffering, the concepts "God" and "sin," will seem no more important to us than a child's toy and a child's pain seem to an old man — and perhaps "the old man" will then be in need of another toy and another pain — still child enough, an eternal child! (5:75; cf. 4: 29-31, Z I: 1)

Along with other outmoded and useless views and ideas, this passage suggests, our most fundamental beliefs are also to be discarded. No matter how seemingly inevitable they are, no matter how deeply necessary they may have been for a long time, no matter how apparently serious they are, they must be seen to be nothing more than a child's toy: of no ultimate consequence, and destined, like all toys, to be cast aside once they have been outgrown.

Nietzsche is careful not to say that these particular concepts or that the religious attitude in general were never needed. In section 188 of *Beyond Good and Evil* he praises the discipline ("tyranny") of Christian morality for being the means "through which the European spirit has been trained to strength, ruthless curiosity, and subtle mobility" (5:109). The third essay of *The Genealogy of Morals* is Nietzsche's most sustained attempt to express his own attitude toward that morality, an attitude which he claims can be found only "here, among us, beyond the bourgeois world and its Yes and No" (5:53, BGE 34). It is his effort to explain how, despite its denial of the significance and value of life, the ascetic ideal is not to be unequivocally condemned: for by finding some ground for value, it was for a long time the best (that is, the only) means available for imposing some interpretation upon the fact of "suffering" and thus for giving human life a purpose and a direction, negative as these happened to be. He believes that the particular interpretation associated with Christianity is now obsolete, that it can no longer serve the purpose for which it was originally designed. It must therefore be cast away like an outgrown childhood toy, the very needs it satisfied now appearing like little more than childhood's pains.

The important thing to notice here is that this discussion would have been the perfect place for Nietzsche to pursue his metaphor in terms of continuing to age and to mature. Following this line of thought, he could have written that we must now give up both childish pains and childish toys altogether, that we must now become able to look at the world as it actually is, with clear and unclouded eyes, without the fears or the wishes of childhood. But this is emphatically not what he writes. Instead, he expresses the hope that "the old man" will still need "another toy and another pain," in relation to which he will be again no more than a child. And when he goes on to characterize this old man as "an eternal child" he implies that the new toy and the new pain are only to be given up in turn and replaced by new ones. As section 94 of *Beyond Good and Evil* puts it, "A man's maturity — consists in having found again the seriousness one had as a child, at play" (5:90).

To the old man, what the child had was only a toy; but to the child, the toy is much more than that: not just representation, but reality.[8] And the old man must in turn take his toys as more than merely that. The metaphor, applied to the topic we have been discussing, implies not merely that in order to come to terms with the world we must inevitably simplify it, but that, in addition, *we must not think that we do* if we are to continue to come to terms with it. Unless one thinks that one's view, interpretation, painting, theory, novel or morality is the truest or the best view, interpretation, painting, theory, novel or morality, one will not be motivated to produce it. In his writings, Nietzsche often insists that truth is not something discovered, but something created (5:144-145, 12:385; BGE 211, WP 522); but he also believes that we must think of it as something we discover if we are to go on to create it (4:50,146; Z I: 8, II:13).

Consider a profound, radical innovation in painterly or writerly style — one-point perspective or cubism, naturalism or stream of consciousness. In speaking of these as styles, we often think of them as means that allow us to depict in novel ways what was there to be depicted all along. But such innovations, it is quite clear, do not simply allow us to represent a pre-existing world in new ways. Equally, they reveal that there are new things to paint or to write about; they create new aspects of reality to which we can now, for the first time, be true.

On one understanding of analytical cubism, Picasso made it possible to represent many sides of a single object at the same time: he made more than the facing surfaces of the world part of the subject-matter of painting. As he himself put it in discussing his *Nude with Draperies* (1907), he hoped that if he had succeeded in that painting, it should be possible to "cut up" his canvas and, having put it together again, "according to color indications...find oneself confronted by a sculpture."[9] Now this is not simply a formal innova-

---

[8] Cf. Gombrich's title essay in *Meditations on a Hobby-Horse* (London: Phaidon, 1963).
[9] Quoted in Douglas Cooper, *The Cubist Epoch* (London: Phaidon, 1970), p. 33.

tion: in a serious sense, Picasso created something in the very act of depicting it. The equivocal manner in which art criticism is compelled to describe Picasso's achievement matches perfectly the ambiguities of Nietzsche's attitude toward the question whether truth is discovered or created. His view (once again dependent on a generalization from the arts) is that great movements in morality as well as in science show, in one fell swoop, that there is something new to be described in the very process of devising a method of describing it. And to the natural question whether the laws of motion did not exist before Galileo described and quantified them, Nietzsche's answer would be that, of course, they did — but no more and no less than all four sides of material objects were there to be painted before Picasso showed us how to do it.

A further question now arises concerning the characters whom Nietzsche describes and praises throughout *Beyond Good and Evil* as "free spirits" and "new philosophers." Are such people capable of going on without the illusions that the rest of us need, in the secure conviction that they are engaged in the continual proliferation of what are "merely" interpretations and nothing more? Is it in such an attitude that "the innocence of becoming" (*die Unschuld des Werdens*) perhaps consists?

There are deep differences between the "free spirits" and the "new philosophers" on the one hand and those whom Nietzsche calls "metaphysicians" or "philosophical laborers" on the other, but I do not think that one of these differences lies in the perfect self-consciousness of the former group. If Nietzsche, as we have seen, thinks that it is desirable to remain "an eternal child," it is not at all clear that anyone can ever be quite free of illusion and falsification. The child confuses representation with reality as (to appeal to another of Nietzsche's metaphors) the inquirer confuses interpretation with text. His view is not that one should go on investigating in the awareness that one is producing "merely" an interpretation. In section 44 of *Beyond Good and Evil* he writes that the free spirits are

curious to a vice, investigators to the point of cruelty, with uninhibited fingers for the unfathomable, with teeth and stomachs for the most indigestible...arrangers and collectors from morning till late, misers of our riches and our crammed drawers, economical in learning and forgetting, inventive in schemas, occasionally proud of our tables of categories, occasionally pedants, occasionally night owls of work even in broad daylight... (5:62-63).

Here, it seems to me, Nietzsche clearly thinks of the free spirits as motivated by the desire, the will, to discover the truth. They may not engage in this endeavor for any ulterior purpose: perhaps their only goal is to engage in it. But their attitude contains nothing of the distance, the irony, that would inevitably be involved in the detached frame of mind which the proliferator of what are "merely" interpretations is bound to display.

On the other hand, the desire to see things as they are, the will to truth, can be seen not as a desire to accomplish once and for all a single overarching task; it can be construed quite differently:

> ...a curiosity of my type remains after all the most agreeable of all vices — sorry, I meant to say: the love of truth has its reward on heaven and even on earth. (5:66, BGE 45)

It can be construed as the will to power. So in the section "On Self-Overcoming" of *Thus Spoke Zarathustra* we read:

> "Will to truth," you who are wisest call that which impels you and fills you with lust?
> A will to the thinkability of all beings; this *I* call your will. You want to *make* all being thinkable, for you doubt with well-founded suspicion that it is already thinkable. (4:146; Z II:13)

And later on in this same section, Zarathustra says:

> ...this is what the will to truth should mean to you: that everything be transformed in what can be thought by human beings, seen by human beings and felt by human beings... And what you have called world, that shall be created only by you: your image, your reason, your will, your love shall be thus realized. And verily, for your own bliss, you lovers of knowledge. And how could you bear life without this hope, you lovers of knowledge? You could not have been born either into the incomprehensible or into the irrational. (*ibid.*, translation slightly modified)

Now, when Nietzsche writes that "that is your whole will, you who are wisest: a will to power," is he saying that we must realize that the will to truth is not really that but something else, will to power, instead? He cannot, for the will to power is not a single reality underlying a multiple appearance: it is itself a multiple phenomenon. The will to truth is not a surface manifestation of what ultimately is only will to power; it just *is* the will to power in the context of investigation.

Construing the will to truth in this manner enables us to look at it from two points of view: from within a particular investigation, and from without. From within an investigation, one is related to that investigation, to truth, and to the world, as the child is related to its toy. The investigation is not pursued in the awareness that it is an illusion. The painter who has adopted a particular style does not work in the knowledge that he is leaving an indefinitely large number of features of his subject out of account. This thought simply does not function in context: the painter paints what he sees, he tries to be as truthful as possible, to get matters right. The detached attitude involved in the view that what one does is merely interpretation is absent from those

Nietzsche calls "the wisest." In fact, such an attitude might even be crippling:

> It is not enough that you understand in what ignorance man and beast live; you must also have and acquire the *will* to ignorance. You need to grasp that without this kind of ignorance life itself would be impossible, that it is a condition under which alone the living thing can preserve itself and prosper: a great, firm dome of ignorance must encompass you. (11:228, WP 609)

The will to ignorance must therefore turn upon itself and become a will to ignore the fact that one is not coming to know many things in coming to know about one, to ignore the fact that one is merely producing an interpretation. Only on this foundation can the will to knowledge function or, as Nietzsche would doubtless prefer it, only thus can the will to ignorance itself function as the very will to knowledge. Such tentative absolutism, as we may call this attitude, is true of morality:

> A morality, a mode of living tried and proved by long experience and testing, at length enters consciousness as a law, as *dominating* — And therewith the entire group of related values and states enters into it: it becomes venerable, unassailable, holy, true; it is part of its development that its origin should be forgotten — That is a sign that it has become master. (13:283, WP 514)

But it is also true of science:

> The presupposition of scientific work: belief in the unity and perpetuity of scientific work, so the individual may work at any one part, however small, confident that his work will not be in vain.
> There is one great paralysis: to work *in vain*, to struggle in vain. (12:206, WP 597)

And it is, finally, true of art:

> Art is the will to overcome becoming, as "eternalization," but shortsighted, depending on the perspective: repeating in miniature, as it were, the tendency of the whole. (12:313, WP 617)

Those who are called "metaphysicians" by Nietzsche are for him people who never want to think that our efforts to understand the world are partial, selective and interpretive — that they all have a specific origin. They remain convinced that either all or a privileged subset of our endeavors are constantly and linearly progressing toward an actual or possible ideal limit, and that at that limit every truth will be known. From an internal point of view, I would like to suggest, Nietzsche's free spirits or his new philosophers may be indistinguishable from such "metaphysicians." The difference between them emerges only when we examine them from an external viewpoint.

Before we look at this difference, however, let us stop a moment and ask whether Nietzsche is correct in insisting that from the inside one is inevitably committed to the correctness of one's enterprise. My own view, though I am not sure that I can defend it very well, is that he is. Such a commitment is not, I think, something over which we have any control; despite various claims to the contrary, it is not in any serious sense a matter of choice. It is manifested in the very fact that we continue to interact with the world and to live in it, and it is presupposed by our commitment to inquiry. Such a commitment is presupposed by inquiry in a way similar to that in which what John Searle has recently called "the Background," a set of stances, habits, skills, and policies, is presupposed by our various intentional states. Such habits, which, according to Searle, include our commitment to the reality of the world and the correctness of our way of looking at it, do not constitute

> a "hypothesis," "belief," or philosophical thesis...my commitment to "realism" is exhibited by the fact that I live the way I do, I drive my car, drink my beer, write my articles, give my lectures and ski my mountains. Now in addition to all of these activities, each a manifestation of my Intentionality, there isn't a further "hypothesis" that the real world exists. My commitment to the existence of the real world is manifested whenever I do pretty much anything.[10]

Searle's personal examples make it perfectly clear that this Background is contingent. There are various modes of life, and our own practices and modes, our most cherished habits and values can and do constantly change. Accordingly, the very world to the reality of which we are committed constantly changes, however imperceptible such change may be to us, from the inside as it were.

Nietzsche's free spirits do realize this contingency, and are therefore unwilling to privilege either the investigations in which they are engaged or the world to which their investigations are committed. They are aware of the fact that they are always in a process of change and development, that nothing about them need remain identical, and they are willing to acknowledge this fact. They are

> at home, or at least...guests, in many countries of the spirit; having escaped again and again from the musty agreeable nooks into which preference and prejudice, youth, origin, the accidents of people and books or even exhaustion from wandering seemed to have banished us... (5:62, BGE 44)

This background, we have said, is contingent; we may prove to be radically wrong about the world; others may, with at least equal justice, come to see things completely differently from us; we ourselves will probably come to see

---

[10] John Searle, *Intentionality* (Cambridge University Press, 1983), pp. 158-159. Searle argues that this set of habits must be in a serious sense mental. One does not have to agree with this point in order to see the importance of the issue in question.

things completely differently from the way we see them now. From none of this does it follow either that any interpretation is as good as any other or that trying to devise better interpretations is impossible or undesirable. Both inferences are instances of the nihilism which Nietzsche constantly attacks; both depend on the assumption that if some single standard is not good for everyone and for all time, then no standard is good for anyone at any time:

The "meaninglessness of events": belief in this is the consequence of an insight into the falsity of previous interpretations, a generalization of discouragement and weakness — not a *necessary* belief. (12:114, WP 599)

Uncommitted to this last assumption, Nietzsche's ideal characters are always willing, and sometimes able, to create new and better interpretations. In creating them they do not see them "merely" as interpretations; on the contrary, as Nietzsche doubtless saw his own thought, they consider them as the best views offered so far, perhaps even as the best that, in the given situation, can ever be offered. But they are also aware of two further points. First, they know that even the most obvious facts are the results of interpretation, and they are consequently always engaged in the effort to show where interpretation has been accepted without our having realized it. They are thus always looking for the contingent basis of their most basic beliefs. Secondly, they also know that if they are able to devise new interpretations, this very act changes the situation in which they are themselves to be found, and that new interpretations, with their attendant new situations, will in turn become necessary. They can thus accept the contingency of their views, when it becomes apparent, and they are willing to part with these views, when this becomes imperative. As Zarathustra says,

there must be much bitter dying in your life, you creators. Thus are you advocates and justifiers of all impermanence. To be the child who is newly born, the creator must also want to be the mother who gives birth and the pangs of the birth-giver. (4:111, Z II:2)

The ever-recurrent imagery of child and childbirth prevents us from construing the process that Nietzsche is envisaging as a linear progress toward a predetermined goal. Just as the members of a single genealogical sequence need not all share a single common feature with all the others in order to belong to that sequence, so there need be no single world which is as real to every child as it is to every other. But just as each child has its toy, each lives in the world.

The realization that all inquiry is partial and perspectival does not therefore enter into one's engagement with some specific project, and to that extent, indeed, "untruth is a condition of life." This realization begins to function in one's willingness to give up any commitment, any belief or any value *if* another, more appropriate one appears. The greatest achievement, of course, is to devise such a more appropriate idea oneself:

What is the greatest experience you can have? It is the hour of the great contempt. The hour in which your happiness, too, arouses your disgust, and even your reason and your virtue. (4:15, Z "Prologue")

Though such new alternatives may appear on their own, it is much more valuable always to be engaged in searching for them, always to *want* to see one's *previous* views as "merely" interpretations, to be able to realize that what we have taken as unquestioned fact has been inherited interpretation. This seems to me to be the very attitude that *Beyond Good and Evil* expresses toward itself at its very end:

Alas, what are you after all, my written and painted thoughts! It was not long ago that you were still so colorful, young and malicious, full of thorns and secret spices — you made me sneeze and laugh — and now? You have already taken off your novelty, and some of you are ready, I fear, to become truths... (5:239, BGE 296)

The book began with the will to truth dictating that it be itself put into question. Motivated by it, and pursuing it relentlessly, and to that extent incapable of putting it completely into question, this text construed the will to knowledge and the will to ignorance as one — as will to power. But at the text's end, the case now apparently made, this very questioning of truth appears itself true. Its author, true to himself, warns against accepting it complacently. He does not disown it, since he cannot do so without a new questioning, and a new text and a new truth, to all of which the same difficulty will once again apply. By the strange artifice of calling his view true, Nietzsche calls attention to its deeply personal nature. And in this interval between presupposing what must not be presupposed and questioning what cannot be questioned, the search for truth takes a giant step — though we still may not be clear in what direction.

University of Pittsburgh

Ran Sigad

The Socratic Nietzsche

My approach to Nietzsche centers upon two primary characteristics of his thought. First, Nietzsche, like Socrates, is not a sceptic even though he maintains a sceptical position toward the knowledge of truth. Indeed, like Socrates, he speaks as a wise man, as if he knew what the truth really is. He even claims that his scepticism leads him out of nihilism. Secondly, Nietzsche's thought is above all critical. This entails that his extreme negative attitude towards reason and the aspiration for truth is not capricious, but grounded on critical speculations that lead to the position where reason is taken to be the falsification of reality. Nietzsche's underlying attitude, then, is that reality should be grasped as it is, hence we should do all we can *not* to falsify it. Here Nietzsche's philosophy is no different from any other. Yet, given Nietzsche's view of reason as a false method of understanding, this implies that there is another way that is superior, that it is possible to grasp reality as it is without falsifying and Nietzsche undertakes to explicate this through his writings. This is simply because otherwise it would be senseless to dismiss reason — any manner of life and thought would be of equal weight and significance. The rejection of reason would constitute nothing more than personal preference, as would the adoption of any alternative.

In fact, Nietzsche himself seems to adopt this relativistic position. He tells us that to choose reason as a way of life is possible as well as legitimate, for it too expresses the Will to Power in a certain form. But if we take this at face value, then Nietzsche's preference for a life ruled by instinct and desire would merely constitute another form, and his choice would reflect personal taste. Nietzsche, however, speaks of a life ruled by instinct and desire as a preference that is not falsifying. According to the very nature of life there is a preference for instinct over reason, for only the former does not falsify reality. Thus, Nietzsche's choice is not simply personal, for at the same time as it is considered one legitimate alternative amongst others, it is also critical, a true description of reality.

Hence in this paper I will argue that contrary to what even Nietzsche explicitly claims, he discloses through his own preference the singular and unchangeable truth about reality. I believe that not only does Nietzsche present us with a positive doctrine in contrast to his sceptical speculations, but that this doctrine is the only necessarily true one. It is the critical nature of his thought that corrects its blatantly arbitrary aspects. Thus, whereas choosing to live according to reason is on the one hand legitimate, it is ruled out on the other. Nietzsche's point of departure is not simply life, rather his starting point, like that of Socrates, is the determination of the good life; and it is from this foundation that he is lead to negate the life of reason.

For Nietzsche, life is a datum to which we attach a value. Affixing the value of instinct to life determines that it is a good one. But why should this be so? I think that the only answer that is found in his writings is that it alone makes life healthy and noble, because such a life is of an inherently critical nature. This way of life does not falsify reality because it accepts life in all its rich multifariousness. Therefore it is true. We shall see that for Nietzsche, the good life, virtue and personal profit constitute a life that is lived according to truth. At this point Nietzsche is essentially Socratic.

If we understand the term 'philosophy' literally as 'love of wisdom,' and not metaphorically as we normally do, we expose the secret of philosophy; that is, that it takes the true understanding of reality to be its necessary product. I think that this literal sense is the original meaning given to it by Socrates. The chief attribute of this view of philosophy is that it requires a total commitment to critical reflection, to criticism that admits only the law of contradiction and consistency to it as constraints, and that is free from the obligations to other values. But such a methodology does not produce a positive system of knowledge. If, then, this process of criticism yields truth, truth cannot be knowledge. On such a view, truth is to be identified as a way of life, the ongoing activity which consists of self-overcoming; the overcoming of anything that is *not* total criticism. In other words, the love of wisdom, itself, when raised to a way of life, constitutes truth. This has the effect of making the lover of wisdom feel as omnipotent as God. I contend that this position is shared by Nietzsche with Socrates. It is this which renders Nietzsche's philosophy so surprisingly akin to Plato's early dialogues. Had Nietzsche distinguished between the Socratic philosophy of the early dialogues, characterized by the Socratic statement "I know that I do not know," and the Platonic Theory of Ideas of the later dialogues, he might have realized that he was following in Socrates' footsteps.

True Will to Truth versus Reason

Nietzsche blames Socrates for being one of the two major causes of falsification of reality that are present within Western culture (the other cause being Judaism). Socrates is taken to be the paradigm of the life of reason. It is a way of life which only prevails due to the weakness of life's powers; it is the evading of a real struggle for life. Human reason is not objective, but on the contrary, it is the expression of the interest to eschew suffering and achieve security through the knowledge of reality. Conceptual knowledge which is but a generalization of similar aspects in the phenomenal world, disregarding everything which is different and incompatible, is an interpretation of reality. Although the interpretation is legitimate, reason usually exhibits its interpretations as the necessary and only manifestation of truth. Therefore reason falsifies reality by contradicting it, for any interpretation that is only partial but exhibits itself as total runs counter to the truth.

When we understand that the ideal of objective truth is but a rationalization turned into an entire culture; when we understand that the aspiration for truth through reason is but an ideology posing as self-consciousness, concealing self-consciousness at the very same time; we then understand that this ideal for truth is not critical. Nietzsche is deeply annoyed by reason's pretension to be capable of revealing truth. Reason presumes to know what Nietzsche's critical speculations show to be impossible to know. In fact, the philosophy of reason does not desire truth at all. It does not aim to reveal reality as it is, but rather has an interest in imposing the values of reason, i.e. of a certain way of life, upon reality. The philosophy of reason does not love wisdom and does not look for truth, but only wants to achieve its self-advancing goal. It is a philosophy obsessed with itself, dissembling to grasp the totality of reality. In fact, Nietzsche contends that it is but a metaphor, its interest being to establish a certain way of life. It is not committed to grasping reality as it is, but favors a particular arrangement of reality that is in accordance with that preferred way of life. So reason is an agent of a psychological purpose, which entails that it is neither critical nor free.

Thus we find that Nietzsche attacks reason for failing to be free. But Nietzsche is not therefore attacking free thinking. On the contrary, free and genuine thinking, being experimental, is for him the supreme value. It is in just such a manner that he viewed his own thought: free, for it was totally critical. The question Nietzsche raises is whether thinking is open to reality or closed within itself. In the context of Nietzsche's terminology, reason represents just such a closed mode.

But does not Nietzsche claim that every act in life is necessarily selfish and arbitrary? How is it then that reason should be rejected for simply fulfilling the necessary demands of its own nature? I think it should be clear that Nietzsche criticizes reason not on account of it being selfish per se, but because this particular form of life is not critical, nor does it seek truth, in contradistinction to all pretense.

Both the life of reason and the aspiration for truth are arbitrary, both are expressions of certain ways of life. But only the aspiration for truth, for revealing reality as it is, i.e. as an unknowable will to power, characterizes true philosophy. This is the way of life of a highly specific sort of man, a man that Nietzsche calls 'noble' and 'superman.' The superman is unique in that he is not interested in a particular way of life, does not defend himself against life, and is not feeble. He is interested, rather, in life as a whole, reality as it is. His instinctive impulse is to open himself to reality at the expense of every other way of life. His desire is to become one with the totality of reality. In what follows we shall see how this can be achieved.

We find then, interestingly, that thinking is critical only when its instinctive impulse is aiming at the one and total truth, which is the disclosing of reality as it is, i.e. as will to power. Reason as rationalization is falsification of this impulse, and this is precisely why it is not critical. Reason is in particular faulted for pretensions to the effect that it can attain total knowledge of reality. True philosophy is based upon the impossibility of this knowledge and the desire to live in accordance with this understanding, a desire that withstands the overwhelming suffering which true philosophy entails. Nietzsche's true philosophy is free and critical thinking, it is an unbounded desire for truth; and thus, it is not a desire for a system of knowledge, for such a system must be based upon self-deception and contradiction: exhibiting reality as known while it cannot be known.

The Ecstatic Identification of Man with God

True philosophy, being a way of life, aims at utility. However, what is useful to Nietzsche's true philosopher is exactly the opposite of what is useful to the ordinary man, namely — suffering. Nietzsche's philosophy is experimental in that it finds suffering to be useful. Suffering as a way of life is a philosophical attitude for it reveals reality as it is, i.e. as a conflict, a struggle of forces which is not disguised by any contrivance of reason. Suffering is useful because it unmasks truth, because it reveals to the philosopher who undertakes it that true utility is the overcoming of ordinary utility; that is, it is the overcoming of the will to find security and resolutions of suffering through reason. The true philosopher turns his back on security and sallies forth to adventure and dangers.

True philosophy is self-consciousness of a radically different order. It is an open and violently individual form of thinking. It represents a destructive process of universal reason. This destruction turns out to be the first expression of freedom and truth, for truth above all is *not* reason. At this point the individual thinker discloses himself, as well as the totality of reality, as meaningless and negative. This entails supreme suffering, for the true thinker sets himself beyond communication and chooses total solitude. Thus, true philosophy results in a disaster for ordinary life. There is no longer any hold of reality, for all the deeds are identical in their meaning. This is a total embarrassment, but it is also for the first time that reality is seen by the true thinker in its entirety. It is no longer seen in the one-sided mode of reason. Therefore the existential catastrophy which the free thinker brings upon himself, is at the same time his critical position towards reality, exposing reality as it is.

Nevertheless, it is impossible to stay passive in suffering, for life means attaching value to suffering. The true philosopher's choice, then, is the opposite of the ordinary one. He does not escape from suffering but chooses it, for he says 'no' to reason, morals, and everyday life, and says 'yes' to his desire to live reality as it is. He chooses himself in his solitary individuality. The belief in this, Nietzsche tells us in the *Genealogy,* is the redemption of man. There can be no other meaning to this statement but a redemption from falsification and openness to the totality of reality. This totality is the instinctive desire of the true thinker. But living according to this desire exclusively constitutes being a different kind of man. One can raise himself to this point only through overcoming the needs and motives of ordinary life, which means self-overcoming. In what follows, this particular quality proves to be identical to reality itself, as well as to truth. The true thinker stands alone in meaningless reality and has to attach a value to it. Hence, he inherits God, for he must give reality a value which is at the same time strictly individual and entirely total. The arbitrary choice to affix such a value is the desire for truth, for understanding reality as it is and not in a partial, one-sided way. Indeed, Nietzsche himself admits (*Gay Science* 344) that he belongs to the cultural tradition as far as searching for metaphysical truth is concerned.

But how can the totality of reality appear as it is within the individual? The individual is but a meaningless member of the things that constitute the totality, not the whole of reality. And moreover, what is the way of life within which reality appears as it is? Now, if everything is interpretation, and every capricious choice legitimate; if we should doubt everything, then we should doubt even logical consistency. Yet Nietzsche never does so. His scepticism remains consistent and subordinated to the process of criticism. Even though he rejects reason as a true criterion, he does not reject rationality altogether; for Nietzsche does not refute his own position, but remains consistent throughout. Hence, Nietzsche must see himself to be committed to rationality which is based on consistency, i.e. the law of contradiction; and this is true despite all that he argues against it, an argument largely located in *The Will to Power*. Thus, we may conclude that although he refutes rationality in the context of reason, he accepts it as total criticism. If this is so, and every position in life as well as in thought by being partial must be overcome, then nihilism too must be overcome. The total 'no' is overcome and so Nietzsche's thought must be ultimately positive, overcoming itself as purely negative criticism. We shall see now how he comes to establish just such a conclusion.

We have seen that Nietzsche's chosen way of life entails suffering and cruelty because of the desire for truth. Self-destruction through suffering means that one criticizes even the most hidden and intimate of values. Everything is exposed to consciousness. Nihilism is then the true philosopher's self-revelation. Everything which brings him satisfaction, pleasure or security is annihilated. Everything which is dear and important is destroyed for the benefit of a noble perceiving of reality, perceiving reality as it is without value or importance. In choosing suffering as a way of life the true philosopher overcomes his own human character and the ordinary life of man. He achieves, thereby, the sense of victory which accompanies such transcendence, a most intense feeling of power. This sense of power increases proportionally to the difficulty of overcoming. Thus the supreme sense of power is achieved by overcoming Man. Self-overcoming generates the true philosopher, and makes him one with the totality of reality. Man and God become identical, since self-overcoming is only achieved if based on a *general principle*, i.e. total reality that is free from inner contradiction that is due to fragmentation.

The deeper and the more profound the suffering, the emptier and more meaningless is free thinking. At this point free thinking is emptied of all content save the struggle and the continuous becoming of reality, that which constitutes the source of suffering. It is here that the power of the true thinker rises to its zenith. The summit of nihilism is to say 'no' both to the struggle and to the becoming of reality. But this time saying 'no' is not an evading of conflict and dissemblance. On the contrary, conflict and suffering are negated by choosing them. Nietzsche says 'yes' to reality as an eternal becoming and as a conflict. The nihilistic 'no' is no longer sufficient for reality is no longer a struggle but as well its overcoming. As long as man suffers there exists a tension between himself as individual and the totality of reality. The true philosopher's self-overcoming abolishes that distinction and so man becomes one with the whole of reality. Man and God are identical, becoming so in the actual conduct of man. Nietzsche's superman says 'yes' to reality as it is, to its rhythm which cannot be grasped by reason. Truth, then, is not a matter of discovery, for there is no state of affairs to be discovered. Reality is a constant becoming. Its real nature is neither fixed nor defined, but is in the process of eternal flux. Hence, truth is not a matter of revealing but of creating. True philosophy, which is the understanding of reality as it is, means the creating of reality, not its discovery. The true thinker turns out to be the creator of reality. Thus, his creation must be such that it would extend over the whole of reality and not a fragment of it, for as we have seen the subject matter of the true philosopher is nothing less than reality as a whole.

Nietzsche argues that this self-overcoming is manifested in the creation of a great style, a style which, alone, exemplifies the supreme power of reality. Having broken all values the true philosopher must decide upon new ones, values that are purely arbitrary and individual. Thus he appears as the legislator of reality who creates it anew. The true philosopher affixes meaning and values to reality by living according to these values. Through his action, his great style, he achieves complete union of private self and the totality of reality, this union being a state of ecstasy.

Creation means giving an individual and arbitrary form to becoming reality. But creation as a great style is the annihilation of reality as it usually appears and the reconstruction of it. The individual subject gives to the whole of reality a purely personal system of values. Yet, in that he lives in accordance with these values, his suffering, which is a consequence of the destruction of the old value system, is transformed to boundless joy, to ecstasy. The true philosopher reveals the whole world within himself. He discovers that his power is infinite.

By forcing a new form upon reality the philosopher is not rejecting reality but says 'yes' to reality as a struggle and its transcendence. Hence, only the true philosopher can accept reality as it is. It is true that all other creatures, as well as the ordinary sort of man, also confine reality within the form of their action in order to overcome suffering. But unlike the true philosopher, they view reality from the standpoint of their own restricted needs. The true philosopher, on the other hand, views reality from *its own* standpoint, as well as from his own, for his personal need is to perceive it as it is. For him, reality is revealed as being of the utmost intimate interest. Thus, when man acts from his arbitrary individuality as if he were the totality of reality, in that action he is God. Here is action that is preconditioned by the desire to experience the whole of reality, a desire which happens to be the one and only motive in man's life.

Strangely enough, it is just such an individual creation of a great style which is manifested paradoxically as objective (as in *Of the Use and Disadvantage of History for Life,* chap. 6), since it is identical with the rhythm of reality itself. Hence, this individual creation is true. The true philosopher, the superman, is an artist in that he gives a great style to reality, i.e., he exemplifies in his very way of life the inner logic of the eternally becoming reality. Reality as such annihilates every datum in order to construct a new one. This new form is true only in its not being old, but it is not true in itself. It is doomed as well. It has been created because of there being a power of life that brought it about, not because of the existence of any special goal that had claimed it. Even a great style appears only to disappear. Creating a great style and living accordingly in Dionysian ecstasy is objective truth in that it is without purpose and does not turn into a law which reason imposes on reality. A great style is the way in which the true philosopher says 'yes' to reality. He asserts in his action that he is the totality of reality to the extent that the Dionysian festivity endures. When there is no longer ecstasy, the great style itself is but a form that has to be overcome. Indeed, a great style expresses in its values only the truth of eternal self-transcendence, and not per se its own values. Hence, true philosophy by creating reality is at the same time discovering it as it is.

We find then that philosophy can only be objective if it is fully subjective. That is, only if it is motivated by the interest to see reality as it is, devoid of egotistic interests, is it objective. The total power of reality emerges when the individual is cleansed of all egotistic interests, and he affirms nothing but the power of negating and destroying. This negating power is identical with the negating power of reality which annihilates everything. The true philosopher is intoxicated by this sense of power, and comes to experience the Absolute. Now the absolute of truth is not knowledge but feeling. In the Dionysian ecstasy we realize that truth is located in the very love of man for reality. Perhaps to put the matter more properly, since man is but a part of reality, we should say that truth is the love of reality for itself (as Spinoza has argued).

It is interesting as well as important to determine the nature of the positive values that Nietzsche, in his own great style, gives to reality. But in fact there are none. His valuating action is no more than refuting the existing values. The change of values is, practically speaking, all negative, so these new values are but the opposite of the old ones; i.e. deduced by the very act of negation. Thus, a great style is no more than affirming reality as it is. The only new value is the discovery of reality as will to power, as self-overcoming. Since reality is constant overcoming, and since the true thinker identifies himself with it in his life and thought, we find that his truth too is in self-overcoming, self-negating and self-creating. It is in this sense that Nietzsche can claim that the Superman loves fate. For fate is nothing but reality as it is, the self-overcoming will to power which eternally recurs. The individual who has only a will to true totality discovers reality in himself as fate, as it is. Hence absolute criticism and negating all values do not leave the true thinker in a position of unbearable suffering, but, on the contrary, give him the power to treat suffering from the standpoint of reality as a whole. Nietzsche's thinking then *must* be positive, since absolute criticism is total negation and total negation must be self-negation, i.e. self-overcoming.

The Rediscovery of Absolute Truth

When the true philosopher realizes all this he reacts with laughter. He realizes that all his unimaginably strenuous effort put into destroying and recreating the world has been for nought. In his openness to reality the true thinker did not discover anything but rather negated everything. Yet he did not fall into a position of nihilism, for he discovered in himself the positive power of reality. His power was due to the fact that he loved it, loved its necessary fate. Total destruction, in view of a new creation which in itself is also destined to be destroyed, is therefore an eternal recurrence. Such a recurrence is to be equated with reality as it is. The understanding of reality is possible only by living in accordance with the process of becoming itself. Hence, reason cannot reveal reality. What we find is rather that reality is disclosed only to the true philosopher, to the one who loves true reality. In the self-overcoming of the true philosopher eternal recurrence, necessary fate, and the will to power are all identical. Such a thinker practices all three of these elements of true reality in the course of his everyday life.

In this love of wisdom Nietzsche is fully Socratic, for it is in this love of wisdom that the overwhelming power of negating makes itself manifest. Without this love Nietzsche's philosophy would have fallen into the meaninglessness of nihilism, since the destructive might of criticism alone leads to nihilism and scepticism. Such criticism is restricted by being solely theoretical. It is limited by real conduct which lies beyond it. But love of wisdom is not restricted to the theoretical. Love of truth makes the lover totally involved in the results of philosophical investigation no matter what they be. Only thus can one be God in his conduct while negating everything else in the world. Truth gives itself totally to whomever gives himself totally to truth. This is how Socrates could be wise without knowing anything. His love of wisdom enabled him not to be a sceptic, although he doubted everything. Socrates, like the Nietzschean true philosopher, was totally engaged in the process of thinking, and overcame anything that might endanger it.

Tel-Aviv University

Eliyahu Rosenow

Nietzsche's Concept of Education

Contemporary philosophy of education ignores Nietzsche's philosophy so much so that there seems to be a conspiracy of silence against it among educationists. Most of them would probably consider a discussion of Nietzsche's concept of education a contradiction in terms. And yet there are few philosophical systems in which the concept of education is of such momentous purport as it is in that of Nietzsche. This disregard of Nietzsche is illuminating of the philosophy of education itself no less than it is of Nietzsche. The discussion of Nietzsche's concept of education serves therefore a double purpose, shedding light not only on an extraordinary view of education, but also on the nature of the philosophy of education as an organized branch of knowledge.

I

Nietzsche characterizes his philosophy in general as an "Attempt at a Revaluation of All Values" (WP, Preface 4). This attribute is pertinent to his concept of education as well, since it is the realm of education in which the problem of values is most salient. Just as it is necessary to understand first the meaning which Nietzsche ascribes to traditional values in order to comprehend the significance of his revaluation of values, so it is possible to understand his transformation of the concept of education only in the light of his criticism of current education.

Nietzsche's criticism of the educational practices of his time appears first in a series of five lectures entitled "The Future of Our Educational Institutions," which he gave in 1872 in Basel. In these lectures education is construed as a device implemented by the state in order to promote its selfish interests. Nietzsche's criticism exposes the idea of the dissemination of general education which the modern "Culture State" ("Kulturstaat") propagates as an ideological deception victimizing those of the younger generation who are really interested in knowledge.[1] The uniqueness of this criticism is due mainly to Nietzsche's strong language and to his biting irony, but substantially there is nothing particularly new about it. His arguments are already present in Rousseau's early essays. Nietzsche's main contribution is their application to the contemporary educational institutions. His lectures on education are therefore of interest mainly as far as they anticipate the criticism in his later writings. In them too education is condemned as a fraudulent and manipulative device but this time from a different point of view. His concern is the inner dialectics of the educational process itself. The object of his criticism now is therefore not the state and its educational institutions, but the educator and his disciple. The ordinary educator appears in Nietzsche's writings as the philosopher.

The philosopher as a rule uses "as a mask and cocoon the previously established types of the contemplative man" (GM III:10) which symbolically represent the different aspects of his being: he is the "ideal scholar," who cultivates the objective spirit and "disinterested knowledge" to such an extent that he annihilates his own individual self (BGE 207) and who lends himself to a skepticism which paralyses his will (208). He is the moralist who subjugates the spirit (188) and who turns man into a slave and a "herding human animal" (202). He is the "religious type" who sacrifices "all freedom, all pride, all self-confidence of the spirit" for the sake of "enslavement, self-mockery and self-mutilation" (46), and he is also the ascetic priest, who hates and negates life and who, haunted by "a ressentiment without equal," practises self-castigation (GM III:10, 11). Thus in his personality the philosopher reflects the paradoxical combination of "inactive, brooding, unwarlike" characteristics mingled with a fierce will to survive and a violent desire to rule, a will and a desire which prevent him from yielding to his passive and inert disposition but which however are not powerful enough to enable him really to live.

The paradoxical being of the philosopher determines his destiny, which is also paradoxical. His weak and softish being and his constant fear because of his inferiority challenge his instincts of survival and force him to endow his existence and appearance "with a meaning, a basis and background" through which others might come to fear him. But this defence mechanism is so contrary to his nature, that he must first subjugate his own consciousness and change himself in order to be able to cut a convincing figure. For this purpose he must learn both to "fear and reverence" himself and to disguise and

---

[1] *On the Future of Our Educational Institutions,* tr. J.M. Kennedy (New York, Russell & Russell, 1964), see esp. Third Lecture.

camouflage his true self. He is therefore like an actor impersonating an alien image who first has to persuade himself that this image is a true one so as to persuade his audience as well (GM III:10).

In this way the philosopher contrives to get a hold on the masses and to dominate them. His means of control are the traditional systems of religious and moral values, through which he imposes his will on them, turning them thus into a herd of docile sheep and obedient slaves. The analysis and criticism of this system of values constitute the main body of Nietzsche's philosophy, and its discussion is outside the present frame of reference. This paper therefore concentrates on the interrelation between the philosopher and the masses on the one hand and between the philosopher and himself on the other, since the distinguishing marks of this interrelation seem to be also those of current education as viewed by Nietzsche.

The object of the philosopher's activity is the man of the masses, who appears in Nietzsche's writings as the slave. The slave too is motivated both by his feeling of inferiority, which is the result of the feebleness and sluggishness of his degenerate nature, and by his instinct of survival, which impels him to develop a mechanism enabling him to keep existing in spite of his insignificance. Possessing no self-esteem, he is capable of confiding in himself only when someone else reassures him that he is worthy, and so he "seeks to seduce him to good opinions about himself," so that he can believe in them afterwards and prostrate himself before them "as if he had not called them forth" (BGE 261). The slave too therefore needs the belief in an illusionary external image in order to survive.

The motive force of the slave is the ressentiment, i.e. those impoverished and degenerate residues of the will to power which motivate the philosopher as well. This force asserts itself by way of negation: since the slave is able to confirm his existence only by negating this world, he negates everything that is "outside," "different" and not himself. He is therefore dependent on a hostile external world. This dependence is reflected in the way he perceives himself: since the slave is unable to accept himself as he really is, he needs an image of his self which is the very opposite of his real self. And since he negates everything that is unattainable for him — life, power, creativity — he condemns whoever represents it as "the evil enemy," "the Evil One." From this basic concept "he then evolves, as an afterthought and pendant," the "good one," i.e. himself (GM I:10).

The same paradoxical mechanism is thus at work in both the philosopher and the slave compelling both of them to negate life and their own authentic selves in order to survive. In both of them the will to power operates as an ambivalent force, concurrently threatening their existence and guaranteeing its continuity. In this way the philosopher and the slave become dependent on each other: each of them needs the other as an object on which he can activate his will to power. This established dependence is dangerous, since it implies that each of them constitutes a threat to the very existence of the other, and therefore to his own existence as well. The dependence is therefore transformed into a symbiosis: the philosopher, disguised as the ascetic priest, alters the direction of the slave's ressentiment. The suffering slave "instinctively seeks a cause for his suffering" and, specifically, some victim "upon which he can, on some pretext or other, vent his affects." The philosopher helps him in this by persuading him that it is he himself, the slave, who is the guilty one, and so he succeeds in directing the ressentiment of the slave against himself and prevent him from an open rebellion and assault which might annihilate the philosopher (GM III:15).

The relationship between the philosopher and the slave is therefore analogous to the relationship between a physician and his patient. But this analogy is also paradoxical: in order to be able to cure his patients the physician "must be sick himself," since only the basic identity of the two enables the philosopher to understand the slave and dominate him. But the philosopher-doctor does not heal the suffering patient: he does not combat "the real sickness," but only "the suffering itself, the discomfiture of the sufferer." He alleviates suffering and consoles the patient by means of cunning tricks which help the sufferer to overcome his agony and survive (GM III:17). But before the philosopher can act as a physician "he first has to wound," and while stilling the pain of the affliction "he at the same time infects the wound," working thus "the self-destruction of the incurable" (16). In this way the mutual dependence becomes permanent: the slave becomes dependent on the philosopher for the alleviation of his suffering, while the philosopher needs the slave to exercise his degenerate will to power upon and so to survive.

Nietzsche's criticism of education in his early lectures exposes education as a manipulative mechanism which serves to distort man's consciousness and to annihilate his self, subjugating him in this way to the absolute authority of the state. It seems therefore that there is a certain resemblance between the state and the philosopher of Nietzsche's later writings. But this similarity is only partial: while the state is presented as an agent acting consciously and expediently, the philosopher is the victim of his own deception and manipulation. The philosopher seems to embody the educator, and the dialectic relationship between the philosopher and the slave is analogous to the relationship which develops between the educator and his disciples in the course of conventional education. This is true also for the value system through which the philosopher takes hold of the slave: it seems to be only a means of control, but actually this system becomes hypostatized so that it is transformed into an independent agent which rules "voluntarily and paramountly" (BGE 62).

Viewed thus Nietzsche's criticism of education is a really diabolic caricature of the educational process. Education turns out to be not merely an instrument of manipulation, but manipulation itself. It not only promotes the selfish interests of a despotic and totalitarian authority, but advances the self-destruction of all: not only of the disciples and the students, but of the educators themselves. The self-deception is complete, the distortion of consciousness is total and the annihilation of the self is final.

"The most distinctive feature of modern souls and modern books," says Nietzsche, "is not lying... Our educated people of today, our 'good people,' do not tell lies — that is true; but that is *not* to their credit! A real lie, a genuine, resolute, 'honest' lie... would be something far too severe and potent for them." Contemporary man is to be characterized by his "inveterate *innocence* in moralistic mendaciousness," a mendaciousness that is "abysmal but innocent, truehearted, blue-eyed, and virtuous" (GM III:19). Nietzsche refers in this passage to Plato for the definition of the genuine and honest lie, but actually Plato defines the innocent lie as well: In his *Republic* Plato makes a distinction between the true and opportune falsehood, i.e. the "noble lie," which is legitimate and useful in the education of the young (377a; cf. 414b-c), and the "veritable lie," which is the "deception in the soul about realities" and the "ignorance in the soul of the man deceived," and abhorred by all gods and men (382a-b). Plato is careful not to attribute this absolute lie explicitly to the tenants of the cave: their world is the world of opinion, in which truth and error are mixed. Nietzsche's case is different; for him man is the captive of his own deception, the victim of himself. Perhaps this is the reason why Nietzsche does not mention the term "education" in the context of his discussion of the philosopher and the slave. The concept "education" seems to be the only one which Nietzsche does not use in the dual meaning which all the key concepts of his philosophy possess: there is no education in the world of the philosophers and the slaves, but manipulation only.

II

Paralleling the two layers of the criticism of education, Nietzsche's writings contain two complementary versions of the true concept of education. The difference is again not in substance but in perspective: in his early writings Nietzsche deals with the educator and the disciple, while in his later writings he analyzes the inner dialectics of the educational process itself.

In the early writings — i.e., in "The Future of Our Educational Institutions" and "Schopenhauer as Educator" — the concept of education is stated in contradictory terms: the educator is characterized as one who exercises authority and demands obedience (Fifth Lecture) — but it is he who delivers man. On the other hand, the disciple is described as possessing a unique and true being which only he himself can reveal[2] — but for this purpose he has to follow the guiding educator. These paradoxes are more apparent than real: they adumbrate Nietzsche's concept of education, fully worked out in *Thus Spoke Zarathustra* which Nietzsche considered to be his central work.

Zarathustra announces his incentive to educate already in the Prologue. Addressing the sun at the beginning of his career he proclaims: "Great star! What would your happiness be, if you had not those for whom you shine!... Behold! I am weary of my wisdom, like a bee that has gathered too much honey; I need hands outstretched to take it. I would like to give it away and distribute it..." (Zarathustra's Prologue, 1). Zarathustra is in need of people, although the origin of this need is not Zarathustra's humanistic or altruistic motive, but an inner necessity. His attachment to men is basically ambivalent: he is simultaneously attracted and repelled by them. At one point in the book Zarathustra dramatically describes himself as a person suspended over an abyss with his eyes raised upwards but his hands trying to find support in the depth. This parable gives expression to Zarathustra's double wish: "My will clings to mankind, I bind myself to mankind with fetters, because I am drawn up to the Superman: for my other will wants to draw me up to the Superman" (Z, Of Manly Prudence). Zarathustra needs people because they are the raw material concealing the form of the Superman, for which he strives. This raw material as such is abhorred by Zarathustra who compares it to the ugliest and hardest of stones (Z, On the Blissful Islands), but he cannot dispense with this abhorrent raw material and go his way without it. He cannot accept people as they are, and therefore shuts his eyes so as not to see their real being: "That my hand may not quite lose its belief in firmness: *that is why* I live blindly among men, as if I did not recognize them." Zarathustra must hide from himself the truth about men and entertain an illusory belief with regard to them, and so he wants to see them disguised and "well dressed and vain and worthy, as 'the good and just.'" For the same reason Zarathustra cannot appear before men as he really is, but has to be disguised too: "And I myself will sit among you disguised, so that I may *misunderstand* you and myself:

---

[2] *Thoughts out of Season: Schopenhauer as Educator,* tr. A. Collins (New York, Russell & Russell, 1964), §1.

that, in fact, is my last manly prudence" (Z, Of Manly Prudence).

Zarathustra has an irresistible drive to educate: he must lavish on others out of his own spiritual superabundance. The act of education is compared to the process of stonecutting. Zarathustra equates himself to a sculptor who sculpts in stone the form he envisions: "But again and again it drives me to mankind, my ardent, creative will: thus it drives the hammer to the stone. Ah, you men, I see an image sleeping in the stone, the image of my visions! Ah, that it must sleep in the hardest, ugliest stone!" (Z, On the Blissful Islands).

Nietzschean education is a really violent process, since Zarathustra works mercilessly, impelled by nothing but his own creativity and devoted only to the form or image he envisions, entirely indifferent to the chips which fly around and fall down in the course of his work. He therefore personifies the image of the uncompromising educator, molding his students according to his vision. No wonder Zarathustra cannot appear in front of his students as he really is; he is in need of an attractive mask. Elsewhere in the book Zarathustra compares himself to a fisherman casting his fishing rod into the sea with a tempting bait on it: "Especially the human world, the human sea: now I cast my golden fishing rod into *it* and say 'Open up, human abyss! Open up and throw me your fishes and glistening crabs! With my finest bait shall I bait to-day the strangest human fish!... For I am *he,* from the heart and from the beginning, drawing, drawing towards me, drawing up to me, raising up, a drawer, trainer, and taskmaker who once bade himself, and not in vain: 'Become what you are!'" (Z, The Honey Offering).

The most remarkable feature of this conception is, that it focuses neither on the disciple nor on society or cultural heritage, but on the educator. Zarathustra is motivated by his overpowering creativity; he is a creative artist. But his artistic drive pushes him not to stone or marble, but to man. Man represents the greatest challenge, since it is he who is a raw material which is most difficult to mold. The encounter with man therefore becomes a most important issue in Zarathustra's life, since man is the only medium for discovering and expressing his true being.

Zarathustra's life is the realization of his will to power, which unfolds itself as a process of legislating and commanding, i.e. as the creation of values (BGE 211; cf. Z, Of the Tree on the Mountainside). He is the "noble type of man," the determiner and creator of values (BGE 260), in constant struggle with the outside world and with himself, who permanently aspires to master and surpass himself. In other words: Zarathustra is the philosopher. But he is not the enfeebled, sly philosopher personified in the images of the scholar and the ascetic priest, but he is a philosopher of "a new species" (BGE 42), a "genuine philosopher" (BGE 211) — i.e. the very contradiction and negation of the false traditional philosopher.

But the new and genuine philosopher is also a play-actor and a misleader, "a pied piper" and "a seducer" (BGE 205), he also appears attired in a disguise and wearing a mask. Zarathustra double-crosses his students, concealing his true personality and his selfish interests. Nietzsche's education seems therefore to bear all the characteristics of manipulation which are the distinguishing marks of current education and to be its afterimage and copy: Just like it, it is "essentially the art of deceiving" (BGE 264).

But this similarity is only an ostensible one. Conventional education presents itself as promoting the individual's well-being, while Nietzsche's education presumes nothing of the kind, but openly declares itself to be what it really is. According to Nietzsche education *is* manipulation, compulsion and deceit, and its driving force is the will to power of the educator, who creates his disciples in order to build up his own self and so as to realize himself. The true educator is therefore indifferent to his disciple's independent personality. It is not the disciples themselves, nor their undiscovered beauty and latent qualities which attract him to them. For the Nietzschean educator the disciple or student is from the very first only a mere object whose attraction lies in the inherent possibilities he opens up for the educator. He therefore does not simply fail to see his disciples as they are, but he does not care to see them: it is not their real selves to which he relates, but an illusionary image which he consciously attributes to them. The educational process as a whole is conceived of as a creative act through which the educator expresses himself and realizes his own potentialities (Z, On Involuntary Bliss). That is why the educator has to assume the role of a tempter.

But this is not all. The philosopher of the new order is not only a play-actor and a misleader, but also "designated as tempter": he leads into temptation (BGE 42). The explicit deceit and manipulation are intended to provoke the student against the educator and incite him to rebel against the latter's domination. Just because the disciple represents untouched raw material and just because it is the process of educational formation and molding itself which is significant for Zarathustra, he has no regard for the passive and submissive student. The disciple is of interest for Zarathustra only as a friend-enemy, i.e. as far as he is a challenge to him (Z, Of the Friend). The climax of the educational process is therefore the rebellion of the disciple against the educator. Zarathustra expects his disciples to rebel against him, and when they do not do so of their own accord, he urges them to rebel or else simply abandons them. "One repays a teacher badly if one remains only a pupil," Zarathustra says to his disciples, and advises them: "Go away from me and guard yourselves against Zarathustra! And better still: be ashamed of him! Perhaps he has deceived you... You had not yet sought yourselves when you found me. Thus do all believers; therefore all belief is of so little account. Now I bid you lose me and find yourselves; and only when you have all denied me will I return to you" (Z, Of the Bestowing Virtue).

This rebellion is essential not only for Zarathustra, but for his disciples as well. The disciple too must learn to stand alone in order to discover his self, and so he has to rebel against the educator. The essence of education is therefore the dialectical tension by means of which both the educator and his disciples each discover their own self: Zarathustra and his disciples must become friends-enemies to each other.

Nietzsche's revaluation of values in education is most striking at this point. Education is explicitly manipulation; but precisely as such it makes rebellion possible: One can rebel only against Zarathustra's ostensible authority, but not against the philosopher's cunning. Zarathustra represents the reversal of the traditional philosopher. The latter must believe in his own mendacity; he must be sick himself and poison the patient so as to perform his task and make the dependence everlasting, and therefore both he and his followers are doomed. The two-fold deceit of Zarathustra is conscious and deliberate and designed so as to incite rebellion. Unlike conventional education the Nietzschean educational situation is a transient one; it constitutes only one stage on the road to perfection. The rebellion is therefore both the climax and the termination of the educational process. At this moment the educator and the disciple separate from each other and start looking for themselves on their own. Rebellion and loneliness are the distinguishing marks of real freedom.

Indeed it is the concept of freedom which epitomizes the contradiction between Nietzsche and traditional education. The philosopher too presumes to liberate man. But this is the normative freedom of the man who is devoted to universal values, and therefore it promotes his basic unity with his fellow-men rather than his unique selfhood. What traditional thinking views as the realization of man's self and freedom is in Nietzschean terms the self-realization of the slave and the perpetuation of bondage. The freedom that Nietzsche promises is the pure and real freedom of a man who creates his values by himself, and whose values are his alone. Nietzsche's principle of freedom in education is entirely new: it is the positive freedom of the realization of man's authentic being. It does not, however, imply an attitude of anarchy and nihilism, but the acceptance of restricting laws and personal responsibility (Z, Of the Way of the Creator; cf. Of the Tree on the Mountain-side). "Man is something that must be overcome" (Of Joys and Passions), says Zarathustra. But whoever follows this maxim finds himself "spun into a severe yarn and shirt of duties" from which he cannot disengage himself

(BGE 226). It is the freedom of the noble man, who never thinks of degrading his duties "into duties for everybody," who is unwilling to renounce or to share his responsibilities and who counts his prerogatives and the exercise of them among his duties (BGE 272).

More than that: since freedom is the realization of one's individual self, Nietzsche only indicates the direction in which the disciple should go in order to free himself and become his own master. Zarathustra helps his disciples peel off the crust of traditional education and human society and helps them emerge from the nihilistic stage. But he does not actually show them the way. Nietzsche does not pretend to actually create the free man, but only to help man to liberate himself; he indicates the way to freedom, but does not actually bestow this freedom, since freedom is by definition something man has to achieve all by himself. At this point there is no longer room for guidance and instruction; this is the end of the educational road. Education merely leads to freedom, but it does not get there. Nietzsche's conception of education includes by its very definition aspects of both external guidance and self education. In this way the paradoxes which characterize Nietzsche's concept of education in his early writings are resolved. Nietzsche's revaluation of educational values starts already at the very point of departure of his philosophy.

The most difficult problem of any educational conception based on the total negation of conventional education is that the radical criticism of the existing social and educational order encloses the critic in a vicious circle, which renders any alternative impossible. A typical example of such a revolutionary conception is Plato's *Republic*. The exit out of the hopeless circle of error in which the tenants of the cave are captured is possible only thanks to what Plato calls "providence of God" (493a). The appearance of the philosopher "who was freed from his fetters and compelled to stand up suddenly" (515c) is nothing short of a miracle. Platonic education itself is possible only thanks to some felicitous but improbable accident by which philosophic wisdom and political power happen to coincide so that the ideal state would become a reality. Plato's educational conception is therefore utopian from its very start. One would expect that such would be the fate of Nietzsche's educational conception as well, since according to Nietzsche all of us are those modern souls infested by our "inveterate innocence in moralistic mendaciousness." Who, then, is the new and genuine philosopher who will liberate us from our "abysmal mendaciousness"? Is his appearance not also a miracle? Is Nietzsche's educational conception not basically utopian?

But Nietzsche deviates radically also from traditional utopian thinking. He does not juxtapose two static systems of existing reality and utopian vision, whose connection is at best a speculative one, but presents one dynamic system which keeps changing shape. The world of the dwellers of Plato's cave is the world of becoming and annihilation, but it is under the rule of a law which guarantees the persistence of its inert existence. Nietzsche's world is governed by a dialectical lawfulness which keeps it in a state of constant flux. The ideological conditioning does not create a hopeless vicious circle, but is governed by a dialectic principle which reduces the deception of both the philosopher and the slave *ad absurdum,* so that it is doomed to annul itself. The accumulation of poison, the aggravation of the disease and self-destruction ultimately destroy the sophisticated mechanism. The inevitable outcome of this process is increasing nihilism. "What I relate," declares Nietzsche in the Preface of his *Will to Power,* "is the history of the next two centuries. I describe what is coming, what can no longer come differently: *the advent of nihilism.* This history can be related even now; for necessity itself is at work here" (WP, Preface 2).

The advent of nihilism seems to threaten European culture and to predict a catastrophe, but in a paradoxical way the opposite is true. "Nihilism represents a pathological transitional stage" (WP 13): Nietzsche believes that it will challenge man's repressed will to power, incite him to rebel against tradition and encourage him to realize his self. The appearance of the new and real philosopher is therefore not only not a miracle, but also a necessity, an unavoidable result of the dialectics of life. Moreover, this new philosopher already actually exists; he is in the midst of us and we hear his voice. It is the voice of none but Nietzsche himself, who is heralding the advent of Superman and who brings deliverance unto the world. From Nietzsche's point of view his philosophy is not only no utopia, but it is operant reality. All we have to do is to open our ears and listen to him.

III

Nietzsche's conception of education is not only original and completely novel in the history of educational thought, but also extremely daring. It states a most militant and bold concept of individualism, which however is neither anarchistic nor nihilistic. But man has to pay an exorbitant price for this radical individualism: it leaves him in abysmal loneliness. The fact that Nietzsche presents this loneliness as the splendid isolation of a chosen few makes it no less of a problem. It is true that Superman is imbued with a deep feeling of responsibility and that he creates values. But these values are completely personal, and therefore they not only do not contribute anything to human communication but, on the contrary, they isolate man. Communication and interaction are for Nietzsche only transitory stages on Superman's way which he must overcome. At the end of his way Superman is asocial, but at its crucial stage he is anti-social: he revaluates not only the concept of freedom, but also the concepts of equality and fraternity. The revaluation of the basic values of democracy and society amounts ultimately to the negation of democratic society altogether. Nietzsche proves that conventional education refutes itself. The unavoidable question is whether Nietzsche's concept of education does not reduce itself *ad absurdum* and whether it does not ultimately refute itself.

Nietzsche was aware of this problem. For him man is "something that should be overcome" (Z, Zarathustra's Prologue 3). For him what is great in man is "that he is a bridge and not a goal," "a rope, fastened between animal and Superman — a rope over an abyss" (ibid., 4). But man's greatness exposes him to a two-fold danger. The first is, that the bridge will lead him to destruction, and the second is, that he might lose his balance and be precipitated into the abyss. The bridge leading to destruction is a symbol of the false interpretation of Nietzsche's teaching, which might be disastrous for both himself and his followers (Z, The Child with the Mirror). But the second danger is much more serious, since it is inherent in Nietzsche's concept of education itself.

Zarathustra's Prologue features an acrobat who starts walking on a rope stretched between two towers and hanging high above the market-place, who loses his head and his footing on the rope and falls down crushing his limbs, after the devil in the image of a buffoon jumps over his head and overtakes him. The devil's speech following this incident explains the moral of this fable: Zarathustra is like a rope-dancer, and the imminent danger he is facing is not so much the hatred of the many but his own collapse (Z, Zarathustra's Prologue 3-8). In other words: the temptation inherent in Nietzsche's teaching is great, but the risk run by whoever succumbs to it is immense. It is exactly this point which Nietzsche has in mind when he speaks about the "philosophers of the future" who "may have a right — it might also be a wrong — to be called *attempters*" — a name which is itself in the end "a mere attempt, and, if you will, a temptation" (BGE 42).

The fact that Nietzsche is hardly ever mentioned in textbooks dealing with the history of educational thought testifies that contemporary philosophy of education did not succumb to Nietzsche's temptation. Nietzsche's concept of education is an integral part of his criticism of conventional education, and both his criticism as well as his new conception present a threat to the very foundations of education. Nietzsche's criticism demolishes current education altogether, and his new concept disqualifies any attempt to justify education. Nietzsche's assertion that education is manipulation, and all its implications — the egoistic motive of the educator, the demand to let man discover and realize his self alone and by himself only, the abolition of communication, and, last not least, the postulate that education is merely a transitory stage which has not only to be surpassed but which has to be terminated by rebellion — all these are ideas which virtually cut the ground from under the feet of any educator.

At the same time, the reluctance to cope with Nietzsche's educational thought is in itself a manifestation of our educational presuppositions. The fact that current philosophy of education prefers to ignore Nietzsche proves, from his point of view, that his prophecy about the advent of nihilism and its inevitable consequences did not come true and that the impoverished will to power of the contemporary educator is still strong enough to help him persist in his inert existence. This educator, who oscillates between the traditional and the radical conception of education, perhaps belongs to the host of the slaves and perhaps to that of the nihilistic Higher Men, and it is hard to tell which of them Nietzsche detests more. Seen from this point of view Nietzsche's educational thought presents a challenge today just as it did one hundred years ago. On the other hand, to anyone trying to reassess it today, Nietzsche's concept of education presents itself not as a solution but as a problem.

Nietzsche gives man the choice of continuing to be a slave or trying to become Superman; but neither of these options offers him a real chance, since the choice of either implies ruin. In other words, Nietzsche lets us choose between the kingdom of God and the kingdom of the devil, between the heaven of utopia and the hell of anti-utopia. Nietzsche's parable, which likens Zarathustra to a rope-dancer walking on a thin rope while a deep chasm yawns below and Satan dances behind him, is therefore applicable not only to Nietzsche himself but to all of us. Even those who are unwilling to acknowledge Nietzsche as an educator can no longer ignore his basic claim, that in our age "education" and "culture" "have to be essentially the art of deceiving" (BGE 264), i.e. that education is essentially manipulation. The question is, what do we prefer — self-deceit or conscious deceit. One way or another, we find ourselves in a trap, the escape from which necessitates an existential decision, i.e. a decision which is purely personal and subjective. And precisely that is Nietzsche's message.

Tel-Aviv University

Eric Blondel

Nietzsche's Style of Affirmation: The Metaphors of Genealogy

An Richard Roos (1923-1984),
dem Philologen, Nietzsche-Leser und Freund.
"Man vergebe es mir als einem alten Philologen..."
(Jenseits, 22)

I. The Conditions of (Im)Possibility

This paper is a *Versuch*. It tries (and perhaps fails) to solve what appears to me as a radical, inescapable dilemma in Nietzsche's thought: How and what can Nietzsche affirm after the death of God, without stumbling into arbitrary and nonsensical speech?

Sure it is, on the one hand, that Nietzsche explicitly wants to pose as an affirmative thinker. In the very climax of his criticism against morality, Christianity and, generally speaking, metaphysics, he says: "In order to remain true to my own way, which is *affirmative* [*Jasagend*] and practises contradiction and criticism but indirectly and unwillingly, I lay down the three tasks for which one needs educators."[1] And this is admittedly no single statement in Nietzsche's work, especially in the later texts, where Nietzsche very often uses the phrase "*Jasagen.*" Indeed, he demands that philosophy, as a problematic of culture, be not so much negation (as e.g. morality, which he brands as "*Verneinung des Lebens*"), criticism and refusal — a cliché imposed on it since Socrates — as a positive disposition, for want of which negation would be sheer reactive weakness. "Dionysus versus the Crucified."

---

[1] *Götzendämmerung,* Was den Deutschen abgeht, 6.
All the quotations of Nietzsche in English are my translation, unless otherwise stated. To avoid equivocal reference keys, they refer to the original German titles. KGW refers to the Colli-Montinari edition (published by W. de Gruyter).

On the other hand, however, how does Nietzsche, or how should we after him, construct this concept of affirmation? In what sense and in what manner does he speak of affirmation? Actually that word, to use Nietzsche's own expression,[2] "deserves quotation marks." Does it mean a confirmation of what *is*? But what is *really,* has a real being? Besides, should that be unadulterated positivity and pure position? Or a kind of new (?) negation of negation in the manner of Hegel? For instance, should decadent morality be affirmed as well as strength, should Christianity be refused as an illusion, as pure *Nichts,* or on the contrary affirmed as a necessary antipode of Dionysiac affirmation? One may wonder whether that word "affirmation" as such would not lead Nietzsche into a pre-critical dogmatism, which would seduce his philosophy into *Schwärmerei* or at least would induce him, ontologically speaking, to a weak, entropic conception of Being and, from the point of view of method, to a resignation of genealogy, appreciation and "war."

If the death of God is no empty, quixotic slogan, but, as I believe it is, a hopeless revelation that the foundation of the highest values of metaphysics and morality is radically unbelievable and unreliable, we must admit that Nietzsche can ground his affirmation neither on Being (as firm identity), nor on Truth (as a communicable object outside the subject), nor on any kind of Subject (whether it were the individual self, or society, or mankind). Besides, Nietzsche cannot have recourse to such *means* of affirmation as language (which he often denounces as essentially metaphysical), or concept and science (which oversimplify and vulgarize reality) — not to mention faith, that is to say morality, metaphysics or religion. Furthermore, to crown it all, if Nietzsche's philosophy does have any contents or tenor of discourse which might be affirmed (and this cannot be denied without complete absurdity), don't we have to admit that it either falls back into the frame of metaphysical unity, systematicity, logical unequivocality (see *Wille zur Macht,* 436), or that it keeps its antimetaphysical impetus only by means of a nightly, underground, almost hypocritical Penelopian unweaving of its own "daily" work? In other words, should we understand the words of *Zarathustra*: "The world is deep, And deeper than day has ever thought" simply as "a night where all cows are black"? If God is dead, are we not obliged to think of Nietzsche's affirmation as an affirmation without concept, without truth, without contents — as an undetermined affirmation which is but nonsensical, ridiculous, and deserves in its turn nothing but a contemptuous smile or shrug? Is Nietzsche a philosophical nincompoop or, what in his own opinion comes to the same thing, a supermetaphysician?

---

[2] *Jenseits,* 11, about German "philosophy"!

To put it bluntly: the question of affirmation necessarily implies an answer to the question: How does Nietzsche philosophize, is he a philosopher at all, and, if so, in what sense? It must be assumed here that, if the word has any meaning, there is no philosophy which does not ask itself about its own conditions and modalities, i.e. its status, aims and terms of affirmation. Now, it should be clearly stated here that, with respect to the definition and conditions of philosophical activity, one cannot read *and* understand Nietzsche as one does other philosophers, (a) because (to put it shortly) the rational, conceptual, unequivocal and more or less logically systematic commentary upon his work is as such *heterogeneous* to Nietzsche's style of *Versuch,* his style of writing, to his ways and styles of progress in thought; and (b) because, as I have just said, Nietzsche is the thinker who has called in question metaphysics as "Reason in philosophy," and therefore cannot be considered simply and unreservedly as a pure rational thinker.

I contend that in fact these two aspects (style of writing and style of thought) are closely bound together in Nietzsche's work. This implies a negative and a possibly positive corollary. Negatively speaking, there appears a dilemma: either one tries to systematize Nietzsche, which leads to leaving out a huge quantity of non-logical, non-"philosophical," "artistic" material, that one tends, in a *dualistic* approach, to discard eventually as irrelevant, purely aesthetic, sensible or, to put it mildly, as rhetorical residue (not to say: waste!). This common attitude among philosophical students of Nietzsche is in fact typically inconsistent with Nietzsche's conception of style and with his antidualistic idea of philosophy. Or, on the contrary, one resigns philosophy as a conceptual activity, and one yields to the temptation (which is *Versuchung* and no more *Versuch*!) of ravelling out and flittering away Nietzsche's thought, thus reducing it to a trivial bauble, a decadent trinket. Is a motley cow better than a black cow at night?

Since there is no chance of finding Nietzsche in the mediocre middle-course between those two extremes, it remains to wonder whether Nietzsche's *style* itself could not help us (speaking now positively) to think out the problem how he affirms. And I think he does so *precisely when* he negates and criticizes. My hypothesis here is that Nietzsche's affirmation can only be what he implies by the phrase "*Ja sagen*," and that "*Ja Sagen*" might be the result of a *displaced* and *displacing,* in other words *meta-phoric* thought, if we understand *meta-phora* both in its rhetorical sense of analogical figure of speech ("as if") and in its etymological sense of displacement. That might help us to define at one and the same time not only Nietzsche's style but also Nietzsche's ways and "contents" of affirmation, *how* he affirms and *what* he affirms, or, in other words, his method of philosophical affirmative philosophizing *and* the ontological nature of the "Being" he affirms thereby.

To say it beforehand, it may happen that in the end we come to the conclusion that Nietzsche does affirm metaphorically (which does not mean at haphazard), but affirms only metaphor itself, or Being as the power of metaphor, that is to say metaphor as the effort of the world itself to pluralize and reinterpret itself, as the structure of the will to power. Metaphor has in charge to let the world be, to make it be, to let the creative plurality of becoming appear and to deepen the world not as a substantial reality, but also as a *sign* of itself. In that philosophy of the will to power, the profundity of the world and of reality consists in their ability to be taken not only as they are or for what they are, but also as signs of themselves, as metaphors of themselves. In the realm of Becoming, Goethe's words which Nietzsche so often discussed and parodied are still true in that sense: "*Alles Vergängliche, das ist nur ein Gleichnis.*" (What is transient is but a metaphor).

I don't pretend here to solve the problems or to decide the preceding dilemma. In fact, I am more and more inclined to insist, when reading Nietzsche, on the tensions upon which his affirmation is built, if ever it *is* so. I simply wish to sketch how, as I read him, his genealogical philosophy, both as a critique of pure discourse (so to speak) and as a philological analysis of culture, is torn asunder between language and body, philology and physiology, strains at saying a metaphorical "yes" to the world, at metaphorically expressing the world and at saying "yes" to a metaphorical reality of the world, that is to say: to life.

II. The Modalities of a Critical Affirmation

Let us read on the text I used as a starting-point for our questioning about affirmation: "The three tasks for which educators are needed" are positively described by Nietzsche as follows: "One must learn to *see*, one must learn to *think*, one must learn to *speak* and *write*." These tasks belong or rather point to two spheres which Nietzsche (can we say: wrongly?) feels as separate and tries over and over again to reunite: life, the body, reality, on the one hand, language, thought and/or reason on the other hand. This can be shown from or traced back to the constant and radical antinomy he sees between philosophy and philology. Anyway, Nietzsche, as a thinker, as a writer, as a philosopher and philologist, settles down *in* the realm of language *and* tries to get out of language, of which his problematic and ambiguous sentence bears this testimony among others: "Nur die *ergangenen* Gedanken haben Wert" (only thoughts *in walking* have a real value) (*Götzendämmerung,* Sprüche und

Pfeile, 34). More precisely, Nietzsche strives at turning language out of itself, so to speak, at making it point and return to its origin or source: the *reality* of life and particularly the *body*. This double movement or trend accounts for his strategy of an indirect, meta-phorical affirmation of the body, in opposition to its denial (as e.g. in Christian morality) and to its direct, intuitive extra-linguistic affirmation (which can be no philosophical affirmation, but a mere extra-discursive, activist position or disposition). Why does Nietzsche take this impossible, dilemmatic course?

Contrary to most of his great predecessors in philosophy, such as Descartes, Spinoza or Kant, Nietzsche is extremely sensible of, not to say sensitive to polysemia, to the interpretative profundity, to the rich and creative enigma of reality, and especially of life and existence. In that sense (and this distinguishes him from Kierkegaard's insistence on the irreducibility of existence to the general concept), Nietzsche's philosophy is that of a *philologist,* i.e. of someone who tends to consider reality as a text (that is to say *not* as a thing which can be intuitively or conceptually seen as it is, but as a set of rich, ambiguous and even mysterious signs which can only be interpreted, deciphered and construed, almost as an enigma), and who therefore never ceases to read more and more in texts. Reality, for him, means always more (and sometimes less), and otherwise than it seems: in this respect, prince Hamlet is one of the symbolic names to which Nietzsche appeals. *But* at the same time, Nietzsche's philosophy is the philosophy of a *"misologist"* (to use Plato's famous phrase in its original and derived sense: opposition to reason and to philology), of someone who tries to let appear the depth and profundity of what exists *outside* the texts, and thence to relate text and language to their hidden origin, to their repressed *alter* ego, to their outside, in short: who strives to relate and refer language to its body as its deeply hidden reality.[3] Here we can find the sense together with the specific dilemma of genealogy as an effort to manifest, through the language, in the language, *that* which the language, being as such metaphysical, tends to hide and deny, and to let the body appear or loom out, whereas the body (taken as an origin of meaning, and of course not as the plain physical, material object) manifests itself *only by*

---

[3] The same problem occurs in psychoanalysis, as an attempt to fill in the gap between the unconscious *Trieb* (originating in the body, properly the *libido* in its Latin psycho-physiological meaning) and the conscious language of the patient talking out his psychic representations. To put it in a short formula: how should one relate the conscious *Liebe* to the unconscious *libido*? Similarly, to use a fashionable phrase (which designates but does not explain), Nietzsche's genealogy (or "psychology") originates in a "psychosomatic" philosophy — or how to know something of the Unknown.

signs.⁴ This is what Nietzsche has in mind when he says that we ought not to take morality at its face value, "word for word," for what it expressly says (*wörtlich*), and describes it on the contrary as a "*Semiotik,*" a "*Zeichenrede,*" a "*Symptomatologie*" which "reveals the most valuable realities of cultures and inner beings who *knew* too little about themselves."⁵

Here should be pointed out that, in saying this, Nietzsche cuts himself off from two opposite assertions, from which two types of possible affirmation could have been derived: (a) that language can *be* or express directly and fully the reality (e.g. of the body): it is only a set of *signs* (*against idealism* of language and of philologists, who tend to see language and texts as realities in themselves); (b) that the body, or ultimately reality, can be *intuitively* seen, directly looked into, known as it is, without the medium of signs and language (*against dogmatic realism*).⁶

In order to illustrate the double and self-contradictory task of genealogy as a kind of philology and physiology, Nietzsche uses three series or sets of very coherent and self-sufficient metaphors:⁷ (1) reading (philology); (2) hearing; (3) smelling. They aim at showing how an *immaterial* set of signs (words, texts, sounds, smells) brings out and betrays the hidden, indirect or distant presence of a *material* origin. That is the way in which Nietzsche's metaphorics of genealogy tend towards what I would call an *indirect referential insistence*.

Let me just point out briefly some main aspects of these metaphorical sets.

---

⁴ As a philosopher, Nietzsche seems to consider that there is nothing to *say* about the "real" existence of the body in itself, apart from language. It apparently can only be felt or lived, and manifests itself in the blank spaces separating Nietzsche's aphorisms.
⁵ *Götzendämmerung,* Die "Verbesserer" der Menschheit, 1.
⁶ I tried to develop this at more length in my Thèse de doctorat: *Nietzsche, le corps et la culture,* and suggested that this double opposition could be described analogically as a kind of Copernican philological revolution (the body *is* in itself, but can be only *known* as speech — *Erscheinung*), which relates Nietzsche both to Schopenhauer's realism (will to life as body) and to Kant's transcendentalism (philologically reinterpreted).
⁷ Since I cannot give here a sufficient number of examples, I must insist that this coherence should rest on a number of samples from Nietzsche's texts, and not only, as is often the case, on the extrapolation from such and such an isolated passage by the unbridled phantasies of the reader himself, or on the misconstruing of German idiomatic phrases into specific and original Nietzschean metaphors. See Richard Roos, "Règles pour une lecture philologique de Nietzsche," in *Nietzsche aujourd'hui?* (Paris: Union générale d'édition "10/18", 1973), vol. II.

1. Reading (philology)[8]

Nietzsche presents himself very often as a philologist (from *Wir Philologen* to *Jenseits,* 22, for instance) and it is as such that he describes himself as a genealogist or, to use another term commonly used by him as an equivalent, as a psychologist and *Rattenfänger* (*Götzendämmerung,* Preface; *Jenseits,* 295). This self-description must be taken literally. It first means that Nietzsche, as a philologist, turns his genealogical object, culture (morality, metaphysics, Christianity, science) into a *text,* or sees it as a text which he has to read, decipher, construe and handle critically. Secondly, the text of decadent culture appears to him in this respect as a defective one, as a text full of absurdities, contradictions, misunderstandings and wrong construings (*Widersinn, Missverständnis*), a text which interprets reality falsely or denies it by inventing a host of fictitious notions (*falsche Übersetzung, Mangel an Philologie,* etc.). Thus Christianity invents (*erfindet*) beings that do not exist (*Antichrist,* 15), translates reality into a false, incorrect, religious language (*Antichrist,* 26), is a false *interpretation* of reality and texts, even of the Bible itself (*Morgenröte,* 84; *Antichrist,* 52). This is not only obvious from the philological terms which Nietzsche uses to discard these interpretations and denials of reality through a false language, but also in his *constant* use of quotation marks (*Gänsefüsschen*) whenever he quotes critically or has to make use himself (in another meaning) of any piece of the moral, metaphysical or religious vocabulary: "soul," "self," "spirit," "God," "Christian," "remorse," "free will," "sin," "nature," "world," "eternal life," "Last Judgment," etc., and even, what is still more interesting, "truth," "being," "cause and effect," "will," etc. (see for instance *Antichrist,* 15, 16, 52 and everywhere in the posthumous papers and *Der Wille zur Macht*). On the contrary, Nietzsche claims that one should distinguish the real text from its interpretations and respect the rules of "philology," i.e. of "honesty" (*Rechtschaffenheit*). He therefore presents himself as a good reader and philologist of texts and of reality (as text), and, what is more, as a good translator, not only of reality but of the incorrect moral texts into their right terms (cf. *Jenseits,* 230 and the very common phrases such as: "As *I* would say," "in my own language," "*auf Deutsch*" etc.).[9] It is along this line that Nietzsche practises or reformulates genealogy as an etymologist (see *Zur Genealogie der Moral,* I,

---

[8] For further detail, see my "Les guillemets de Nietzsche," in *Nietzsche aujourd'hui?*
[9] See also "My task is to translate the apparently emancipated and denatured moral values back into their nature — i.e., into their natural 'immorality'" (*Der Wille zur Macht,* 229, trans. W.A. Kaufmann in *The Will to Power*).

and especially his explicit linguistic and etymological question in the final remark at the end of the first Essay) and refers it to interpretation and grand style.

Now it appears that, if Nietzsche's philology implies a *formal* aspect as regards his criticism of the "moral" language, it also and, perhaps primarily, has a *referential* intention, insofar as it tries to display, *in* the language and the text, precisely that which refers to their *physiological* origin (style: see *Jenseits,* 246, 247; *Ecce Homo,* III, especially 4; *Götzendämmerung,* Was ich den Alten verdanke) or to their *history* (etymology, history of language, translation: *Genealogie* I), that is to say, generally speaking, to their "outside." Thus it is literally true that "in my writings a psychologist speaks" (*Ecce Homo,* III, 5). In that respect, genealogy should be in the first place a kind of stylistics, according to the following principles of style: "The important thing is *life*: style ought to *live*. Style must prove that one *believes* in one's thoughts, and not merely *thinks* his thoughts but *feels* them" (KGW, VII, I, 1(109), 1 & 7).

2. Reading-listening[10]

That the style of a text reveals something of the body and instincts appears more clearly from the metaphors which Nietzsche links with philology. Reading, according to Nietzsche, should not be understood as simply understanding thoughts and meanings, but also as *hearing* the physical and physiological conditions in which a number of sentences are written, articulated and spoken out (see again *Jenseits,* 246 & 247) In the Preface of *Götzendämmerung,* Nietzsche refers to his philosophy as an auscultation and sounding (*Aushorchen*), and talks about his "wicked ear" (*böses Ohr*). I want to stress in the first place that this substitution of the sense of hearing for the sense of sight is perfectly consistent with the image of twilight in the title, which suggests the fading out of Truth and Being as light in the philosophical tradition (Plato's Cave, the light of the world in the Gospel, Descartes' description of God at the end of the Third Meditation) and the correlative disparagement of knowledge described as vision (*eidos, évidence, theoria,* intuition are all terms which relate to the sense of sight and imply light (God) as their cause). What does

---

[10] I dealt with these themes more at length in my "Götzen aushorchen," in *Perspektiven der Philosophie* 7 (1981) (repr. in *Nietzsche Kontrovers,* I, Würzburg: Königshausen & Neumann, 1981), which is mainly a detailed commentary upon the metaphors to be found in the Preface of *Götzendämmerung.* See also my translation and commentary of the same book, *Crépuscule des idoles* (Paris: Hatier, 1983).

Nietzsche do instead? Since night has come, his genealogical method cannot rely on the sense of sight, but must have recourse to the sense of hearing.

But what is the result of this new type of method? Provided one "has a second pair of ears,"[11] one can guess the nature or the condition of the body which resounds, and "hear that famous hollow sound which betrays something of flatulent bowels" (*Götzendämmerung,* Preface). In that case, the philologist is therefore an acoustician, a musicologist as well as a physiologist. Whereas most metaphysicians are deaf (*ibid.,* Streifzüge eines Unzeitgemässen, 26), the genealogist, like Nietzsche, is musical, for he perceives what is unheard (*Unerhörtes*) or almost inaudible for common ears, even "events which creep on with dove feet" (*Zarathustra*; see also *Genealogie,* I, 14 and *Jenseits,* 10), even the meaning of "silent events" and the imperceptible difference between the affirmative "*Ja*" and the donkey's submissive "*I-A,*" between "*gerecht*" (just) and "*gerächt*" (avenged) (*Zarathustra*).

This also implies that the philologist-genealogist is a phonologist and physicist: a sound is a sensation produced in the ears by the vibrations of air caused by the movements of a *living* or inanimate body; it is uttered by a chest, a tongue, a throat, lips, or sent out by any object that is hit or set in movement. Any sound therefore reveals the quality, nature and physical condition of that which sends it out: what we call its *tempo* (a frequent word in Nietzsche's texts) and its ring (*Klangfarbe*) betrays the physical state of its origin: bronze, wood, steel, stone, etc.; hollow or full; ill or sound; solid or cracked, etc.

Lastly, this set of metaphors accounts for the real function of the "philosophizing with the hammer": the latter is but seldom and secondarily a sledgehammer or any such instrument used to destroy or break (and sculpt), but a "music" instrument, a *Stimmhammer* (tuning hammer), compared with a *Stimmgabel* (tuning-fork), a piano hammer, a medical sounding-hammer (for percussion of the body), or a metallurgic instrument (test hammer or jeweller's hammer). It should help the genealogist to "oblige to talk out that which precisely wishes to remain quiet" (*Götzendämmerung,* Preface).[12]

Through sound, the body as a *physical* being is affirmed by Nietzsche.

---

[11] "*Ohren hinter den Ohren,*" or "a third ear," as Nietzsche writes in *Jenseits,* 246, and as psychoanalyst Reik not surprisingly entitled his book: *Listening with the Third Ear* (New York, 1948).

[12] This conception of the idols is reminiscent of the biblical description of the idols as "dumb." It has been remarked that Luther's translation of the Bible insists more particularly upon the acoustic and olfactive images than on the visual ones (L. Febvre). The same applies to Nietzsche, a regular Bible-reader.

3. Smelling[13]

But if we now turn to the set of metaphors of smelling, which Nietzsche frequently uses to describe the method of genealogy, we find that they not only intend to insist on the relation of the symptom to a hidden or distant body (as can be the case for both sound and smell, but remarkably *not* for sight, which is again instructive), but this time also point out the *physiological* nature of the *living* body (*Leib* as opposed to the general *Körper*). "*Ich höre und rieche es,*" I hear and smell it (*Zarathustra*, III, 8, 2): hearing and smelling means to guess something of the living body, although it is not exposed to the sight, although it is hidden, distant, obscure and deep — unconscious. The genealogist, like the psychoanalyst (as Freud explicitly says) should have a fine sense of smell (or nosing out: *Witterung*): "What fine instruments of observation we have with our senses! The nose, for instance, which no philosopher ever spoke of with respect and gratitude, is even, in the mean time, the most delicate instrument we dispose of: it is able to ascertain infinitesimal differences of movement which the spectroscope itself is not even sensitive to" (*Götzendämmerung,* Die "Vernunft" in der Philosophie, 3).

Just a few examples here: we may call to mind Nietzsche's insistence on the bad smell of churches and of the New Testament (*Genealogie,* III, 22; *Götzendämmerung,* Die "Verbesserer" der Menschheit, 3), on the "*Stubenrauch*" of Christian life (*Antichrist,* 52), on the confined, sickly and stinking atmosphere of the idealistic "den" (*Genealogie,* I, 14) — and, on the contrary, Nietzsche's desire and longing for fresh air, windy places (the mistral), pure air of the high icy mountains where ideals are "deep-frozen" (*Ecce Homo,* III, *Menschliches allzu Menschliches,* 1 and Preface).

This valuation of the sense of smell should remind us that genealogy is in the final account anti-idealistic, medical and "medicynical," that even in the "pure" would-be disincarnate ideal, we can smell out the carefully hidden traces of a diseased body, or traces simply of blood, breath, bowels and matter of a living and sensible body.[14]

The otorhinological, so to speak, genealogy in Nietzsche is thus a derivation from philology to physiology and indicates a referential insistence, an

---

[13] More about this range of images in my Thèse de doctorat, *Nietzsche, le corps et la culture* (Paris, PUF, forthcoming).

[14] Bachelard, who beautifully analyzed these metaphors of air in Nietzsche's works, does *not* relate them to their genealogical, bodily origin (*L'Air et les Songes,* chap. V). Nonetheless, he rightly stresses the metaphorical unity of Nietzsche's thought "*as a poet,*" in a true anti-dualistic insight.

indirect affirmation of the body. Hence the question asked by Nietzsche in *Ecce Homo*: "Why philologist and not rather medical doctor?"[15] takes its real and full meaning. Since the body cannot be a simply somatic, mechanical, physical thing, distinct from the "soul" (*psychē*), as in the dualistic view, but a "psychosomatic" whole (*grosse Vernunft*), *what* is indeed that body which Nietzsche thus affirms indirectly, negatively, when he genealogically points at its transcriptions in the text of ideals?

III. The Metaphorical Affirmation of the Body

Unexpectedly, though in fact explicably, Nietzsche gives no positive and conceptual physiological doctrine of the body as a counterpart to his genealogical criticism of idealism and as a foundation for his genealogy leading indirectly to an ontological affirmation. Nietzsche affirms the body, he holds that the body *is* the reality of ideals: but *how* is it so, and *what* is it, *what* is thus *affirmed,* which could play the role, either of Being (*eidos,* substance, *hypokeimenon,* subject, self, will, God, etc.), or at least of a transcendental constitutive point of will to power, and thus replace, in Nietzsche's thought, the dead "God" (whether it were essential or substantial Being or any kind of *ego cogito, ich denke,* etc.)?

To put it briefly: it looks as if Nietzsche left us at a loss in this respect, for he eventually leads us, not to a definition and description of the body, but to the ultimate notion of interpretation, in the sense that (a) the body in the end is an interpretative constellation (naturally as far as meaning and knowledge of "being" is concerned, the body as an "object" to which genealogy refers, as its "*Leitfaden*"); (b) interpretation itself is not otherwise described than through metaphors of the body.

I will just sketch here how Nietzsche has recourse to another set of metaphors in order to describe the body (*Leib*).

---

[15] *Ecce Homo,* II, 2. See particularly the details Nietzsche gives in this latter book, chap. II, about his regime and his numerous "medicynical" remarks: most of them refer to a smelling body: "All prejudices arise from the bowels," "German spirit arises from disturbed bowels," etc. Incidentally, he writes there that all places fit for geniuses have a remarkably dry *air,* and quotes some famous towns: he is right about Jerusalem, *not* about Paris!

1. Digestion. What is the body? Since Nietzsche views it as an inseparably psychic *and* somatic whole, he describes it in terms of drives (*Triebe*), which unceasingly try to increase their own power and to absorb or digest each other. This first range of digestive metaphors is very common and constant in Nietzsche's texts, from e.g. *Morgenröte,* 109 & 119 down to the *Genealogie,* II, 1[16] and the posthumous papers until 1888: *Assimilation, Einverleibung, Ernährung, hineinnehmen, Verdauen, fertig werden, Durchfallen, Appetit, hinunterschlucken* (*Ecce Homo,* III, Der Fall Wagner, 1). There are hundreds of passages in the texts where Nietzsche describes the mutual relations of the *Triebe* in the "body" (as *Selbst,* as a *grosse Vernunft*) in terms of nutrition, swallowing, digestion, elimination, rejection — a set of metaphors which is extended to the whole kingdom of life and to culture as a struggle for domination between forces. The sense of this is that power tends to reduce plurality and diversity to sameness and unity (*Assimilation* as *ad simile reductio*).

2. Politics. But how does this assimilation proceed? As before, we can see that another set of metaphors relays the former in order to interpret it (what I call a process of concatenation-transference). We ought to pay attention to this mode of interpretative explanation of the description, since it warns us that Nietzsche is quite conscious of giving no descriptively explanatory definition, but seems to imply that the body can *only* be described in terms of interpretative metaphors, i.e. only interpreted: "Auslegung, *nicht* Erklarung," interpretation, *not* explanation.[17] In the present case, the relaying set of metaphors is politics, which tends to show how and according to which rules the drives fight, absorb and reject each other. One of the most typical texts in this respect is to be found in 599 of volume XIII in the Kröner edition (KGW, VII, 3, 3(74), in which Nietzsche compares the conscious self with the stomach and describes the "body" as a plurality of "*Bewusstsein*" (consciousness) to be compared with a political society: a reigning collectivity, an aristocracy, where the conscious selves in turn obey and command, elect a dictator, constitute a regency council, etc. The "body" is a stomach, which

---

[16] Many of these images are in fact borrowed from Schopenhauer, *World as Will and Representation,* Supplements to Book I, chap. XIV, *in fine.*

[17] KGW, VIII, 1, 2(82), (78) & (86); see also *Wille zur Macht,* 492. This should be compared with the similar problem of the "description" of the unconscious by Freud: we eventually *can* have nothing more than a metaphorical in-sight, i.e. an interpretation of it (or else, would it be unconscious?). Freud has recourse to the metaphors of hydraulics, of war, of a boiler and, once, of the ... stomach (*New Introductory Lectures on Psychoanalysis,* chap. IV).

could be in its turn compared with a political collectivity: how is the self to make *one* will from a *plurality* of voices, in a body which Nietzsche elsewhere describes as "a herd and shepherd"?

3. Philology. But this metaphorical description needs again to be interpreted. How do the selves choose, elect, command over each other? "Every one of these voluntary actions implies, so to speak, the election of a dictator. But that which offers this choice to our intellect, which has previously simplified, equalized, interpreted (*ausgelegt*) these experiences, is not that very intellect [...]. This choice [is] a way of abstracting and grouping, a *translation (Zurückübersetzung)* of a will..." (*ibid.*).[18] We have therefore but signs of the body as a kind of text which we see on the *conscious* level as arranged, simplified, falsified, translated, abbreviated: in short, interpreted. The body "is" a world of signs — or at least we can only see it as such, because commanding is "a way to take possession of facts by signs," to "abbreviate," to "master by means of signs" (*ibid.*).Commanding (and what else do the wills to power inside the body do?) is interpreting: therefore, the body, as will to power, a stomach, a fighting-place "is" that which interprets signs.

Here we find ourselves eventually brought back to our initial philology metaphor. This means first that the body cannot be strictly defined in terms of explanation, of mechanism, or as any sort of substance (and we have seen that Freud has to deal with the same problem when he tries to define and describe the unconscious — a notion very closely akin to Nietzsche's conception of the body as mostly unconscious and instinctive "great reason").

In the second place, it should be emphasized that this anti-substantialist description precludes any temptation to biologize Nietzsche, as was often done in early interpretations of his thought.

Now, without entering further into the difficult questions implied by my second remark ((b) above), saying that interpretation is never explicitly defined by Nietzsche, but only "described" again by metaphors (and so, in a circular way, interpreting is like digesting — the famous "ruminating" — like fighting, choosing, simplifying, multiplying, etc.), I would just like to state a few points about the initial question of affirmation.

(1) Nietzsche *affirms indirectly* insofar as he reveals the will to power of the body as the hidden principle of the ideals (genealogy) and refuses its denial in idealistic culture (morality, religion, metaphysics).

---

[18] We can find the same interpretative concatenation of metaphors in *Der Wille zur Macht,* 492 (KGW, VII, 40 (21)).

(2) But, first, *what* does Nietzsche affirm? Not the body as an assignable and definable essence, or being, but as the central(?), fundamental(?) and anyway *plural* location of interpretation. No *ego cogito* — rather a *cogitatur,* as Nietzsche suggests in a fragment (Kröner, XIV, 7, see *Wille zur Macht,* 484) — no originally synthetic unity of aperception, but a multiple center of interpretation of reality, a reality which however cannot be taken hold of and apprehended as a substance, but only through it, and perhaps is partly made up by the body. Nietzsche thus is *displacing* the affirmation.

Secondly, *how* does he affirm? Since the body is, as a multiple center, essentially hidden, distant (hearing and smell), this "great reason," this interpretative reality cannot be explained but by signs, i.e. metaphorically, in a displaced way. In that sense, Nietzsche is a *displaced* (and displacing) thinker, a thinker of signs, and not of a real "Being" which could be in the end unified, totalized and equalized. Now, at this point, the question may be asked whether this is not a failure on his part: to which it might be also answered that this kind of failure is the condition *sine qua non* of his non-metaphysical affirmation and taking into account of the body and, through it, of a richer affirmation of Being, of the metaphorical power of life than had ever been the case in the rationalist tradition of metaphysicians, "those albinos of concept," as he calls them. Or, in other words, Nietzsche's final lesson might be that thought *has* to fail, in a certain way, when confronting life and the body (which is also, though differently, Kierkegaard's and Freud's lesson, if one takes their mistrust towards philosophy and metaphysics into account).

But Nietzsche's own original metaphoric way is also instructive as such, philosophically speaking — for he never gives up philosophy. Between the *negation* of the real body in idealism and the realistic *affirmation* of Being (Will, Body...)[19] leading to an eventually entropic activism, Nietzsche seems to affirm that, for us, what should be *affirmed* can be neither a substantial Being (to be ultimately known), nor sheer nothingness, but, taking the word in its literal sense, "*Selbstüberwindung,*" an overcoming of identity and sameness (*selbst*), an interpretative meta-phor (transference), a dis-placement (*Übertragung*) of Being opening on into a world of signs. Nietzsche writes: "'Truth' is therefore not something there, that might be found or discovered — but something that must be created and that gives a name to a process, or rather to a will to overcome that has in itself no end — introducing truth as a *processus in infinitum,* an active determining — not a becoming-conscious of something that is in itself firm and determined. It is a word for the 'will to

---

[19] As for instance in Schopenhauer's thought.

power.'"[20] "Truth" (and "Being") therefore differ from themselves: whereas, in Hegel, Time was that which made Being and Truth unequal to their own substance, I would suggest that, in Nietzsche's conception, it is the sign, i.e. signification, interpretation. Reality, for Nietzsche, *is* not, it signifies (itself). So, God is dead, but Nietzsche believes in signification: only it is lost and even wasted in the empty space, since God is missing: "There are far more languages than one thinks; and man betrays himself far more often than he would wish to. Everything speaks (*Alles redet*)! But very few are those who can listen, so that man, as it were, pours his confessions out into the empty space; he lavishes his own "truths" as the sun lavishes its light. Isn't it a pity that the empty space has no ears?"[21] Ambiguity, obscurity but also richness and infinite plurality of signs therefore replace the stability and transparent unity of Being. Hence: "Interpretation, *not* explanation. There is no state of things, everything is fluent, incomprehensible, receding. What is most durable in the end: our opinions. To project sense into things (*Sinn-hineinlegen*) — in most cases a new interpretation thrown over an old one that has become unintelligible, that is itself now only a sign."[22]

Such a kind of "Truth" and of "Being," as we suspected from the beginning, cannot properly be *affirmed,* that is to say "solidified," "made firm," considered as a "firm" object (*ad-firmare*), i.e. seen, handled and finally grabbed. To a "text," to an interpretation, to a world of signs that is continually "in the making," one can only, as Nietzsche puts it quite precisely and coherently, "*say* 'yes'": "*Ja sagen.*"

University of Nancy

---

[20] *Der Wille zur Macht,* 552, trans. W.A. Kaufmann (KGW, VIII, 2, 9 (91)). Notice here the quotation marks!
[21] Kröner Grossoktavausgabe, XIII, 363.
[22] KGW, VIII, 1, 2(82).

Shlomo Pines

Nietzsche: Psychology vs. Philosophy, and Freedom

I

Many texts can be adduced to show that Nietzsche considered himself to be a philosopher, and this is what he is currently held to be.

Heidegger, for instance, thinks of him as the last metaphysician, the man with and through whom the deviant road struck out by Plato, Aristotle, and many others came to its inevitable conclusion.

Nietzsche also used to call himself a psychologist or rather a *Psychologe* — the German term has some connotations lacking in the English one.

In the first part of this paper I shall try to show that Nietzsche the philosopher and Nietzsche the psychologist may be said to be at odds in a significant way, although admittedly, he himself in certain moods would have dismissed this view out of hand. Thus he refers, rather complacently, to the psychological method (*die Psychologie*) of the philosopher, meaning himself.[1] To start with I shall try to indicate or illustrate at the level of rudimentary semantics the meaning of the term *Psychologe* as used by Nietzsche.

In the first place a possible misconception should be avoided. Nietzsche usually gives the term *Psychologe* the meaning which it had in current non-specialized usage before the advent of the age of "Psychology" with a capital letter, that is before Freud and his peers and rivals. In the 19th century, in spite of the fact that psychology was already a constituted science, the term *Psychologe* was in ordinary parlance applied to a person — it was often a

---

[1] Cf. for instance, *Ecce Homo, Warum ich so klug bin* 3, in: K. Schlechta (ed.), *Friedrich Nietzsche in drei Bänden* (Munich 1960). References to passages in works of Nietzsche are made to this edition, identified by book and section numbers; references to posthumous notes are identified by volume and page number of this edition. See also *Götzen-Dämmerung* 45.

writer, particularly a novelist — who was interested in, and capable of discerning, sometimes by empathy, workings of the human psyche that are camouflaged by words and outward appearance.

In his reading Nietzsche encountered through what he regarded as a lucky chance, two psychologists with whom he felt an affinity, Stendhal and Dostoevsky; the latter he refers to as the only man who taught him something in psychology.[2]

An interesting point Nietzsche mentions in two letters, one to Peter Gast (March 7, 1887) and one to Overbeck (Feb. 23, 1887), is that the first work of Dostoevsky, which he read in a French translation, was *l'Esprit souterrain*. The edition contained according to him two stories. This may refer to the two parts of Dostoevsky's work, usually known in English under the title: *Letters from the Underworld*.[3] At all events there can be no doubt that the second story included in this edition was either this work or its second part. Nietzsche describes this story as "a psychological *Geniestreich* ["a stroke of genius" in an inadequate translation] a terrible and cruel mockery of *gnōthi sauton*, written with such an easy boldness and sense of happiness originating in great strength that I was intoxicated with pleasure."[4]

---

[2] *Götzen-Dämmerung* 45.
[3] Its Russian title is: *Zapiski iz Podpolya*.
[4] The parallels which may be drawn between Nietzsche and certain characters in "the polyphonic" novels of Dostoevsky are more than curious, as the following example may show. Kirillov in the *Devils* (part I, chap. 3, section 8; cf. also part III, chap. 6, section 2) speaks of God having been destroyed (or annihilated) and Nietzsche (in *Die fröhliche Wissenschaft,* III:125, and elsewhere) of His having been killed, and both believe that this deed may lead to a profound transformation of the human race; men will — or must — become gods. The similarity between the two utterances is as evident as the difference between their opinion and a mere denial of the existence of God, a negation which was as current in nineteenth century Russia as in other countries. Yet Nietzsche does not refer here to the freedom of man resulting from the destruction of God, whereas Kirillov insists upon this consequence of the event: man liberated from the fear of God and the fear of afterlife — the two are clearly regarded as going together — dares to kill himself because it is indifferent to him whether he lives or dies. However, as far as Kirillov himself is concerned, the demands of his terrible freedom are evidently as absolute as those of the most rigorous moral imperative: he is required to manifest his freedom by committing suicide. *The Devils* was published in Russia in 1872, *Die fröhliche Wissenschaft* in 1882, four or five years before Nietzsche was aware of the existence of Dostoevsky. It may have been Thomas Mann's sense of Nietzsche's kinship with some characters of Dostoevsky's that led him to crib from Ivan Karamazov's conversation with the (or a) devil some important traits that are found in the scene in *Doktor Faustus* in which this personage addresses Adrian Leverkühn, who, though a musician, is to a great extent modelled upon Nietzsche (see G. Bergsten, *Thomas Manns Doktor Faustus,* Tübingen 1974, p. 87 f.). Perhaps — I am not quite certain

Now this story of Dostoevsky, which some critics and philosophers, Shestov for instance, regard as his most quintessential and revealing work, certainly is concerned, if one wishes to put it in this way, with the Delphic and Socratic maxim "Know thyself."

It seems to me that such conceptions as the *Übermensch* or *Zarathustra* tend to lose their lustre if Dostoevsky's story is taken seriously. I am, of course, not claiming that this story had by itself this effect on Nietzsche. What I wish to say is that the affinity which he obviously feels with Dostoevsky's attitude, as reflected in this story, shows how right Nietzsche was when in a passage of the *Nachlass,* entitled "Zur Psychologie des Philosophen," he makes the following remarks concerning the danger (clearly for himself) of introspection:

Quite the first indication in a great psychologist of the instinct of self-preservation is that he is never in search of himself (*er sucht sich nie*), he has no eye for himself, no interest in himself, no curiosity about himself. (III:790-791)

Further on he says:

We are no Pascals, we are not interested in saving our soul or in our own happiness or virtue. We have neither enough time, nor enough curiosity to turn in this manner around ourselves. If one looks more deeply there is also something else; we mistrust the contemplators of their own navel, because we regard self-observation as a degenerate form of the psychological genius, as a question-mark with regard to the instinct of the *psychologist.*

The danger of self-observation for Nietzsche, the catastrophic effect which self-knowledge had, or might have had, upon him is expressed in one of the *Dionysos-Dithyrambien,* entitled *Zwischen Raubvögeln.*

The theme of this dithyramb is the contrast between Zarathustra, who in this context may safely be identified with Nietzsche, as he was when he was a philosopher, or rather a certain kind of philosopher, and Zarathustra-Nietzsche when he is delving into the depths of his own self.

I shall quote some of the verses:

O Zarathustra, / grausamster Nimrod. / Jüngst Jäger noch Gottes / [...] Der Pfeil des Bösen.
O Zarathustra, / most cruel Nimrod / You who were not long ago the Hunter of God / [...] The arrow of evil.

---

about this — the following autobiographical note, supposed to have been written by Nietzsche in the autumn of 1868 or in the beginning of 1869, should be quoted in this context: "Was ich fürchte ist nicht die schreckliche Gestalt hinter meinem Stuhle, sondern ihre Stimme, auch nicht die Worte, sondern der schauderhaft unartikulierte und unmenschliche Ton jener Gestalt. Ja, wenn sie noch redete, wie Menschen reden" (quoted in C.P. Janz, *Friedrich Nietzsche Biographie,* Munich 1978, I:265f.).

Jetzt von dir selber erjagt, / deine eigene Beute. /
Now / you have been hunted down by yourself / your own prey / having bored deep into yourself. / Now / solitary with yourself, twofold / in your own knowledge / false before yourself / among a hundred mirrors. /

And further on:

you who were not long ago / alone without God [*der Einsiedler ohne Gott*] Or in a solitude of two with the Devil [*der Zweisiedler mit dem Teufel*], Who were the Scarlet Prince of all high-spiritedness / Now twisted between two nothingnesses / you are a question-mark, / a tired riddle, a riddle for birds of prey.

The concluding verses read:

O Zarathustra!... / Selbstkenner!... / Selbsthenker!...
O Zarathustra!... / Knower of yourself!... / Hangman of yourself!...

The wise Zarathustra, who was Nietzsche's idea of himself as a philosopher, is thus reduced by introspective psychology to toil, bowed down, in the quarry of his own self. Nietzsche sometimes uses in a derogatory sense the term "*der böse Blick,*" the glance of malice which picks out the evil or weakness in the person at which it is directed.

Let us now turn to the philosopher, or rather one characteristic philosopher as Nietzsche conceived him and also to what differentiates the new philosopher of whom he speaks in *Jenseits von Gut und Böse* 2 from the old.

The characteristic I have in mind is the tyrannous disposition of the true philosophers, their wish to be lawgivers and tyrants. In *Menschliches allzu Menschliches* (I:261) he ascribes this disposition in the first place, though not exclusively, to the Greek philosophers, every one of whom was according to Nietzsche a violent tyrant, who had a firm belief in his own truth and tended to suppress by means of this truth his neighbours and predecessors. The Greek philosophers were also lawgivers or would-be-lawgivers, law-giving being a sublimated form of tyranny.

In *Jenseits von Gut und Böse* 207 Nietzsche refers to the philosopher in general, not only the Greek philosopher, as the Caesarean breeder (*Züchter*, one who is engaged in effecting the breeding and education of men or peoples) and a man of violence within culture. He speaks also of their being lawgivers, they command and create new conceptions of value. It should also be noted that in *Jenseits von Gut und Böse* the philosophers whom Nietzsche has in mind, the new philosophers, the philosophers of the future, or in other words he himself, differ greatly from those described in *Menschliches allzu Menschliches*.

When reading *Menschliches allzu Menschliches* one is struck time and again by a certain affinity between the attitude of the author and that of Spinoza in the *Ethics*: the tendency to self-preservation referred to in *Menschliches allzu Menschliches* (I:104, 109, 517) recalls to some extent Spinoza's *conatus,* and both works give expression to a similar conception of truth. These points, as well as the denial of evil and various other points mentioned by Nietzsche in a postcard he sent to Overbeck three years after the publication of *Menschliches allzu Menschliches,* can account for the delight with which he describes to his correspondent his having discovered "a forerunner and such a forerunner."[5]

However in *Die fröhliche Wissenschaft* criticism of Spinoza sets in. Thus Nietzsche objects to Spinoza's phrase, *non ridere, non lugere, non detestari, sed intelligere,* "not to laugh, not to be sad, not to hate, but to cognize." According to Nietzsche cognition merely reflects the way various impulsions (*Triebe*) act upon and react to one another; cognition is a resolution of the struggle between them. This means of course a denial of the idea that man can cognize the truth.[6]

This modification of Nietzsche's point of view goes together with his ceasing to emphasize the tendency to self-preservation. In the new phase his thought is centred, as far as this point is concerned, on the struggle for power rather than on the struggle for mere existence,[7] and on the excessive, wasteful expenditure of force which appears to him to be characteristic of men he holds exceptional or whom it gives him pleasure to understand.[8] Spinoza has stated in a letter that he does not claim that his philosophy is the best philosophy; his claim being that it is true. The differentiation between true and good goes back to Aristotle, but the sort of opposition between the good and the true which this statement of Spinoza's implies was taken from Maimonides.[9] Nietzsche, for his part, in a phrase clearly directed against Spinoza, speaks of men transcending the dimension of humanity who are endowed with freedom not only from good and evil, but also from truth and falsehood.[10] With a

---

[5] The postcard, dated July 30, 1881, seems to have been written by Nietzsche after having read Kuno Fischer's account of Spinoza's doctrine. *Menschliches allzu Menschliches* was published in 1878.

[6] *Die fröhliche Wissenschaft,* IV:333; for other passages which are critical of Spinoza, see I:37, V:372.

[7] *Die fröhliche Wissenschaft,* V:349. In this passage Nietzsche establishes a connection of some kind between the importance attributed in the Darwinist teaching, which he rejects, to the struggle for existence, with Spinoza's doctrine. Cf. also *Der Wille zur Macht,* III:650.

[8] Such as the pre-Socratic or pre-philosophical Greeks, see, for instance, *Götzen-Dämmerung, Was Ich den Alten Verdanke,* 3, and *Nachlass,* III:748.

[9] See S. Pines, "On Spinoza's Conception of Human Freedom and of Good and Evil," *Spinoza — His Thought and Work* (Jerusalem: The Israel Academy of Sciences and Humanities, 1983), pp. 147-159.

[10] *Der Wille zur Macht,* II:244.

naivety due to their superabundant force the new philosophers play with and turn into play all that up to their time men held to be holy.[11] They may think that the value attributed to truth, to the will to be truthful[12] and to unselfishness is perhaps only due to these qualities being seen from a certain perspective from below and that their opposites may be of greater value for life.

These new philosophers are, as I have already said, simply Nietzsche, and what to my mind sets them apart within the context of Nietzsche's view of history is that they and only they are exempt from being judged by his psychological sense of smell, as he puts it.

In this connection a curious inconsistency may be remarked upon. While he tends to deny the validity of human knowledge in general, and the possibility of anything held to be a truth corresponding to something in reality, because there is no reality *per se,* he never seems to be in doubt as to the validity and correctness of his own psychological insights.

He claims that the hidden history of philosophy, the psychology of the greatest names in it, were revealed to him.[13] On the basis of this remark, the supposition seems to be justified that he held that there may be a true knowledge of the history of philosophy, and that his comprehension of the psychology of the greatest philosophers gave him this true and valid knowledge.

The comprehension, the psychological insights he claims to have, may be illustrated by his remarks concerning various philosophers, some, though not all of them, are severe. Thus Plato has according to him an actor-like nature,[14] the phenomenon Plato is a superior kind of swindle,[15] and there are various scurrilous observations concerning Kant. I may add that in using the adjective 'scurrilous' I do not mean to imply that there is no truth whatever in these observations. In *Jenseits von Gut und Böse,* 25, it is suggested that Spinoza's

---

[11] *Die fröhliche Wissenschaft,* V:382; *Jenseits von Gut und Böse,* 2; cf. *Ecce Homo,* on *Also sprach Zarathustra* 2.

[12] *Wahrhaftigkeit.* In the context "the will to be truthful" rather than "truthfulness" seems to be the appropriate rendering.

[13] *Ecce Homo,* Vorwort, 3.

[14] See *Jenseits von Gut und Böse* 7. In this passage Nietzsche interprets Epicurus' description of Plato and the Platonists and it is evident that he agrees with Epicurus.

[15] *Götzen-Dämmerung, Was ich den Alten verdanke,* 2: "Zuletzt geht mein Misstrauen bei Plato in die Tiefe: ich finde ihn so abgeirrt von allen Grundinstinkten der Hellenen..., dass ich von dem ganzen Phänomen Plato eher das harte Wort 'höherer Schwindel' oder, wenn man's lieber hört, Idealismus — als irgendein andres gebrauchen möchte." Many derogatory remarks of Nietzsche concerning Plato could be mentioned. In a letter to Overbeck dated January 9, 1887 (III:1247-1248) he calls him "Europe's greatest misfortune."

desire for revenge may have been at the bottom of his ethics and theology.[16]

This psychological perspicacity is, as has been already said, in general not applied by Nietzsche to Zarathustra or to himself. Zarathustra generously reveals all his secrets. He has no unrevealed and shameful thoughts and impulses which a psychologist whose glance is full of malice could unearth and bring to light. Nor has Nietzsche, if one is to judge by *Ecce Homo,* a piece of hagiographic writing about himself, in which his diseases and physical weaknesses are proved to be conducive to a higher form of health.

It seems to me that from time to time Nietzsche may have been aware of this, perhaps deliberate, refusal to let his own philosophy be publicly tried by his psychological flair. The dithyramb I have quoted is an exception in this respect; so are perhaps letters written in the last period before his final breakdown in which he says of himself that he is perhaps a clown.[17]

In *Jenseits von Gut und Böse,* 289[18] he states that the writings of solitary men — and all philosophers are perhaps that — (he himself certainly considered himself to be condemned to an almost complete solitude) never express their true opinions; in fact a man of this sort has in his psyche caves behind caves, what he writes is in a way only a façade.

Such ideas as the *Übermensch* and the Eternal Recurrence, or rather the moments of what he thought of as inspiration in which he conceived these ideas, may have seemed to him too precious for their connection with the underground world to be laid bare.

However, whatever allowances may be made because of various possible reasons and motivations, the fact remains that Nietzsche does not subject his own philosophy to his own psychological judgments, the acid test by means of which he evaluates other philosophies. This privileged position is of course an inviduous one; all the more so because many of Nietzsche's psychological judgments seem to be valid. The adoption of Nietzsche's psychological method necessarily leads to a perhaps destructive critique of Nietzsche's philosophy.

---

[16] "Diese Ausgestossnen der Gesellschaft, diese Lang-Verfolgten, Schlimm-Gehetzten — auch die Zwangs-Einsiedler, die Spinozas oder Giordano Brunos — werden zuletzt immer, und sei es unter der geistigsten Maskerade, und vielleicht ohne dass sie selbst es wissen, zu raffinierten Rachsüchtigen und Giftmischern (man grabe doch einmal den Grund der Ethik und Theologie Spinozas auf!)..."

[17] *Hanswurst.* He also uses other expressions to convey this view of himself. Cf., for instance, E.F. Podach, *Nietzsches Zusammenbruch,* Heidelberg 1930, p. 78 ff.

[18] Cf. also 40, and 278, and Lou Andreas Salomé, *Friedrich Nietzsche in seinen Werken* (Dresden, no date, a reprint of the first edition, published in Vienna in 1894), p. 19 ff.

II

In this part some suggestions are made as to a possible "genealogy of certain conceptions of freedom." Nietzsche's notions of the slave insurrection in the sphere of morals and of bad conscience are connected with resentment, and the relation of this insurrection to Nietzsche's psychological insights and judgments are also discussed.

In the second essay of *Zur Genealogie der Moral* (16 and 17) Nietzsche dwells upon the profound transformation which the primitive man, the savage, underwent when he found himself deprived of liberty, imprisoned by the inexorable organization of state and society. This man, beating against the walls of his cage, revolting against the way of life imposed upon him, with his instincts and drives turned against him, invented bad conscience (*das schlechte Gewissen*), a strange and uncanny sickness through the instrumentality of which man, with his soul at war against itself, became something new, mysterious, directed towards a future in which great promise may be hidden. Owing to this sickness man may be counted as one of the luckiest turns of the dice thrown by Heraclitus' Great Child, the God Zeus, or perhaps chance. Now this sickness, the bad conscience to which man owes all the interest and fascination he possesses, is not characteristic of the conquering hordes, which Nietzsche professes to admire. It is the sickness of the conquered, and is — Nietzsche was certainly at times aware of this fact — akin and very close to the *ressentiment* which he so often vilified.

A conquering horde, in organizing its rulership with the unconscious egoism of an artist, brings about, according to Nietzsche, the seeming disappearance of a great quantum of freedom. The instinct of freedom becomes latent, is internalized, turns into bad conscience, and thus the transformation of man which Nietzsche found so fascinating comes about.

In the passage I have just summarized Nietzsche appears to have had in mind a primitive society. Now there was a period in history when, in a society which was by no means primitive, something similar to this schema (in spite of significant differences) did occur. Moreover it was a period with which Nietzsche was intellectually concerned and emotionally involved, in the sense that he had a strong antipathy to one of the main protagonists in this dramatic sequence of events. The historical period I refer to is that of the genesis of Christianity, the protagonist in question being Paul. As far as I can see, Nietzsche failed to perceive this similarity.

This failure was perhaps partly due to his getting his facts wrong. Nietzsche describes the Jewish people in Palestine in the 1st century C.E. as a wholly apolitical community, which had some kind of parasitical existence within the

Roman Empire.¹⁹ In fact, it was a thoroughly politicised community, as communities sometimes are a short time before a catastrophic war or revolutionary upheaval, events which cast long shadows before them. It is rather surprising that Nietzsche, the classical philologist, in writing about this period, did not consult the only detailed historical source for it, namely Josephus, to whom he never refers. (Perhaps by that time he has already decided against reading many books.)²⁰

The slogan — the *idée-force,* to use a somewhat dated French expression — adopted by the activist part of the Jewish community in Palestine in order to prepare the uprising against Rome was a new one in the context of this society. This slogan was liberty, namely liberty from foreign rule: God alone was to rule Israel.²¹

The term liberty does not occur in a political or theologico-political context in the Hebrew of the Bible, nor was it used in the course of the Hasmonean insurrection. In my opinion, it was taken over from the Greco-Roman culture. In spite of the fact that a great part of the Orient was hoping for the end of Roman rule and seething with apocalyptic agitation, the Jews were apparently the only oriental people to have adopted a slogan calling for liberty.

However, the liberty they called for had a different meaning or shade of meaning as compared to the *eleutheria* of the Greeks and the *libertas* of the Romans. These two peoples valued and fought for a liberty they were conscious of having. For the Jews, who were in a state of political servitude, liberty was something to be won; it was liberation which is a more dynamic concept than liberty.

The Jewish war that resulted in the destruction of the Second Temple by the Romans, can be used to illustrate this dynamic nature. "Liberty," in the sense of liberation, was one of the main slogans of the activists during the politico-religious ferment preceding the Jewish insurrection and during the insurrection itself. This is a noteworthy fact. For it was perhaps the first time in history that a literate population, which had an ancient culture of its own, and which had been for a considerable time under foreign rule, struggled against this rule in the name of liberty. It was not to be the last. An ideology that could be used in other struggles for liberation was created.

---

¹⁹ *Nachlass,* III:578-579. Cf. *Der Antichrist,* 27.
²⁰ *Ecce Homo, Warum ich so klug bin,* 8.
²¹ Some of the sources that can be adduced to support this thesis are given in my article on "The Historical Evolution of a Certain Concept of Freedom," *Iyyun, A Hebrew Philosophical Quarterly* 33 (1984):247-265.

However, at about the same time another event, which was at least as momentous, took place.

In a text of the *Mishnah*[22] three kinds of "yokes," that is servitudes, are mentioned; one of them is the "yoke" imposed by the government, another the "yoke" of the *Torah,* the Law.[23] This could suggest that liberation might consist not in political emancipation, but in throwing-off the yoke of the *Torah*. In historical reality Paul did conceive liberation in this way. Liberty or freedom is an idea, an objective, which is mentioned again and again in his Epistles as something desirable, something to be aspired to and achieved. And to his mind it meant freedom from the Law[24] (which amounted of course, *inter alia,* to revolt against the Jewish establishment). Paul was aware that this might be construed to mean the rejection of all morality, and he opposed this interpretation; but freedom, if once admitted, cannot be easily kept within bounds.

To go back to Nietzsche, the freedom enjoined by Paul corresponds, I think, fairly closely to what Nietzsche calls the internalization of freedom, which according to him generates *das schlechte Gewissen,* bad conscience, a phenomenon which, as we have seen, Nietzsche found fascinating and full of promise.

Paul is one of his *bêtes noires,* and he coined a special disparaging term for the religious movements and currents of thought, the most influential, widespread and extreme forms of which can be traced back to Paul; in Nietzsche's view they represent the *Sklavenaufstand in der Moral,* the slave insurrection in the sphere of morals,[25] "which starts with the ressentiment becoming creative and generating moral values (*Werte*)."[26] According to Nietzsche this insurrec-

---

[22] *Pirqei Abot* (The Sayings of the Fathers), III:4-5.

[23] The third "yoke" is, according to the current interpretation, the servitude imposed by the need to earn one's living.

[24] See for instance, Galateans, II:4; V:1 (in this verse the word "yoke" also occurs; apparently the yoke of the Law is meant); I Corinthians, X:28-30.

[25] See *Jenseits von Gut und Böse,* 195; *Zur Genealogie der Moral,* I:7-10.

[26] *Zur Genealogie der Moral,* I:10. According to Nietzsche, the slave insurrection in the sphere of morals begins with the Jews, whose prophets have made an amalgam of the words rich, violent, evil (*böse*) and sensual, and have given the term "world" (*Welt*) an opprobrious meaning; only the poor, the miserable, the powerless, the deseased, are regarded as the good. Christianity went even further, negating even the last reality that subsisted in Judaism; for it negated "the holy people," "the people of the chosen." Jesus incited the outcasts, "the sinners" within the Jewish community to rebel against the established order that prevailed in that community (*Der Antichrist,* 27). Paul annulled Christianity as it was at its origin and falsified the life and death of Jesus. What was important was not the life of Jesus, but his resurrection (see *Der Antichrist,*

tion and the values it imposes play a major part in the emergence of European nihilism.[27]

On the other hand, the suspicious attitude towards human actions and virtues, which the Pauline conceptions of Christian freedom and of original sin generate, account for the "moral scepticism," which Nietzsche approves of in Christianity.[28] According to him, this Christian scepticism has rid every individual of belief in his own virtues. It is owing to it that we feel both superior and amused when we read the works of Seneca or Epictetus. We (meaning Nietzsche himself) have, however, extended this scepticism also to all religious notions or states of mind, such as sin, repentance and so forth. In the letter to Overbeck, dated February 23, 1887, in which Nietzsche refers to Dostoevsky's story *l'Esprit Souterrain,* he remarks, *inter alia,* that the entire European science (*Psychologie*) suffers (*krankt*) because of Greek superficiality (*Oberflächlichkeiten*). He adds "and without the bit of Judaism etc. etc." (*und ohne das bisschen Judenthum usw. usw.*), obviously meaning that the Jewish element in European civilization made up to some extent for the inadequacy of the Greek psychological insight and knowledge. In this context Judaism may possibly stand for Pauline Christianity.[29]

42, cf. *Nachlass,* III:656). Paul understood that a conflagration spreading over the whole world could be started with the help of the small Christian community, that all the elements in the Roman Empire that had in secret rebellious tendencies could be united by means of the symbol: "God on the cross" (*Gott am Kreuze*) and transformed through their union into a most powerful community (*Der Antichrist,* 58). In *Zur Genealogie der Moral,* I:8, in a context in which Nietzsche treats of the slave insurrection in the sphere of morals he remarks concerning the symbol "God on the cross" (which, as we have just seen, he states in *Der Antichrist* to have been set up by Paul) "that *sub hoc signo* Israel with its vengeance and its transmutation of all [moral] values (*Umwertung aller Werte*) has up to now again and again triumphed over all other ideals, over all ideas of a nobler quality (*vornehmere*)."

[27] Cf., for instance, *Der Antichrist,* 6 and 7; *Nachlass,* III:634 f.

[28] *Die fröhliche Wissenschaft,* III:122. In a passage of the *Nachlass* (III:881) Nietzsche states that Christianity will be destroyed by the will to truth (*Wahrhaftigkeit*), which it has furthered. For the will to truth brings about disgust with the falsity and mendacious character of all Christian interpretations of the universe and of history.

[29] In a passage of the *Nachlass* (III:432) Nietzsche states that the Greeks misunderstood the tragical element (*das Tragische*) because of their "moralistic superficiality." In other passages, in which Nietzsche does not directly refer to the inadequacy of the psychological comprehension characteristic of the Greeks, he speaks of the latter being superficial because they were profound, *oberflächlich aus Tiefe*; cf., for instance, *Die fröhliche Wissenschaft,* Vorrede 4 and *Nietzsche contra Wagner,* Epilog 2. In these passages he praises the Greeks for their ability or their courage to keep to the surface of things. It may be maintained — though like all broad generalizations, which cannot but be approximations, the thesis is open to innumerable objections — that insofar as

The impact of the Pauline notion of freedom, freedom from works, i.e. in its extreme form, freedom from morality, cannot be easily overestimated. Luther's revolt against Roman Catholicism may be considered as an instance of this impact. It can be easily understood that because of his reaction to his Protestant upbringing, Nietzsche was in general inclined to dismiss with repugnance the notion of *evangelische Freiheit*.[30]

Another rather surprising instance of the influence of the Pauline notion may possibly be found in Spinoza. As we have seen,[31] this philosopher radicalizes the opposition, formulated by Maimonides and others, between the notions of good and evil on the one hand, and the notions of truth and falsehood on the other, and, as a result, affirms in *Ethics* IV:58 that the free man has no concept of evil.

In the terminology of this statement two sources may be distinguished. One is a medieval philosophical source; but the term "free man" does not have this origin. Human freedom, *libertas humana,* is for Spinoza the highest degree to which man can accede. Now in one sense the attribution of great value to human freedom is a philosophical, particularly, Stoic, truism; freedom being a pleasant and enviable state peculiar to a man who is not dominated by his passions and affects. For Spinoza, however, as we have seen, human freedom does not have this meaning only. It is also freedom from the notion of evil, that is, specifically from moral and religious prohibitions. Spinoza, as we know, entitled the last part of his *Ethics "De Libertate Humana."* This emphasis put on the notion of human freedom can by no means be explained by a reference to the philosophical tradition. In my opinion, the importance which Spinoza attaches to this notion may be due to the influence of Pauline Christianity. In the *Tractatus Theologico-Politicus* there are numerous quotations from the Pauline writings, most often from the *Epistle to the Romans.* Some of these quotations indicate, as Spinoza points out, that man is not required to observe the religious Law (i.e. the commandments of the *Torah*). Spinoza was, of course, also familiar with later manifestations of Pauline Christianity.

In the postcard to Overbeck of July 30, 1881 mentioned above, Nietzsche lists five points on which he agrees with Spinoza, one of them being the denial

---

Nietzsche considered himself as "*Psychologe,*" he was aware, at least sometimes, that he derived from the Judeo-Christian tradition, whereas as a philosopher he often felt a profound affinity with some of the Greeks. He had this feeling with regard to Heraclitus even in his later period when he wrote *Ecce Homo* (See *Ecce Homo* on *Die Geburt der Tragödie,* 3).

[30] Cf. *Nachlass,* III:825f., III:614.
[31] Cf. my article on Spinoza referred to above in footnote 9.

of evil (that is the adoption of Spinoza's conception of the free man). In one sense however Nietzsche extends freedom further than Spinoza. As has been already observed, it is most difficult to set limits to freedom, if the desirability of freedom is accepted. In our times, as we know, the obligation to be free is sometimes felt to be the only moral imperative that is valid. This is the impression that is conveyed by certain works of Sartre.[32] In a crude form it is formulated in a slogan of the so-called French student revoution of 1968, which proclaims: *il est interdit d'interdire,* it is forbidden to forbid.

This was not Nietzsche's style, nor did it correspond to his way of thinking. He would not have explicitly recognized freedom as a moral obligation. Politically he was opposed to the revolts of the oppressed and to their aspiration for liberty. It seems to me, however, that, as far as he personally is concerned, one may speak of what he called internalized freedom, a notion which, as I contend, corresponds to a great extent to what Nietzsche contemptuously designated as the slave insurrection in the moral sphere, one of whose main initiators was Paul. As has been mentioned Nietzsche (or the "new philosophers") is — unlike Spinoza — prepared to jettison the belief in the value of truth and of the quest for truth. This may be because Nietzsche, in his rôle of philosopher-lawgiver, may think that error can be more conducive to a superabundance of life and energy. However a passage in *Zur Genealogie der Moral* (III:24) lends colour to the suspicion that this willingness to sacrifice the very concept of truth is due to a compulsion exercised by "internalized freedom" on those whom Nietzsche calls "the free spirits," "*die freien Geister.*" According to this passage, the freedom of people who may be sceptics, atheists, nihilists, immoralists, antichrists (or anti-Christian), but believe in knowledge, is not complete; as Nietzsche says: "das sind noch lange keine *freien* Geister, *denn sie glauben noch an die Wahrheit*" ("these are far from being *free* spirits, *for they still believe in truth*"). Freedom, internalized freedom, does not permit such a limitation. The logic of freedom demands liberation from truth.

The Hebrew University of Jerusalem

---

[32] There is a logical contradiction between this imperative, which is quite evidently posited in many of Sartre's writings, and his contention that whatever a man does, he is condemned to be free. In *l'Etre et le néant* (Paris, 1973, p. 635) Sartre considers the case of a chained slave; the latter is free to choose to get rid of his chains or to choose to remain a slave. Both choices are founded on the slave's freedom to choose. In the passage referred to, Sartre does not explicitly state which choice is according to him preferable, but there can be no doubt as to what his attitude in such a case would be. For him, and not only for him, the moral imperative to be free is of so absolute a nature that it needs no justification.

Jacob Golomb

Nietzsche's Enticing Psychology of Power

I. The Objective of Nietzsche's Philosophy

Gradually it has become clear to me what every great philosophy so far has been: namely, the personal confession of its author...also that the moral (or immoral) intentions in every philosophy constituted the real germ of life from which the whole plant had grown. Indeed, if one would explain how the abstrusest metaphysical claims of a philosopher really come about, it is always well (and wise) to ask first: at what morality does all this (does he) aim? (BGE 6)

Both Nietzsche's "moral intentions" and the practical objective of his philosophizing have to do with helping us recognize our power and use it creatively in authentic patterns of life. His moral theory of power ultimately turns out to be the hub in which all his earlier and later views "become...more and more firmly attached to one another,...entwined and interlaced with one another" (GM V:2). This logical and ideational interrelation of central Nietzschean concepts and motives transforms what would seem at first to be a loosely connected and aphoristic work into a positive and comprehensive philosophy and psychology of power — one which can be discussed coherently.

Nietzsche's new psychology — which unlike others "dared to descend into the depths" and became what he called "*the doctrine of the development of the will to power*" (BGE 23) — unmasks the basic instinct of the human-all-too-human soul: *Macht*.

In the early *Birth of Tragedy* Nietzsche had already sketched the cardinal objective of his philosophy: attaining a mental state which would allow us to "gaze" courageously into the horrors of the "*tragic insight*" (BT 15). The same fundamental motif recurs later in the distinction between such weak, "gentle, fair...skepticism" as paralyzes the will and results in a nihilistic denial and "another and stronger type of skepticism" that "does not believe but does not lose itself in the process" (BGE 208-209).

Nietzsche's philosophy and the psychological means he employs purport to lead us to this skepticism of positive power and reach the state of the "great spirits" (A 54) who — like Zarathustra — are skeptics out of an abundance of power and sustain their skepticism in all vitality and creativity. In Nietzsche's terms, to dance "even near abysses" (GS 347) is the only alternative left after the "Death of God"; it is the ability to embrace this alternative that is the "proof of strength" and an indication of the "free spirit *par excellence*" with its positive power.

Thus Nietzsche's ultimate objective is to provide modern man with an intellectual therapy by preparing him for a creative life in a world without dogmatic beliefs. The death of dogma will not lead to the end of man and his culture, but will rather liberate his creative resources that have been suppressed till now by repressive morality. It will open new horizons to new beliefs, but these will function now solely as life-enhancing "perspectives." Once they lose their usefulness, such beliefs will be discarded and painlessly exchanged for other perspectives.

Nietzsche's own psychology is to be regarded as just such a belief — a temporary perspective, to be left behind once it has fulfilled its therapeutic mission. This explains, among other things, why so much of the psychological passages in Nietzsche's writings read as the self-diagnosis of a desperate physician who proposes to us a pattern of mental health, while suffering himself from a serious malady.

Hence, Nietzsche's psychology is to be a means: "a mere instrument" (BGE 6) to entice us to reach and freely employ our positive powers. In view of this, Nietzsche unquestionably belongs to "these philosophers of the future" who may have a right to be called "*versucher*" (BGE 42). The appropriate aphorism concludes with the words: "Dieser Name selbst ist zuletzt nur ein Versuch, und, wenn man will, eine Versuchung."[1]

Nietzsche describes the essence of this "Versuchung" or enticement: "One has to test oneself to see that one is destined for independence and command — and do it at the right time" (BGE 41). That is, it is an "experiment," an

---

[1] See also the statement that the genuine philosopher "fühlt die Last und Pflicht zu hundert *Versuchen* und *Versuchungen* des Lebens" (KSA 5: 133, BGE 205). Nietzsche's play on the words "*Versuch*" (hypothesis or experiment) and "*Versuchung*" (seduction or enticement) is far from unintentional as, for example, Walter Kaufmann calls it in his translation (*Beyond Good and Evil,* New York, 1966, pp. 52-53). It clearly points to one of the most significant features of Nietzsche's philosophy, namely, that it is a sophisticated mode of enticement; see my "Nietzsche's Phenomenology of Power," *Nietzsche-Studien* 15 (forthcoming).

"enticement" and a "hypothesis" that direct man's efforts toward positive power and test his ability to reach and activate it in his life's endeavors. These "experiments," "tests" or "enticements" are the psychology of power, which becomes Nietzsche's principal "instrument" for attaining his philosophical and existential goals.

The method of enticement is indeed a valuable means, since it seeks to draw us into embracing positive patterns of life — positive according to Nietzsche's psychological analyses and valuations. Indeed the word "enticement" in itself has no negative connotations but signifies rather a neutral process. Its positive or negative value depends solely on its purpose. Nietzsche is consistent in carefully distinguishing between the positive enticement to pathos — or the pattern of positive power which he calls *Versuchung* — and the negative seduction used by Christianity to suppress positive expressions of power, which he calls *Verführung*: "This Jesus of Nazareth, the incarnate gospel of love...was he not this seduction (*die Verführung*) in its most uncanny and irresistible form...?" (GM I:8).

Hence we understand why Nietzsche calls himself the "Anti-Christ."[2] He is like Christ insofar as he uses the same method of enticement that Christ used to divert mankind toward negative ideals. But Nietzsche is also Christ's opponent, since he uses the same enticing tactics to re-activate and intensify the positive powers of man and his culture. Against the Christian gospel of salvation from the hardships and maladies of life by means of seduction towards negative power (*die Verführung*), Nietzsche posits its antithesis: salvation from this negative salvation by psychological enticement to power (*die Versuchung*).

I have said that this psychology of power becomes, in Nietzsche's hands, the principal instrument of enticement. It is not, however, the only one, since from this psychological perspective we can now view some of his other so-called metaphysical ideas — especially the eternal recurrence of the same — as additional devices for the positive enticement and transformation of the reader.

The metaphysical hypothesis of the eternal recurrence appears frequently in Nietzsche's writings, not as an absolute dogma but more as an "experiment," which is also a test and an enticement. The acceptance or rejection of this hypothesis becomes an important indication of man's mental resources

---

[2] EH III:2 and see Jörg Salaquarda, "Der Antichrist," *Nietzsche-Studien* 2 (1973): 91-136 on other meanings of this term in Nietzsche's thought.

and powers.³ Thus, a quasi-metaphysical doctrine becomes a sort of Darwinian-psychological test, designed to distinguish between different patterns of power. It is important to emphasize here that in the passage where this thesis is first introduced — in the "as-if" version, by the testing "demon" — Nietzsche leaves room for only two possible responses:

Would you not throw yourself down and gnash your teeth and curse the demon who spoke thus? Or have you once experienced a tremendous moment when you would have answered him: 'You are a god and never have I heard anything more divine.' (GS 341)

Nietzsche does not allow for the indifferent or objective reaction which is the appropriate response to a scientific or metaphysical hypothesis. The strongly emotional reaction which he expects only corroborates my contention that the "eternal recurrence" was not really meant to be a metaphysical thesis, but rather a sort of *gedanken Experiment,* whose strong existential and psychological impact is manifested in either succumbing to it or in escaping from its consequences. This impact spells a significant change in the life of the man who faces the idea: "If this thought gained possession of you, it would change you as you are or perhaps crush you" (GS 341).

The motif of temptation and transformation involved in this idea explains why Nietzsche does not trouble to provide, in his published writings, any rational basis for the "eternal recurrence." What really matters to him is not the validity or truth of this thesis, but whether one possesses enough positive power to believe in it and to change accordingly. Since there is no logical connection between the truth of any idea and willingness to believe in it — Nietzsche is not required in this context to metaphysically or rationally substantiate his thesis, the superior aim of which is to entice the reader to reach and activate his positive power. This is why Nietzsche regards his Zarathustra, who personifies the educative and tempting aspects of his psychological philosophy, as "the teacher of the eternal recurrence,"⁴ and defines

---

³ See, e.g. *Musarionausgabe,* 14: 187. Thus I am here proposing a reconciliation between what Bernd Magnus aptly calls the "normative interpretation of recurrence" (*Nietzsche's Existential Imperative,* Bloomington, 1978, p. 142), which stresses the psychological consequences of this doctrine, and Magnus' own interpretation, emphasizing the existential-heuristic role of this teaching. Thus the introduction of the concept of "enticement" in this context is an attempt to capture the psychological importance of this doctrine without attaching it too narrowly to its truth-value — as does, e.g., the normative interpretation.
⁴ Z 3 "The Convalescent" 2 and Cf. Haim Gordon, "Nietzsche's Zarathustra as

his educational goals according to the existential demands of this idea.

Nietzsche is aware of the fact that enticement — his therapeutic means *par excellence* — is not intended for everyone. In fact he considers our reaction to his therapy as an additional criterion of distinction between different patterns of power. He implies that if we fail to respond to his enticement, this is not because of any inner flaws in the therapy or because it lacks appeal, but because of our own inability to raise ourselves to the level of its demands; and because we do not possess the positive power for it to become manifest and allow us to rise to the Nietzschean challenge:

> What serves the higher type of men as nourishment or delectation must almost be poison for a very different and inferior type... There are books that have opposite values for soul and health, depending on whether the lower soul, the lower vitality, or the higher and more vigorous ones turn to them: in the former case, these books are dangerous and lead to crumbling and disintegration; in the latter, herald's cries that call the bravest to their courage. (BGE 30)

It is possible to distinguish in this passage three kinds of responses to enticement. The challenges stand in direct correspondence to the psychological type at whom they are directed: the "inferior type" of negative power rejects the enticement, is confused by it and escapes from its consequences; the "higher type" of adequate positive power accepts it and becomes more powerful, independent and authentic; the *Übermensch* of optimal power does not respond to this enticement since he does not require it. He is endowed with the highest capacity for auto-creation, and thus is able to go his own way, overcoming even this Nietzschean enticement by creating his own perspective and values. Here the rejection of Nietzsche's challenge does not stem from cowardliness or weakness (as in the first case) but, on the contrary, out of a surplus of power and an abundance of self that is not in need of such psychologistic crutches.

By viewing Nietzsche's philosophical psychology as an educative means for the enticement of the reader we can explain various peculiar characteristics of his writings. It accounts first of all for the sub-title of *Zarathustra* (where the eponymous sage personifies and symbolizes this enticement) as "Ein Buch für Alle und Keinen," and for Nietzsche's belief that his books are not intended

---

Educator, *J. of Philosophy of Education* 14 (1980): 181-192. This article emphasizes the educative aspect of Zarathustra, seeking to arouse his students to accept the example of the *Übermensch*, but ignoring the enticing side of this education to adopt the patterns of positive power. See also my "Nietzsche's Early Educational Thought," *J. of Philosophy of Education* 19 (1985): 99-109.

for all, that only a few will really understand them. It also explains the poetic style, the powerful pathos and the provocativeness which he deliberately introduced in his messages. Not only the specific content but also the external form of Nietzsche's psychology aim at softening and reducing our resistance to its therapy. Thus it is not by accident that in several places Nietzsche insists on the close interrelations between his goal as a psychologist of morality and his peculiar personal style.[5]

"Whatever is profound loves masks" declares Nietzsche, and whatever educates loves the enticing mask behind which lies "so much graciousness in cunning" (BGE 40).

Nietzsche clarifies his task as the enticing psychologist in a retrospective passage in *Ecce Homo*: "To give an idea of me as a psychologist, I choose a curious bit of psychology from *Beyond Good and Evil*" (3:6).

This passage runs as follows:

> The genius of the heart, as that great concealed one possesses it, the tempter god (*der Versucher Gott*) and born pied piper of consciences whose voice knows how to descend into the netherworld of every soul; who does not say a word or cast a glance in which there is no consideration and ulterior enticement; whose mastery includes the knowledge of how to seem — not what he is but what is to those who follow him one *more* constraint to press ever closer to him in order to follow him...the god *Dionysus,* that great ambiguous one and tempter god...this type of deity and philosopher...often reflect[s] how [he] might yet advance man and make him stronger, more evil, and more profound than he is. (BGE 295)

In brief, the "teacher" is endowed here with a more powerful pathos of the positive power, what is called elsewhere the "Yes-saying pathos *par excellence*" (EH, Z 1) or "The pathos of nobility and distance" (GM I:2). The main ploy of this Nietzsche-Dionysus is his psychology and all its components. Psychology becomes here again "the path to the fundamental problems" (BGE 23) or, in my terminology, *the path to the fundamental patterns of positive power*. However, this being only a path, it is naturally abandoned once it has come to an end. Nietzschean psychology will have become then a sort of temporary scaffolding, a provisional hypothesis or a metaphoric structure (in the original meaning of the term *meta-phora*), to be abandoned once it has served its purpose.

---

[5] E.g.: "This sounds harsh... But why stroke the effeminate ears of our modern weaklings? Why should *we* give way even one step to their tartuffery of words? For us psychologists this would constitute a tartuffery in *deed*... For if a psychologist today has *good taste* (others might say, integrity), it consists in resistance to the shamefully *moralized* way of speaking..." (GM III:19; see also EH III:5).

An illuminating analogy (apart from Freudian psychoanalysis) that may help us understand this unique function of Nietzsche's psychology, is the early Wittgenstein's concept of the ladder that, at the end of the *Tractatus Logico-Philosophicus,* his reader is asked to "throw away...after he has climbed it."[6] This ladder is metaphysics as conceived and portrayed by Wittgenstein in that book.

The enticing ladder of Nietzsche the psychologist is composed of four distinctive steps: psychologization, positive psychology of power, phenomenology of power, and genealogy of power.

All the components of Nietzsche's psychology confront us with tragic insight and Dionysian skepticism. In the process of this psychologization, in this unmasking of illusions and peeling off of defensive mechanisms (such as religion, science, philosophy, etc.) — the positive power of man is exposed. The more this power is unleashed, in the qualitative sense, the better it will work, vitally and creatively, without intellectual defense mechanisms — until it reaches the optimal point at which it will no longer need the psychological ladder and can dispense with it. In other words: Nietzschean psychology is at the same time an instrument for freezing repressive ideologies and a means for enticing and intensifying the will which assists man to endure this very process. In the preliminary stages of maturation, power still needs therapeutic and psychological crutches. But with the full ripening of power — with the attainment of autonomy, Nietzsche's "auto-creation" — man's authentic power must shed off its supports and prove its authenticity by being able to thrive without them. So the way leading to power must already include this very power; it carries this power as a potential for full actualization through a painful and gradual process of reactivation. The psychological ladder does not create the power or its positive patterns and pathos *ex nihilo*; it merely explicates and activates this power. This is the main meaning of Nietzsche's conception of the philosopher's confession and of his focal statement that the philosopher's "thinking is, in fact, far less a discovery than a recognition, a remembering, a return and a homecoming to a remote, primordial, and inclusive household of the soul"; and therefore that "philosophizing is to this extent a kind of atavism of the highest order" (BGE 20).

This explicative aspect of the ladder also includes a personal meaning

---

[6] 6.54, trans. D.F. Pears & B.F. McGuinness (London, 1961). A different sort of analogy between Wittgenstein and Nietzsche may be found in Erich Heller, "Wittgenstein and Nietzsche," in: *The Artist's Journey into the Interior* (New York, 1959), pp. 201-226, which discusses several similarities between Nietzsche and the later Wittgenstein of the *Philosophical Investigations.*

clearly indicated by the terms *das Selbstbekenntnis* and *mémoires* (BGE 6). Here we have not only a theoretical explication of *Macht,* but also Nietzsche's own existential explication of a man who by his philosophizing strives to express his positive power, towards which he seeks to lead us, and which he seeks to expose and intensify within his own "household of the soul." This instrumental psychology is intended to fulfill not only our needs but also Nietzsche's. His explication of power thus becomes a kind of self-psychoanalysis. Freud was probably well aware of this. [7] Nietzsche's analysis of power and self-analysis are parallel and complementary processes but they are not derived from one another. For while it is true that in his enticing psychologizations Nietzsche himself is enticed, and that in giving directives for our maturation Nietzsche himself matures and becomes powerful, nonetheless these two processes are not causally connected. They are both separate manifestations of Nietzsche's one "common root," of his *"fundamental will"* (GM V:2). The "common root" is always power, whether used for self-overcoming or for the overcoming of one's epoch. Or, more precisely, this power is used to overcome all these patterns of life and their cultural rationalizations that hinder the spontaneous and creative employment of positive powers hidden in Nietzsche and his contemporaries.

This self-psychoanalytic, subjective component, interwoven with the theoretical elements of Nietzsche's thought, explains, among other things, why he did not elaborate a philosophical, non-personal system; why he resisted the ideal of philosophy as science, and objected to the notion of the autonomy of reflexion. The subjective component also accounts for Nietzsche's personal way of writing and for its partially aphoristic and associative form, very much

---

[7] Witness his biographer Ernst Jones, who in describing the meeting of the Vienna Psychoanalytic Society of 28 October 1908, devoted to the analysis of *Ecce Homo,* remarks that Freud "several times referred to Nietzsche as to the man who had a more penetrating knowledge of himself than any other man who ever lived or was likely to live" (E. Jones, *Sigmund Freud: Life and Work,* London, 1955, II:385). Coming from the founder of psychoanalysis this is no small compliment. Moreover, Freud and his followers believe that man is able to reach self-knowledge only by following a long and intensive psychoanalysis. Thus, Freud implies in this passage that Nietzsche, who possessed self-knowledge "more than any other man who ever lived" (including Freud himself, who, as is well known, performed self-psychoanalysis while writing *Die Traumdeutung*), had acquired such knowledge as a result of a painful process of introspection, similar to Freud's. That this is so appears from some comments made by Freud at the same meeting: "He makes a number of brilliant discoveries in himself. The degree of introspection achieved by Nietzsche had never been achieved by anyone, nor is it likely to be reached again" (*Minutes of the Vienna Psychoanalytic Society,* New York, 1967, II:32).

resembling the psychoanalytic treatment, which employs spontaneous outbursts of "primary associative processes" (to use Freudian terms), as well as more objective interpretations and theoretical reflections upon these processes. Both evoke and nourish these processes and are in turn elicited by them again and again.

This consideration of Nietzsche's psychology from a therapeutic perspective assists us in approaching the problem of the apparent vicious circle between his positive doctrine and his skeptic-perspectivist epistemology. The emphasis upon enticement in Nietzsche's thought clearly shows that there is no logical reason for rejecting his enticing psychology since it does not stand in any contradiction to criteria of objective truth — "frozen" in the preliminary psychologizations. If his skepticism is regarded as one of the vital components in the therapeutic attempt to expose and to activate the positive powers of man and his culture, the problem of the circularity between Nietzsche's anthropology and epistemology becomes less acute than is generally considered.

II. The Phenomenology of Power

Nietzsche's psychology of power is not an inductive theory or an empirical hypothesis, as Kaufmann claims.[8] Apart from the speculative method of psychologization it also clearly contains a tendency which we can call phenomenological, without, of course, identifying it with Husserl's phenomenology "as Rigorous Science." Here the use of "phenomenology" is not intended to equate Nietzsche's descriptions with Husserl's apodictic and idetic analyses.[9] However, for didactic purposes, the term is useful in stressing the most conspicuous feature of Nietzsche's psychology — its explicative and typological dimension — in contrast to the constructive and explanatory aspect of the empirical sciences. This dimension is vividly expressed in Nietzsche's analyses of the different patterns of power and his distinction between its two central manifestations: the positive and the negative. The explication of a given phenomenon does not include its rational justification and foundation, but the former may surely function as a necessary introduction for the latter. This is what Nietzsche has in mind when he says that all philosophers so far have "wanted to supply a rational foundation" for prevalent morality, but they

---

[8] Walter Kaufmann, *Nietzsche* (Princeton, N.J., 1968), pp. 92; 183.
[9] See my "Psychology from the Phenomenological Standpoint of Husserl," *Philosophy and Phenomenological Research* 36 (1976): 451-471.

have completely ignored its vast variety and immense richness. Thus they were involved in providing a justifying philosophy, a "science of morals," namely, a rational ethics, and did not deal with the preliminary "typology of morals" (BGE 186). Because of this exclusive preoccupation, the philosophers "left in dust...the task of description," and were not at all concerned "to collect material, to conceptualize and arrange a vast realm of subtle feelings of value and differences of value which are alive, grow, beget, and perish." Thus they completely neglected "attempts to present vividly some of the more frequent and recurring forms of such living crystallizations," forgetting thereby that "the real problems of morality...emerge only when we compare *many* moralities" (BGE 186). Nietzsche dealt extensively with such comparisons and with descriptive typology and the "subtle" distinctions between different moralities in his works and thus the phenomenology of power and its derivatives were laid bare.

The phenomenological dimension reveals that Nietzsche, in explicating various moral patterns, is not searching for new, esoteric values. Nor does he intend to establish a new ethics. What he aims at is crystallizing, intensifying, re-activating a number of values that are regarded by most of us as good and useful, securing the social order and fostering our mental health.

This can easily be seen by looking at some of the characteristics of positive power that Nietzsche describes in his writings. Among the many positive predicates of the man endowed with power we do not find any original or new values but rather concepts such as self-sufficiency, heroism, creative sublimation of instincts, intellectual tolerance, generosity, nobility, dynamic vitality, courage, the will to life, self-control, faith in oneself, the ability to accept contradiction, the lack of bad conscience, and the like. Most of these values appear in traditional philosophical ethics, such as the theories of Plato, Spinoza and Kant, to whom Nietzsche frequently refers. In using the term "ethics" I mean a doctrine aiming at a rational foundation and justification of moral norms. Nietzsche, however, does not believe that our reason is capable of providing any such rational foundation. This, of course, raises the question: why should we prefer the morality of positive power and reject the various expressions of the morality of negative power, if neither can be transcendentally justified? Why should we prefer the *Übermensch* to the ordinary man? Why should we choose creativity and sublimation and reject repression, which over a couple of millenia has brought about Christian-moral culture with its glorious tradition? Or, to put it more bluntly: why be a moral agent at all?

Nietzsche was well aware of this meta-ethical question, which in the above-cited aphorism he calls: "The problem of morality itself." It is implicitly answered in his explicative attitude towards morality as such. He emphasizes psychology as much as he does just because he does not believe in the possibility of a philosophical justification of morality. However, even psychology at its best can do no more than offer us good reasons for the adoption of this or that pattern of life; but it is unable to provide the ultimate justification for the adoption of such a pattern.

Nevertheless, providing reasons for adopting the morality of positive power is not the only function of Nietzsche's psychology. Its other important role, as I have indicated above, is to be an enticing, persuasive tool, an heuristic and therapeutic means for helping us to discover and actualize our power. In Nietzschean terms, it can be said to be a *monumental psychology,* functioning in a way similar to his heuristic "monumental history."

Now, it is impossible to entice someone and persuade him to act in some specific manner, unless he does already possess the inherent ability to meet the challenge or yield to it. Positive power must already be hidden in mankind (and its expression in everyday life and culture must be possible). As in Freudian psychoanalysis, so also in Nietzschean psychology it is not assumed that we could be injected with patterns of positive power. These must lie within us and it is the task of psychology to activate them creatively. Therefore, there is no contradiction between the fact that Nietzsche has no esoteric, ideal prescriptions, and his insistence in calling on us to live creatively, to widen our intellectual horizons and to lead original lives. Originality, Nietzsche believes, springs from the inherent sources of power and lies in the manner in which it is operated, not in its external manifestations.

By enticing us to exhibit and courageously operate our positive power, Nietzsche strives to assist us in overcoming the impediments that have inhibited the spontaneous manifestation of that power. The enticement will help us to uncover the origins of creation. Nietzsche supposes that these origins of power are rooted deeply within ourselves, but because of various psychological handicaps (such as cowardice, for example), we have repressed them and have prohibited their free operation. These handicaps have been projected as an ideological network with patterns of negative power, and Nietzsche uses his psychologistic method (his "hammer") to shatter such prohibiting "idols," to overcome them while freezing our faith in them — all in order to evoke creative-instinctive positive power.

The very process of "freezing" our belief in most of the prevalent values of negative power is founded on the assumption that the "frozen" individual will reject certain values and accept others, which already exist both in his social surroundings and within himself.

An illuminating example of such a "freezing," explicative and psychologistic process, based upon an implicit set of values latent within ourselves, can be found in Nietzsche's analysis of the ascetic ideal, to him the ultimate expression of negative power:

> It is my purpose here to bring to light, not what this ideal has done, but simply what it means; what it indicates; what lies hidden behind it, beneath it, in it... And it is only in pursuit of this end that I could not spare my readers a glance at its monstrous and calamitous effects, to prepare them for the ultimate and most terrifying aspect of the question concerning the meaning of this ideal. (GM III:23)

There is a striking similarity between the procedure of "coolly placing on ice" (EH, HH 1) and the aporetic tactics employed by Socrates, whom Nietzsche ambivalently admired. Socrates "froze" by logical means whereas Nietzsche does this solely by means of genetic psychologizations. In his dialogues, Socrates is seeking to freeze the listener's belief in x, for examply, by showing him that this logically entails a belief in y. The listener is not ready to endorse belief in y because of his belief in the set of values $p, s, t \ldots$ which he shares with Socrates.

Nietzsche employs almost the same method. He shows his readers that their most "sacred" values are rooted in negative power and the psychological "effects" of their endorsement are stagnation, repression, inhibition of creativity, depression, regression and so forth. Now, most of us consider these effects to be undesirable, and we all wish to be rid of them. The enticing psychological arguments for the morality of positive power, therefore, are not presented directly and prescriptively. Rather, the process of "freezing" is employed indirectly by means of a genealogy, which shows that most prevalent norms originate in negative power and that the effects of our accepting these norms are psychologically and existentially destructive for the individual himself and, in the long run, for the whole culture.

All this is closely connected to Nietzsche's phenomenology, since in order to evoke positive power he must first overcome the inhibiting forces. Both the positive enticement and the negative freezing assume that men possess an implicit set of values that drive them to reject negative patterns. Therefore, along with his enticing psychology Nietzsche must explicate these implicit norms. He must elaborate what I have called the phenomenology of power.

In the very process of phenomenological explications a strong heuristic element is inherent. This is because Nietzsche's description portrays a sublime pattern of life which evokes our reverence (what Kant calls our *Achtung*), and indicates that the power in question is attainable, since it hides at the base of our mental and cultural life, and since it has already manifested itself frequently in history — in the noble moral patterns of the "masters."

By focusing on a phenomenon hidden yet implicit in our culture — scattered in various patterns of life and in different philosophies of morality — Nietzsche's phenomenology of power functions like a lighthouse, showing the way and enticing us to follow it. Hence the phenomenology of power is — like most of his psychology — a monumental phenomenology that has its beginning in "Schopenhauer als Erzieher," where Nietzsche portrays several models of ideal human beings. The heroic presentation in itself, Nietzsche assumes, may tempt us to aspire to the sublime level of the heroes.

Another crucial passage stresses this explicatory feature of Nietzsche's discussion of the phenomenon of power:

Wandering through the many subtler and coarser moralities which have so far been prevalent on earth, or still are prevalent, I found that certain features recurred regularly together and were closely associated — until I finally discovered two basic types and one basic difference.

There are *master morality* and *slave morality* — I add immediately that in all the higher and more mixed cultures there also appear attempts at mediation between these two moralities, and yet more often the interpenetration and mutual misunderstanding of both, and at times they occur directly alongside each other — even in the same human being, within a *single* soul. (BGE 260)

Nietzsche describers his investigations of different moral patterns as a search for "certain features [that] recurred regularly together." This is obviously a description of the explicative method, which seeks to expose the definitive and essential features of certain phenomena. The two moral phenomena presented are actual cultural patterns, and are far from being *a priori* constructions of our minds. "Master morality" and the pattern of the *Übermensch* are historical phenomena,[10] which Nietzsche defines more closely in order to avoid confusion with the "slave morality." Let us emphasize that in Nietzsche's own view his originality is not expressed by the establishment of a new and unique moral set, but rather by elucidating already existing moralities and by giving them new names, throwing new light on their essential features: "What is originality?" — Nietzsche asks, and answers: "To *see* something that has no name as yet and hence cannot be mentioned although it stares us all in the face" (GS 261). As long as the moral phenomenon "stares

---

[10] This contention is confirmed not only by the phenomenological-explicative dimensions of Nietzsche's thought, but also by his thesis of the "eternal recurrence of the same." If we accept this idea literally — what has been will be again — the historical types of *Übermenschen* are of course included. The *Übermensch,* therefore, is not a new element but an already existing person, who will reappear in the future. Indeed, Nietzsche maintains that in the figure of Napoleon: "the problem of the noble ideal as such made flesh" (GM I:16).

us all in the face" without being named, and without undergoing the most sustained explication and classification, it cannot influence or move us. In other words: it cannot become an operative ideal.

This is how we should grasp Nietzsche's statement that "Never yet has there been an overman" (Z 2). This is so, since there is no complete and concrete picture of the moral pattern of positive power. Such a pattern is given in the fictitious figure of Zarathustra, who consolidates the positive values scattered in the various patterns of negative power. Thus the explicit moral ideal of positive power has been wanting. If we want such an ideal to move us, to entice and inspire us — we must bring it to a full and conscious explication, distinct from opposing ideals and freed from contradictory features. However, once the phenomenology of power has provided the necessary, full explication of this implicit ideal, it will refine this ideal and transform it from an historical phenomenon into a regulative and influential idea — the theoretical distinguishing features of which cannot be materialized on the empirical level.

The heuristic explication of the positive and negative moral patterns of power is especially needed since Nietzsche, observing the cultural history of morality, discovers "the interpenetration and mutual misunderstanding of both" (BGE 200). Moreover, the phenomenological view of history discloses the slow, gradual progression from the "morality of the herd" to a morality that increasingly stresses the value of the individual. The gradual emergence of the morality of positive power is already taking place in the history of mankind, Nietzsche claims (GS 117-120). Thus the main goal of his phenomenological explications is to speed up this process of emergence and provide it with an operative and effective power.

It follows that we must understand Nietzsche's basic idea of the "transfiguration of all values," not as abolition but as a gradual transfiguration of the morality of negative power into the morality of positive power. Of course, this is not a radical change, *ex nihilo,* beginning with the complete lack of positive power. In order for a significant change to take place, the changing element must already contain, at least implicitly, the seeds of this change. The process of "transfiguration" is well established both in our cultural history (GS 117-120) and also "within a single soul" (BGE 260), fluctuating between the opposing vectors of positive and negative powers.

The phenomenology of power thus reflects upon the "single soul" of the individual. Nietzsche, like Freud, occasionally delineates parallels between phylogenesis and ontogenesis — between the development of cultural patterns and their evolution in individual souls that partake of that culture. Thus, after claiming the interpenetration of the two moralities on the wider, historical level, Nietzsche goes on to make an ontogenetic statement, namely that such moral processes "occur directly alongside each other — even in the same human being" (BGE 260). Since with reference to the "*single* soul" it is difficult to speak about morality, which requires the social context, it seems that what Nietzsche is describing here is the more transitory, fluctuating, emotional and mental state of the individual, "the true pathos of every period of our life" (GS 317). Such an individual "pathos of life" crystallizes into a social formation of moral patterns and positive/negative ways of life.

It is very likely that Nietzsche, in speaking of the "single soul," actually also had his own personality in mind and was referring to the negative and positive sentiments intermingling in it. Here is added to the phenomenology of power another aspect — that of Nietzsche's self-psychoanalysis, uncovering the conflict within himself between the powerful, healthy, vital and spontaneous life pathos, on the one hand, and the weak, sick, repressed, destructive and passive pathos, on the other. Such rapid and acute transitions from one type of pathos to another characterize, in psychoanalytic literature, the neurotic personality. In his writings, letters and the autobiographical essay *Ecce Homo,* Nietzsche frequently describes such "neurotic" swings between ecstatic creative periods and prolonged repression, dejection and malady. According to his own testimony, his neurosis (to which Freud frequently referred) facilitated his psychological insights and enabled him to make fine-drawn distinctions, both phenomenological and psychological, between good/evil and good/bad. Nietzsche finds intimate connections between sickness and philosophy, and claims that someone who has not experienced the pathos of negative power, the "disgust...gloominess and loneliness" is not "predestined for knowledge" (BGE 26). Only a person who experiences such a neurosis and overcomes it is able to "go inside" and to possess an "inborn fastidiousness of taste with respect to psychological questions" (GM V:3). This ability to "go inside" and overcome the states of negative pathos is regarded by Nietzsche as the foremost indication of the existence of positive power in a person, daring to explore the darkest recesses of his soul and explicate them for the sake of health and vitality.

It is easy, then, to see how Nietzsche's power philosophy contains the component of self-psychoanalysis, by means of which the thinker seeks to overcome his own negative power. His philosophy, as he testifies on several occasions, is "written with his blood" — with the blood of his distress and struggle against his neurosis and negative power. However, what is first required for such a self-overcoming is a "confessions," a self-explication of the patterns of negative power. This is the phenomenology of power, and in delineating it Nietzsche means not only to entice and direct *us* toward healthy morality, but also to guide himself in the same direction.

Although Nietzsche is mostly preoccupied with the pathos of negative power and its numerous cultural expressions, the very fact of the confession and the will to overcome the negative pathos by its means are clear indications of the existence of positive power in the confessing man. At the time of his confession, this man already stands within the boundaries of positive pathos, firmly rejecting the negative accretions. This is similar to the state of the man who decides to undergo psychoanalytic treatment, for this very decision constitutes a recognition of positive power with an implicit set of values and a will to reject the elements that inhibit it, choosing mental health rather than sickness, creative vitality rather than repressive *akrasia*.

Thus Nietzsche's phenomenological psychology is directed at all those people, in whom, as in the neurotic, the opposite vectors of positive and negative powers are in constant fluctuation and "interpenetration." The goal of this psychology is always the same: to assist these people to creatively actualize and exhibit their vital resources.

III. Nietzschean versus Husserlian Phenomenology

We must now deal more critically with the epistemological status of Nietzsche's phenomenology — especially against the background of his theory of perspectives and its skeptical meaning. I have already implied that despite some similarity between the phenomenology of Nietzsche and that of Husserl,[11] an essential difference remains, which even calls the validity of Nietzsche's "phenomenological account" into question. This marked difference stems from the different objectives of the two phenomenologies. Whereas Husserl, by means of his phenomenological analyses, strives to attain the scientific ideal of the apodictic and "pure" consciousness, Nietzsche regards the scientific ideal as just another, and redundant, "shadow" of the dead God. Philosophy, he holds, must assist us in attaining a specific pattern of life by revealing our personal power and helping us to overcome the obstacles in its way. Nietzsche's ideal is not rational but existential. He does not wish to achieve "pure knowledge," for he does not even believe in its existence, but

---

[11] Thus, for example, another parallel might be found between Husserl's noetic-intentional acts, which bestow meaning upon the stream of consciousness, and the similar function of Nietzsche's concept of power, which by its interpretations and Apollonian projections forms meaningful structures in the chaos that confronts it (WP 604-605). From this point of view Nietzsche's power has the same constitutive status as Husserlian consciousness.

rather to attain a way of life with the moral pathos of positive power.

Nietzsche's skeptical attitude toward the validity of intuitive knowledge, whether discursive or phenomenological, stems directly from his perspectivistic doctrine. If a perception is the product of an interpretation and of a perspectivistic mold, it includes the immediate perception as well. Hence it is nonsense to speak about "immediate certainties; for example, 'I think'...as well as 'absolute knowledge.'" This is "the seduction (*Verführung*) of words!" (BGE 16). Nietzsche thus wishes to undermine the Cartesian foundation of the phenomenological attitude and the validity of its introspective reflexion, which, however, actually lies behind Nietzsche's own phenomenology of power. From this point of view it can be said that for Nietzsche even the explication is merely another interpretation.

Moreover, Nietzsche, out of his skeptical attitude repeatedly rejects the main assumption of Husserlian phenomenology — the autonomy of reflexion — among other reasons because of his suspicion "of all thinking," which is solely a matter of "perspective estimates and appearances" (BGE 34). In Husserlian terms, Nietzsche rejects the very possibility of the "phenomenological reduction," since it is impossible to perform upon reason — which is another expression of power — " unselfing and depersonalization"; hence it is nonsense to speak about "disinterested knowledge" and the "objective person" (BGE 207). The very impossibility of Husserl's phenomenological-psychological reduction brings about the impossibility of the Husserlian "epochē," of putting "the external world" (BGE 4) within the phenomenological brackets.

All this brings Nietzsche to a serious methodological contradiction. The phenomenological means for the explication of power is invalid, since this same power, which also operates the "perspectivistic" method, is not purely rational, and therefore it introduces an opaque, non-cognitive element into the explicative method, thereby losing its validity. The object and the methodology of the investigation stand in basic contradiction to each other. Hence, Nietzsche is unable to explicate power by phenomenological-psychological, or, for that matter, by any rational means. Unable to validate power rationally he must posit it dogmatically as a subjective and arbitrary expression of his own will to power, accepting the resulting circularity: "Supposing that this also is only interpretation — and you will be eager to make this objection? — well, so much the better" (BGE 22).

Why then does Nietzsche use this phenomenological, explicative method at all, notwithstanding his belief that it is no more valid than other possible methods? Perhaps it can be said that he adopts the phenomenology of power since it efficiently serves as an enticing means for positive power. This pragmatic, psychological, reason for the employment of any theory or research method is relevant to the theoretical distinction between the act of accepting *x*, which is an immediate act of the will (or in Nietzschean terms — of personal power), and the act of rationally judging whether this *x* is true or false (which in Nietzschean terminology is also an expression of power, but this time of a negative, "Socratic," and discursive power). Because of Nietzsche's will to express his positive power and to entice us to follow in his steps — he employs the phenomenological attitude, although he believes that it lacks real validity in the classical sense. In any case this phenomenology is only a provisional tool employed on the way toward attaining power, and after it has served its purpose, it may be discarded together with all the other means used along the way.

But why should we employ the phenomenological or any other method, if none of these are any more "true" or valid than any other? Now, life of a certain moral pathos, although it lacks objective validity, expresses the person's positive power. In the same manner the acceptance of the psychological scaffolding, in spite of the fact that it is devoid of any rational foundation, expresses "the ability to accept criticism and contradiction" (GS 297). For Nietzsche, this ability is always the sign of the positive power of "the liberated spirit" (*ibid.*) and the sign of a powerful, vital skeptic who is not crushed under the weight of his burden. Further, even if we are not enticed to climb the phenomenological ladder or to take any other step on the road, we must still distinguish clearly between the different reasons for this unwillingness. If the enticement fails because of rational reasons or any reason derived from prevalent morality — this is an indication of a person of negative power, in whom the positive elements are completely suppressed; the enticement is void then because it lacks an object. Since in this case there is no possibility of, or condition for, the achievement of the "transfiguration of our nature," it would be nonsensical to attempt to evoke this transfiguration. However, if we reject Nietzsche's enticement because we have our own original way (in the double meaning of autonomous origin and unique content), then he would say that we have already employed our autonomous positive powers, characteristic of such a unique individual who overcomes both social and moral predicaments and the teachers of his age. We would thus not need Nietzsche's enticement, since we would already be taking the path toward which he wishes to direct us.

Other objections, not stemming from the perspectivistic doctrine, may be made to the phenomenological aspect of Nietzsche's psychology. First, there is the general contention that a lack of any explicit methodology (a lack which is compatible with Nietzsche's skeptical perspectivism), leads to a confusion among his various methodological means — the several psychological steps that should lead to the attainment of his philosophical objective: the pathos of positive power. The grounds for this objection are well illustrated here. Nietzsche has not explicitly clarified the nature of the relation between his psychology and his phenomenology. Thus, in contrast to Husserl's phenomenological method, which aspired to be presuppositionless, Nietzsche, in his psychologizations and explications, applies various psychological presuppositions which sum up his mental theory. I have in mind especially the presupposition of the unconscious, which aims to explain why we are not always conscious of our positive power, of our will for maturity and of a whole set of values that motivate us and shape our judgements and way of life. The lack of such consciousness justifies the phenomenological explications of the phenomena of power, since it is possible to uncover something if and only if this 'something' is implicit and concealed from our eyes. Apart from the idea of the unconscious which Nietzsche frequently uses in his explications, there are several theoretical psychological concepts, such as sublimation, repression, internalization, self-overcoming, etc., that obviously have importance beyond the limits of explication alone.

Not only is there a confusion among the different methodological steps in Nietzsche's psychology of power, there is also confusion between the provisional means and the moral-philosophical objective of that psychology. This can be regarded as a severe defect, especially by commentators who distrust the psychologisms of which Nietzsche may be accused.

Husserl is committed to the neutral attitude of the *epochē*, which purports to abstain from any evaluation or expression of personal attitude toward the explicated content of the phenomenological analysis. In contrast, Nietzsche, from the beginning, expresses a definite acceptance of some valuable patterns of positive power and their moral pathos, and an unequivocal rejection of the many expressions of the negative power. Nietzsche's writings are saturated with value judgements and criticisms that presuppose a complete set of values. His works are polemical and adopt definite attitudes toward significant cultural issues. The title itself of the work in which his typological phenomenology reaches its peak, *Beyond Good and Evil,* indicates that Nietzsche has moral commitments and preferences.[12]

Not only does Nietzsche *not* abstain from holding a definite system of values in his phenomenological stage, but he actually argues for the theoreti-

---

[12] See also a later composition, where Nietzsche presents his moral code: "What is good? Everything that heightens the feeling of power in man, the will to power, power itself. What is bad? Everything that is born of weakness" (A 2).

cal impossibility of such an abstention. We cannot close ourselves up within some neutral attitude towards phenomena, because our cognitive relations themselves are driven by the actions of our power. Indeed, it is impossible to conceive of a cognition which is completely severed from any perspective formation, and the perspectivistic interpretation itself is controlled by the will to power. Where we speak about man's will, it is possible in principle to evaluate and judge the effects of this will, including Nietzsche's *perspectivistic* effects. Nietzsche, therefore, does not believe in the ideal of "the *ideal* scholar," who "places himself too far apart to have any reason to take sides for good or evil." He does not believe in such an ideal since behind any philosopher and behind any cognition and explication there hides "power, self-reliance," the will "to be master" (BGE 207). Hence, Nietzsche intentionally mobilizes his phenomenology for the sake of the moral ideal which is the *raison d'être* of phenomenology in his writings. As a result, the tenuous border between the "is" and the "ought" becomes ill-defined, even indistinct.

IV. Nietzsche against Psychologism

We now come to the obvious question of whether this moral commitment on the explicative level is enough to justify the charge of moral psychologism that may be levelled against Nietzsche.

According to Husserl in the *Logical Investigations,* psychologism is an attitude that strives to derive normative rules in logic and ethics from empirical psychological laws. To derive moral norms in this way means to justify and ground them rationally upon the natural laws of the *psyche.* In *Philosophy as Rigorous Science* Husserl describes such psychologistic procedure as "the naturalizing of ideas and consequently of all absolute ideals and norms."[13] Nietzsche (in one sentence) links both these aspects of psychologism — the rational justification of morality by psychological norms and the naturalization of its values: "Every morality is...a bit of tyranny against 'nature'; also against 'reason'; but this in itself is no objection..." (BGE 188).

Here at least it seems that Nietzsche would have rejected the criticism of moral psychologism had any such charge been brought against him. Yet, what reasons could he give for rejecting this criticism?

He is clearly against the naturalization of morality. Morality to him is not something given but something created and constructed. He opposes the

---

[13] Husserl, *Phenomenology and the Crisis of Philosophy,* trans. Quentin Lauer (New York, 1965), p. 85.

tendency of most philosophers to anchor and justify ethics on objective and rational grounds. This opposition stems not only from his skeptical perspectivism, which rejects absolute truth — according to which it would be possible to justify morality metaphysically — but also from several psychological reasons:

> What the philosophers called 'a rational foundation for morality' and tried to supply was, seen in the right light, merely a scholarly variation of the common *faith* in the prevalent morality; a new means of *expression* for this faith. (BGE 186)

If we do not find "psychologism" in the strong sense of the word, as a rational derivation of values from natural laws of the *psyche,* it is because, as we have already seen, Nietzsche's psychology does not constitute or create new values. Nietzsche's psychology does not function as a theoretical basis for the constitution and justification of an ethos or ethics. Rather, it explicates and assists by enticement and persuasion to activate powers and values that have already implicitly existed in us and in our society. This psychology is a therapeutic and heuristic means and not a constituting and founding discipline. This is so also because Nietzsche rejects out of his perspectivistic attitude the independent validity of psychological laws and the certainty of introspection. Therefore he has no psychological norms from which to derive moral ideals. It follows that if there is psychologism in Nietzsche, it is solely in a weakened form as a reasoning and enticement, not in the strong form of a justification and constitution. Can such an approach still be called "psychologism"?

If there is only an element of persuasive explication in Nietzsche, we might still ask whether he is not himself open to the accusation that he brought against the philosophers who in their ethical discussions expressed "the common *faith* in the prevalent morality"? Surely Nietzsche cannot be so accused since he does not justify the prevalent morality. But it is perhaps still possible to contend that on the level of psychologistic reasoning and enticement, in explicating what actually exists, some belief in the prevalent is nonetheless retained. In other words: is there not some tension or contradiction between the explicative level and Nietzsche's rejection of Naturalism (propounded e.g. in BGE 9)?

I do not believe this to be the case since Nietzsche rejects only psychological, crude and simple Naturalism which bases its values on raw drives and instincts such as those for self-preservation, pleasure, etc. He affirms psychological power not as it is actually given, but only after it has passed through the sublimative and rational process of transfiguration and self-overcoming. In short: the "is" becomes "ought" and desirable only if it undergoes an intensive elaboration and transformation.

However, even if there is no apparent contradiction between the explicative dimensions of Nietzsche's thought and the rejection of Naturalism, it may be claimed that such an inconsistency does subsist between his explications and his ideal of positive power, that is, between the means and the end of attaining this power, which is essentially an incessant overcoming of the given. What *is* — including prevalent or implicit values — becomes an obstruction to the activity of power; yet the explicative method assumes the existence of value or the wish to materialize these values.

If positive power is a process of dynamic, continual becoming in a Heraclitean chaos without *logos,* then no eternal value is capable of expressing it. Indeed, this power does not attach itself to fixed values. Rather, it is determined by impermanency, which is its positive pathos.[14] It seems however that an explication may be possible only for static and permanent elements of logos and ethos; or must we claim, paradoxically, that we are actually giving an explication of the dynamic pathos and the incessant overcoming? Here, however, we are reaching the limits of our capacity to speak rationally in a world of chaos and pathos without logos. And perhaps Nietzsche intended to bring us to this ultimate border in order to help us transcend his own thought as well, and thus assist us to reach the real maturity of positive power: standing ultimately on our feet and throwing away all the crutches, including Nietzsche's.

Thus he says to us through his hero, Zarathustra: "'This is *my* way; where is yours?' — thus I answered those who asked me 'the way.' For *the* way — that does not exist" (Z 3). This is also the way Nietzsche speaks about the philosophers of the future, the "free spirits," amongst whom he wishes to be counted: these philosophers "will certainly not be dogmatists. It must offend their pride, also their taste, if their truth is supposed to be a truth for everyman..." (BGE 43).

Finally, does not this hypothesis — that Nietzsche wants to assist us to overcome even his own thought — stand in clear contradiction to my contention, that he actually means by the use of his psychology to entice us toward the way of positive power? Not necessarily, since we are speaking here about one of the final steps on the road of this enticing psychology. A vital part of the work of a good psychologist is to check, at any stage of therapy, whether

---

[14] See BGE 41, where Nietzsche draws a model of a man with positive power (of the really free spirit), who does not adhere to any permanent value, since such a fixation hinders the dynamics of power. Therefore only a conditioned, detached life is possible for the one who "tests oneself" but does not adhere to the concrete results of these tests.

his patient can continue on his own, whether enough power has been released to enable the patient to function without psychologistic crutches. Therefore, Nietzsche, at every stage of his enticing psychology, tries to entice us to overcome even his own thought and influence. This is the real meaning of his saying: "It is a humanistic virtue of the teacher, to warn his student also against himself" (Dawn 447).

The Hebrew University of Jerusalem

Yirmiyahu Yovel

Nietzsche and Spinoza: *amor fati* and *amor dei*

Amor fati — love of fate — is the defiant formula by which Nietzsche sums up his philosophical affirmation. The term, never before used in philosophy,[1] is clearly a polemical transformation of Spinoza's *amor dei intellectualis,* rejecting the primacy of the intellect and positing *fatum* (fate) instead of Spinoza's nature-God as the object of love.

The pair *amor dei* and *amor fati* can provide an adequate verbal representation of the complex relationship between Nietzsche and Spinoza, the two enemy-brothers of modern philosophy. Perhaps no two philosophers are as akin as Spinoza and Nietzsche, yet no two others are as opposed as they are. If Spinoza has started the modern philosophy of immanence and underlies it throughout, then Nietzsche brings it to its most radical conclusion — and, as we shall see, turns this conclusion against Spinoza himself.

Nietzsche explicitly recognizes his debt and kinship to Spinoza. Speaking of his "ancestors," Nietzsche at various times gives several lists, but he always mentions Spinoza and Goethe — and always as a pair.[2] This is no accident, for, as Nietzsche tells us, he sees Goethe as incorporating Spinoza and as anticipating his own "Dionysian" ideal.

Goethe, Nietzsche says, was a "magnificent attempt to overcome the eighteenth century by a return to nature," an endeavor in which he "sought help from history, natural science, antiquity, and also Spinoza..." Goethe,

---

[1] See William S. Wurzer, "Nietzsche und Spinoza" (doctoral dissertation, University of Freiburg i. Br., 1974) p. 84. This study seems to contain all the quotations in Nietzsche where Spinoza is mentioned or alluded to, as well as many useful comments. Wurzer reports having failed to find a precedent to *amor fati* in all the philosophical handbooks and encyclopaedias he had perused.

[2] Nietzsche mentions "Heraclitus, Empedocles, Spinoza, Goethe" (*Gesammelte Werke,* Musarionausgabe, XIV: 109); or also "Plato, Pascal, Spinoza, and Goethe" (XXI: 98); in HH 408 he mentions "three pairs" as follows: "Epicurus and Montaigne, Goethe and Spinoza, Plato and Rousseau."

Nietzsche adds, wanted "totality" (of sense, reason, feeling, will); he "disciplined himself in wholeness," and he "created himself."

> Goethe conceived a human being who would be strong, highly educated, skillful in all bodily matters, self-controlled... who might dare to afford the whole range and wealth of being natural, being strong enough for such freedom; the man of tolerance, not from weakness but from strength... the man for whom there is no longer anything that is forbidden — unless it is *weakness,* whether called vice or virtue. (TI, "Morality as Anti-Nature," 49)

This Spinozistic ideal of Goethe Nietzsche then turns in his *own* direction:

> Such a spirit who has become free amid the cosmos with a joyous and trusting fatalism, in the faith that only the particular is loathsome, and that all is redeemed and affirmed in the whole — *he does not negate any more.* Such a faith, however, is the highest of all: I have baptized it with the name of *Dionysus.* (ibid.)

In this revealing passage Nietzsche attributes his own idea of *Übermensch* to Goethe while painting it in milder and more harmonious colors. In a certain respect, indeed, Nietzsche is a kind of intemperate Goethe, a stormy cultural radical who lacks Goethe's delicate artistic balance and is carried away by contradictory drives and by the more ferocious aspects of his naturalistic revolt. But, at bottom, as he looks upon Goethe's ideal, Nietzsche recognizes himself in it, assimilates this ideal to his own Dionysus — and traces it partly back to Spinoza. Spinoza has thus a privileged role in forming Goethe's position which Nietzsche sees as the kernel of his own.

The extent of their kinship came as a flash to Nietzsche in the summer of 1881 when, probably after having read Kuno Fischer's book on Spinoza (where the concept of power is especially emphasized), he exclaimed in a postcard to his friend Overbeck (Sils Maria, July 30, 1881):

> I am utterly amazed, utterly enchanted. I have a *precursor,* and what a precursor! I hardly knew Spinoza: that I should have turned to him just *now* was inspired by 'instinct.' Not only is his over-all tendency like mine — making knowledge the *most powerful* affect — but in five main points of his doctrine I recognize myself; this most unusual and loneliest thinker is closest to me precisely in these matters: he denies the freedom of the will, teleology, the moral world order, the unegoistic, and evil. Even though the divergencies are admittedly tremendous, they are due more to the differences in time, culture, and science. *In summa:* my solitude, which, as on very high mountains, often made it hard for me to breathe and made my blood rush out, is at least a dualitude (*Zweisamkeit*).[3]

Nietzsche in his enthusiasm tends to minimize the divergencies between

---

[3] I used Kaufmann's translation (*The Portable Nietzsche,* p.92) but rendered *Einsamkeit* as "solitude" (not "lonesomeness") and the pun *Zweisamkeit* as "dualitude" (not "twosomeness").

himself and Spinoza, which the attributes to the distance in time, culture, etc. On other occasions, however, he disputes with Spinoza quite bitingly. What had incited Nietzsche's enthusiasm was, above all, Spinoza's strict naturalism, with its various derivatives, including the abolition of good and evil, the denial of a built-in moral world order, and Spinoza's emphasis on self-interest and power as the basis of life and the lever for ethical advancement.

Nietzsche also singles out their common tendency "to make of knowledge the most powerful affect," meaning that knowledge is no longer seen as an autonomous interest, but as determined by the affective and instinctual part of life; and also that, as affect, knowledge retains its role in liberating life. But here a major difference arises. Nietzsche, in a more Socratic stance, attributes to knowledge the salutary affective power in the critical, not the doctrinal sense; it is the kind of "knowledge" that is gained through disillusionment. This knowledge teaches no fixed positive truth, but purifies the individual of decadent images and false metaphysical consolations, preparing him (or her) for the final self-overcoming assent of *amor fati*. In Spinoza, the immediate affective tone of knowledge is joy, the sensation of the enhanced power of life; Nietzsche, on the contrary, incessantly stresses the painful nature of knowledge and measures the power (and worth) of a person by "how much truth he can bear." Knowledge, in the sense of disillusionment or critical enlightenment, is a source of suffering and a temptation to despair — which the Nietzschean man will overcome and transform into Dionysian joy. *Gaya Scienzia* — joyful knowledge[4] — is a task and a goal in Nietzsche, not the normal outcome; and even when this goal is achieved, the conquered temptation to despair remains an inevitable component of the Dionysian joy. Joy is not the natural outcome but the product of self-overcoming.

This already hints at some of the crucial differences between Nietzsche and Spinoza. Indeed, if Spinoza, as Nietzsche puns, redeems him of his solitude into a state of "dualitude," he also faces him with a powerful alternative. Nietzsche and Spinoza offer two rival options within the same radical conception, that of total immanence. Both declare the "death" of the transcendent God, and see life within immanence as all there is. This-worldliness is coextensive with being in general. Moreover, the universe, *pace* Hegel, is devoid of any subject-like features or inherent teleology, and thus offers man no consoling semblance of his own image engraved in the nature of things. Man himself is fully an immanent (or, in Spinoza's terms, natural) being, with no supernatural gifts, obligations — or deficiencies; he neither *lacks* something more elevated residing in a superior world, nor is he *endowed* with special

---

[4] I render this term according to its philosophical meaning, not its literal translation, which is, of course, "gay science."

powers emanating from such a transcendent domain. Man has no separate, eternal soul,[5] no "transcendental self" to replace it, or an *a priori* reason demanding to impose itself externally upon nature and life. As a finite mode, man is however but a drop in the immanent universe and as such is inescapably bound and constrained by it; this fact (or destiny) he must interiorize, understand, and assent to with the full intensity of his life, if he is to endow his bare existence with a worthwhile meaning compatible with the boundaries of immanence, such as freedom in Spinoza, or authentic existence in Nietzsche. This involves some form of "love of necessity"; yet the crucial question is how to interpret this necessity, whether as a self-justifying system of rational laws or as opaque and indeterminate *fatum* which nothing can justify or capture by rational categories, causes, or laws. This question is the watershed at which, upon the common ground of immanence, Nietzsche and Spinoza stand in conflict and each argues, indeed pleads and seduces, towards a totally different *experience of immanence.*

In Spinoza the immanent world inherits the divine status and many of the properties of the defunct transcendent God. Self-caused and self-justified, it is eternal and infinite (both in quantity and in perfection). Its existence follows necessarily from its essence, is governed by fixed and eternal laws, and is rationally intelligible throughout. As for man, he exists "in God" and shares in the same universal rationality by which eventually he can rise above his finitude and realize eternity within his temporal existence. By contrast, Nietzsche's experience of immanence leaves no room for order, permanence, fixed laws, inherent rationality, or truth; it presupposes a mode of existence from which not only God, but, as Nietzsche says, "God's shadows" have also been removed. Man exists here in an ever-transient flux of (cosmic) "will to power," without redemption, without fixed truth, with nothing to explain his life or justify his death. As for the concept of *necessity* — the object of love — it signifies in Spinoza that existence flows from the essence of God and is rational and divine throughout, whereas in Nietzsche necessity is opaque and unintelligible *fatum,* devoid of essence or rational ground and pressing upon all creatures as an inescapable burden.

These are two radically opposed experiences of the world, one securing order, permanence, and even, in a new pantheistic mode, the sense of cosmic meaningfulness and shelter provided by the old religions (although it denies

---

[5] In Spinoza, the alleged eternity of the soul, discussed in the last part of *Ethics* V, is impersonal; it is the eternal idea of myself in the "infinite intellect" which exists without the body. The mind-body parallelism is not broken but the problem is shifted to another duality; that of eternity and duration.

their historical form); whereas the other leaves man in a metaphysical wasteland, a world of conflict and transience which cannot be captured by rational categories and from which all metaphysical consolation is banned. Consequently, the assent and celebrating acceptance of immanent existence in Nietzsche's *amor fati* must take the defiant and self-overcoming form of a "nevertheless." *Amor fati* is based upon a fundamental dissonance between the individual and the world, as against their agreement and semi-mystical identification involved in Spinoza's *amor dei intellectualis*.

Nietzsche's attitude may be construed as a more radical Spinozism. Spinoza, Nietzsche maintains, did not carry his battle against anthropomorphism far enough. He denied the Hegelian idea of a subject-like universe and insisted that man confront reality as the *non*-humanized being it is. But in maintaining the law-like and eternal organization of the universe Spinoza went on projecting a human-like and human-made form upon a world that inherently lacks any permanence. This, to Nietzsche, puts Spinoza back into the camp of Hegel, their classic dispute notwithstanding.

Nietzsche denies not only Hegel's view of immanent being as Subject, but equally Spinoza's construal of it as Substance — that is, a non-humanized system enjoying permanence and fixed rational features. This is yet another form of man-made projection and false metaphysical consolation, since order and permanence exist only in our human desires and illusions but cannot be objectively attributed to reality.

Personal Affinities

Later we shall return to these differences in more critical detail. But first, the striking *personal* kinship of Nietzsche and Spinoza cannot pass without comment. When Nietzsche speaks about their "dualitude," he throws into relief the picture of two independent and solitary thinkers, each living in relative isolation, their lives consumingly submerged in their philosophical work, and both making unsettling discoveries which alienated them from most of their contemporaries (who saw them as cultural villains), and from the major bulk of tradition. (Nietzsche, however, already had Spinoza to lean upon — and compete with — in building a new counter-tradition.) The objects of shock and horror, they were denigrated as "atheistic" or "nihilistic" (depending on the abusive idiom of their respective ages) and shunned as socially subversive and grossly anti-moral. However, both Nietzsche and Spinoza, although they rejected the concepts of good and evil, were profoundly moral philosophers, not in the sense of prescribing duties or grounding moral obligations, but in setting a perspective of human ascendance and perfectibility and trying to draw and seduce their audience toward it.

The highly esoteric nature of their ideal reflects both men's existential isolation and aristocratic frame of mind. Spinoza, unlike Nietzsche, was partly equipped to deal with the problem of esoterism, since he had worked out a distinct moral perspective for the multitude, and distinguished it categorically from that of the happy few. Not so Nietzsche, who sometimes seems to suggest that his aristocratic psychology should apply to everyone within the new culture. This is both incoherent and dangerous, a potential for inevitable abuse.

Linked to their isolation and revolutionary message — and also, in Nietzsche, to his sense of depth and aristocracy — is both men's taste for mask and equivocation. "Every deep spirit loves masks" says Nietzsche, who abundantly illustrates this preference in his work. His complex, aphoristic utterances, intentionally equivocal, loaded with allusions and ironic twists, exaggerating, pretending, over- and understating, leaving crucial points half said while lingering upon others of lesser importance, etc., provide the naive reader with a wealth of insights as well as of pitfalls. This way of writing does not only reflect the nature of Nietzsche's literary gifts, or his conscious choice of unsystematic style, or his need to divert, shock, and seduce his readers, but also, I think, betrays an existential need for masks *per se*. Depth cannot disclose itself directly but must use the roundabout route of hide and seek, overwhelm and retreat, which also includes irony as a necessary ingredient. Nietzsche's depth is frequently dramatic but rarely pompous; and, like Heine, it recognizes the uses of good style not only in passing on a message but also in drawing a protective screen. Self-exposure borders on bad taste, and sincerity is the virtue of the vulgar.

Spinoza, with his geometrical method, had obviously no qualms using a direct, unequivocal style, at least for strict philosophical purposes and when communicating with the initiated. Yet Spinoza was also a great *connoisseur* of masks and a master of equivocation. Few had excelled him in running a discourse on several levels simultaneously — a practice he used primarily for reasons of prudence and persuasion, but in which he clearly also revelled as an intellectual and aesthetic pleasure. It was to him not only a strategic necessity but also a *laetitia* (if not an outright *amor*) *intellectualis*.

The mask had yet another function for both philosophers. Experts in using it, they were equally sensitive to its use — and abuse — by others, especially when the mask was not put on by deliberate intention. In this they share with thinkers like Marx and Freud who set out to unmask accepted notions and established personal and social facades by digging into the unavowed motives and mechanisms behind them. True, Spinoza still lacks a sophisticated apparatus for explaining the varieties of self-deception and ideological mystification, but he shares, and indeed triggers, the modern trend of educating the mind to be suspiciously attentive to itself and its projected images, and to seek a deeper, perhaps a *darker* kind of enlightenment of itself and its world than the one provided by the overt process of reasoning.

That such a trend of "dark enlightenment" (as we may call it) is tied up with a philosophy of immanence will be attested by the list of its major representatives: Machiavelli and Hobbes, Spinoza, Darwin, Marx, Nietzsche, Freud, perhaps Heidegger, and Sartre were all bound by some version of naturalism or philosophy of immanence which challenges the "divine part" in man and its alleged origin in a transcendent realm; each had worked to shatter complacent self-images and comforting illusions and claimed to have discovered something about the structure of man and his world that seemed dark and unsettling to their contemporaries, and also to posterity. This kind of "knowledge" — always painful, as Nietzsche repeatedly says, with its critical, "dark" side and disillusioning cure, and the unrelenting drive to gain it, to make it a powerful and salutary affect — is also the common ground which Nietzsche seems to have discovered in both Spinoza and himself.

Morality and Self-Overcoming

Although Nietzsche and Spinoza reject good and evil as values embodied in nature or imposing themselves upon nature from without, we have said that both are deeply moral philosophers, in the sense of designating a perspective of human perfectibility. Each inspires his readers to seek a rare ethical achievement — *amor dei* in Spinoza, *amor fati* in Nietzsche — or, at least, to rise to some degree of existential liberation. Ethics, however, cannot be based upon extra-natural powers, norms, categories, transcendental precepts, and other similar candidates to usurp the role of the transcendent God. Nor can ethics take its cue from some latent structure of the universe, as if there existed a "moral world-order" imprinted upon things, which has to be copied or read off them as a guideline for moral obligation. The very notion of moral obligation (or moral duty) has no sense in a strictly immanent system, and must, in both Spinoza and Nietzsche, make place for *self-overcoming* as the key ethical concept.

Ethical achievements must have nature as their sole source, substrate and principle. As strict naturalism goes hand in hand in both Nietzsche and Spinoza with a powerful ethical project, the latter must be construed as an ethics of self-overcoming, whereby the immanent natural principle (*conatus* in Spinoza, *will to power* in Nietzsche) shapes itself into something higher than its raw givenness, producing a value that does not conflict with nature or transcend it toward some supra-natural norm, but resides in the new organization and quality of the same natural principle and the mode of life to which it gives birth.

Self-overcoming thus differs radically from what may bear a similar name in Kant, the Stoics, or Christian morality and asceticism. It does not impose external constraints upon life and the emotions, but lets life re-shape and sublimate itself, with one strain of emotions working on and giving shape to another. Not reason versus life, but life molding itself and enhancing its own power, is the generator of the self-overcoming involved in both these philosophers of immanence.

This is also the new or alternative interpretation given by them to the age-old concept of "spirit" or "spirituality," although they do not use these words in order to avoid the adverse connotations of Christian asceticism and priestliness. Restraints that depress life by subduing it to a superior principle over and above life itself are liable to produce a morbid and self-denying asceticism which Spinoza shuns as much as Nietzsche despises. Spirit, or what should serve as its adequate substitute, is not a separate principle stemming from another world or from man's "pure" and autonomous consciousness and serving to depress or subdue life. Rather, Spirit (or, in Nietzsche, "free spirit") is life itself, with its full-blooded dash and affective power, as it shapes and gives meaning to itself by that mode of self-overcoming which enhances rather than reduces its vital and creative powers. On this understanding, the Dionysian way of life is also the most "spiritual."

In Spinoza this envigorating self-overcoming is informed by reason and objective knowledge, hence it has definite rules and universal patterns by which to proceed. Not so in Nietzsche, who conceives of the life of his *Übermensch* as an open existential experiment and recognizes no objective knowledge but only perspectival interpretations. Self-overcoming has therefore a hermeneutical aspect in Nietzsche; it is linked to a personal mode of self-interpretation whereby the individual projects meaning to his life from his or her own immanent resources.

Conatus vs. Will to Power

Another necessary consequence of the philosophy of immanence which Nietzsche shares with Spinoza is their adherence, in their theory of man, to a strict naturalistic monism. For both philosophers, there is a single natural principle active in man and constituting his or her individual existence (as it does everything else in nature). This principle is not a static being but a dynamic thrust, a striving, or desire; as such it is also the unique principle underlying all the affects and drives and the diverse forms of human bahavior. Spinoza calls it *conatus;* Nietzsche *will to power.*

Conatus in Spinoza is basically the striving for self-preservation. "Everything... endeavors to persist in its being" (*Eth.* III 6) is the first principle from which the rest is derived, encompassing all human affects from the most common to the highest philosophical degree. To Spinoza, the mode of being of individual things is *duratio* (duration), defined not in temporal but in modal terms. It is the mode of being of a thing whose existence does not follow necessarily from its essence. As such, it needs external causes in order to come into existence, and it will endure in existence as long as external causality will permit, constantly resisting its assault and the dangers it represents. This resistance, the negative aspect of the *conatus,* is not an attribute or an added quality of finite things but their very mode of being; it constitutes their individuality as distinct entities.

In defining humans by their self-centered desire, the *conatus* is (as Nietzsche recognizes with approval) the very opposite of disinterestedness. Yet its offsprings include not only the common passions and desires but also the drive for rational knowledge (*conatus intelligendi*) as well as the supreme emotion and life-form of *amor dei intellectualis.* Both aggression and empathy, violence and mutual help will issue from this single, natural principle, depending on circumstances, the laws of psychology, and one's degree of knowledge (that is, of emancipation). This monism is, of course, a necessary corollary of Spinoza's strict naturalism or principle of immanence. Since there is no transcendent world, no moral world order, no *a priori* norms and obligations, and no purposive organization of the universe, but only a world governed by a play of mechanical forces, therefore the individual's *total* life must be explained and grounded in a strictly natural principle of desire which also individuates him or her as a single entity. *Conatus,* as the striving of every natural being to persevere in existence and, for this purpose, to enhance its power to exist, is thus made by Spinoza into the single principle from which all human behavior and all civilized phenomena are derived.

This monism agrees with Nietzsche as well — and for similar reasons. Nietzsche's will to power, like the *conatus* it replaces, is conceived as "the primitive form of affect, that all other affects are only developments of it" (WP 688), Nietzsche writes in a note to himself, naming Spinoza as his specific framework of immanence. "It can be shown most clearly that every living thing does everything it can not to preserve itself but to become *more*" (WP 688), Nietzsche writes in a note to himself, naming Spinoza as his specific opponent. Elsewhere he insists: "A living thing seeks above all to discharge its strength — life itself is will to power; self-preservation is only one of the indirect and most frequent results" (BGE 13). What especially disproves Spinoza's thesis are the frequent cases (which Spinoza was unable to explain except as "folly") in which one is ready to risk one's life for the sake of expanding and transcending oneself:

The wish to preserve oneself is the symptom of a condition of distress, of a limitation of the really fundamental instinct of life which aims at the expansion of power and, wishing for that, frequently risks and even sacrifices self-preservation. (GS 349)

It is true that Spinoza, too, speaks of enhancing the power of existence (and of action) as his goal.[6] Frequently he conjoins this goal with self-preservation (either as its implication or even as its equivalent), and at least on one occasion he seems to suggest they are independent concepts.[7] But despite this (slight) ambivalence, the only coherent way to construe Spinoza's theory is to see the one goal as subservient to the other: enhancing the power of existence and of action is desirable because it increases the prospects of self-preservation. In Nietzsche, however, power is not an instrument of life but defines and encompasses it; we do not first exist and then seek to prolong our existence by augmenting its power; rather, we exist from the start *as* will to power, that is, as the dynamic projection of our being and as the built-in thrust to enhance and expand it, for which life as merely given may sometimes be jeopardized.

Will to power is thus a drive toward self-transcendence which is *natural* to all humans (and to all other beings as well). Nietzsche (correctly, I think) sees no contradiction in the idea that immanent entities — the only kind there is — strive by nature to go beyond their boundaries and "become more." This does not infringe upon the principle of immanence, because in transcending themselves they are not necessarily guided by a transcendent realm or by *a priori* norms, but express and project their *own* existence and constitution. Hence we

---

[6] For example: In *Eth*. III, 13, Spinoza shifts from the original *conatus* to the concept of "the power of activity" of the body and/or the mind.

[7] In the *Preface* to *Eth*. IV (in the last two paragraphs), Spinoza rejects the usual concept of perfection and imperfection, then gives them a new use: greater perfection means that "the power of activity" has increased (meaning self-originating activity, or freedom). And that, he goes on to say, is independent of duration: one cannot say that a thing is more perfect because it has persisted longer in existence. Hence, the goal of "increasing the power of activity" of the individual is here dissociated from self-preservation and linked directly to freedom.

need not assume a separate world in order to think that all this-worldly entities exist by *nature* as this self-transcending drive.

Heidegger later adopted this Nietzschean idea of self-transcendence within immanence into his own account of human existence (*Dasein*) and of the meaning of being-in-the-world. But Heidegger restricted his analysis to human beings alone, to whom he accorded a privileged ontic position in being; thereby he aligned himself to the *Hegelian* strand within the philosophy of immanence and, like Feuerbach, performed an inner critique within it. Nietzsche, on the other hand, sides with Spinoza's anti-Hegelian view that humans have nothing special that distinguishes them ontologically from the rest of being, to which they are assimilable and uniform.

This uniformism leads Nietzsche and Spinoza to apply their respective principles even to physical entities. In Spinoza, the physical side of *conatus* is the resistance a body shows to external causes that threaten to dispossess it and take its place;[8] it thus displays a "defensive" posture (so to speak): the effort to resist external invasion and preserve what is physically the self. But in Nietzsche, characteristically, the physical idiom of will to power states the exact opposite: "every specific body strives to become master over all space and to... thrust back all that resists its extension" (WP 636).[9]

The monism of *conatus* and will to power requires a theory to explain *how exactly* the diverse and opposing forms of mental and cultural phenomena spring from the same primordial principle. But only Spinoza provides such an account; Nietzsche leaves us wondering how the will to power takes the various forms it does, especially those forms which Nietzsche considers devious, alienated, or otherwise non-genuine. Will to power can be "healthy" or "degenerate," Dionysian or decadent; in its negative form it underlies the morality of *ressentiment,* the Christian culture, and the attempt of the rationalists to dominate the world by subjecting it to an imaginary web of fixed categories. What is to distinguish between these "negative" forms of will to power and its "positive" or healthy expressions? What will explain how the one can be transformed into the other (as Spinoza explains the transforma-

---

[8] This contrast remains significant even if we choose to read Nietzsche's words metaphorically rather than literally. Such a reading is invited because the crude physicalistic translation of will to power runs into grave difficulties, not the least of which results from Nietzsche's own critique of the concepts "matter," "body," and "quantifiable space" as "fictions."

[9] This corresponds roughly to what non-Cartesian philosophers (such as Locke and his followers) called "impenetrability," namely, the ontic quality which constitutes materiality. (In Spinoza and Descartes extension alone is sufficient for this purpose, but Spinoza, in the physical side of the *conatus*, implies a form of impenetrability as well).

tion of a "passive" into an "active" affect) — and why do we go on calling "weak" a form that has dominated human life throughout two millenia of their history? Nietzsche would have been greatly served by a theory of "alienation" of some sort, accounting for reversals in the mode of will to power (from genuine to devious and vice versa) and explaining *how* it becomes a hindrance to itself and how this can be resolved.

Finally, it may be noticed that Spinoza's insistence on self-preservation is in accordance with his metaphysics of self-identity and permanence, whereas Nietzsche's will to power, in attributing self-transcendence to all immanent entities, agrees with his general theory of flux which denies self-identity of any sort. Thus, their differences over *conatus* and will to power falls well within the broader Spinoza-Nietzsche controversy over the nature of the immanent world.

The Nature of Immanence and the Problem of Truth

How does Nietzsche's *positive* picture of immanence, the basis for his *amor fati,* distinguish itself from Spinoza's? Before resuming this problem in some detail, a crucial problem must be mentioned, however succinctly. Nietzsche recognizes no facts but only interpretations, no objective truth, only "perspectives" relative to existential interests and drives. Yet he gives detailed accounts of the nature of the universe as the *Übermensch* will recognize and experience it. Do these accounts have only the value of a metaphysical fable, or is there a "Dionysian truth" which escapes perspectivism and applies to the world prior to all interpretation?

This is perhaps the hardest problem is Nietzsche scholarship. Neither the text nor the logic of Nietzsche's work can furnish, I think, a satisfactory answer. On many occasions Nietzsche seems to suggest that there is a sober, painful view of the world and life which deserves the name of truth *simpliciter.* The more we can take and accept of this truth, the stronger we are and the freer we may become. Frequently Nietzsche also speaks of those who shun tragedy, transitoriness, or the multi-facial character of existence as fearing "truth" or fleeing from it; and he calls the opposite beliefs, the postulates of rational science and metaphysics, by the outright name of "errors" and "fictions." It seems to me that this tendency betrays Nietzsche's more spontaneous mind, when his "gut-philosophy," so to speak, expresses itself without the critical restraints which, however, he *should* have obeyed because of the nature of his philosophical method. For on Nietzsche's official view of philosophy, nothing can evade the hermeneutical process; there can be no "bare" facts or truth prior to a value-laden interpretation; and perspectivism is the universal rule.

If so, one may wonder, what is the status of the latter pronouncement? Is not this theory itself yet another perspective — a *meta*-perspective, perhaps, but one which also depends upon an existential commitment? Yes, a Nietzschean might answer, this is the cognitive counterpart of the Dionysian way of life, which it makes possible and to which it is relative. Existential options come together with their corresponding cognitive images; but the latter depend on the former, not the other way around.

Whether Nietzsche would have lived in peace with this relativization of what he sensed as his painful and dramatic discoveries about the universe is an open question. In the final analysis, I think that Nietzsche can neither accept nor reject the idea that the Dionysian world-view is a truth unbound by perspective. But this important question has little bearing on our present discussion; for we are contrasting two rival experiences of immanence and there is no doubt that, on whichever interpretation, *the Dionysian world-image enjoys in Nietzsche a privileged position as the view which he pleads for and values most*. Whether his reasons are partly also cognitive or only existential is a secondary consideration for our present purposes.

With this in mind we may now summarize the Spinoza-Nietzsche confrontation on the image of the immanent world.

In Spinoza the immanent world is a rational *causa sui*, having its reason, meaning, and justification within itself. Eminently intelligible, it is illuminated, as it were, from within by the light of reason, which pervades and constitutes every entity. The universe inherits the role and status of God and omnipotent reason takes the place of the divine presence or grace of the religious tradition. As for man, in living within the immanent universe, he exists within God and may rise to a detailed knowledge of this relation — with all the mental repercussions that such a consciousness would entail. God, in other words, is not dead in Spinoza. He does not disappear from the horizon of his philosophy but is, as Spinoza sees it, correctly identified for the first time. All the sublimity, the infinity, the supreme "wisdom" (intelligibility), the omnipresence, and the divinity of the old personal God are here attached to what is claimed to be their true and only legitimate subject — the universe or the nature-God. Spinoza, as has been said, does not only naturalize God, he thereby also deifies nature.

In addition, God's "shadows" (as Nietzsche calls them) are indeed present everywhere. The world as "substance" is eternal and self-identical, governed by strictly rational laws which express its divinity. And although there is transience in this world as well — every particular thing is limited in its duration — the process is fully intelligible and has a necessary ground in God; and every individual thing has also an eternal aspect to it, by which it is grasped (and exists) "from the standpoint of eternity." Individual things are self-identical and fully determined through cause and effect; and this causality, far from expressing something arbitrary or "opaque" about the universe, embodies its supreme rationality — and divinity. Mechanism is the only type of relation between things, yet the mechanical necessity expresses a logical necessity and is supposed to be identical with it; even things which do not exist by the nature of their essence (i.e., particular things) are, from the standpoint of eternity, *logically* and not just factually necessary.

In Nietzsche, on the other hand, the immanent world has no inherent reason, order, or justification. Even its natural necessity — the basis for *amor fati* — cannot be construed as a rational system of cause and effect. To Spinoza's banning of teleology Nietzsche adds the abolition of mechanical causality, as yet another form of anthropomorphism. As there is nothing fixed and capturable in the world, there are no identical and even no self-identical cases and events, and thus no basis for permanent universal laws. The major categories and postulates by which we understand the universe are but fictions. Even logic has been exposed as an illusion, an imaginary fixation of what in itself is indeterminable flux, evading all forms of "correct" or "true" picturing.

If Spinoza's rational substance continues the tradition of Parmenides and his Eleatic schoool, Nietzsche sides with their opponent, Heraclitus, but goes much further than this Pre-Socratic master, since he also denies the *logos,* or fixed rational order, which in Heraclitus underlied the world-flux.[10] Thus man has nothing constant to hold on to in Nietzsche's world; his experience of immanence is that of a metaphysical desert, a yoke, the everlasting undoing of all transitory forms and the constant slipping of Being from under his feet.

The theory (or rather, the myth) of the eternal recurrence does not impose a fixed order on the universe; rather it indicates, or dramatizes, the inescapability of immanence. There is no perspective of life either outside the world or within it (in some better future) which is supposed to redeem life in the present, guide it, or give it meaning. As life has no source of meaning beyond itself, it must be endowed with meaning on the basis of its instantaneous character.

---

[10] Nietzsche would agree with Cartilus, who radicalized Heraclitus in saying that one cannot enter the same river even *once,* since flux undermines self-identity and there is no such thing as the *same* river. But even Cratilus did not deny — as Nietzsche does — the eternal logical order of the universe which the flux constitutes and reproduces.

Eternal recurrence, says Nietzsche, is the chief doctrine taught by his Zarathustra (EH III: 6, 1). Therefore it deserves attention, especially as a clue to *amor fati* in its opposition to Spinoza's *amor dei*.

Eternal Recurrence

I shall not discuss the question whether eternal recurrence is a full-fledged cosmological theory, but take it as an *existential fable,* expressing the kind of self-overcoming which *amor fati* involves. Seen in this way, eternal recurrence serves to better explicate the content of *amor fati* and also to test its existence.[11]

Eternal recurrence takes its primary meaning in Nietzsche from being the theme of a major act of affirmation. Whether in joy, routine or suffering, and although he does not see an inherent purpose or ready-made meaning in existence, the Dionysian man will say "yes" to his life as it is by wishing this life to repeat itself over and over again, exactly as it has been, without any novelty, betterment or "progress." In *Gay Science* Nietzsche puts this idea in terms of an acute temptation and test:

What if one day or night a demon were to sneak after you into your loneliest loneliness and say to you, "This life as you now live it and have lived it, you will have to live once more and innumerable times more; and there will be nothing new in it, but every pain and every joy and every thought and sigh and everything small or great in your life must return to you — all in the same succession and sequence... Would you not throw yourself down and gnash your teeth and curse the demon who spoke thus? Or have you once experienced a tremendous moment when you would have answered him, "You are a God and never have I heard anything more Godly"?... How well disposed would

---

[11] I share Schacht's view that eternal recurrence appears primarily as a test for the Dionysian life; only later did Nietzsche also try to see "whether it might as well be true" (Schacht, *Nietzsche,* Routledge & Kegan Paul, 1983, p.260). This attempt powerfully tempted Nietzsche (its peak occurs in WP 1066) but is overridden with problems, both *within* the theory itself and concerning its status as metaphysical "truth". On this last issue it ties in with the general problem of truth we sketched above. But even as a perspectival hypothesis it has its problems of coherence, both within the rest of science and concerning its postulates. (How can identical states recur if there is nothing identical in the world?) This in itself should have undermined all efforts by Nietzsche to canonize his existential fable of recurrence (Magnus calls it a "counter-myth") into a semi-scientific theory. Fortunately, however, the existential and ethical function (and meaning) of this fable does not depend on its being also a full-fledged cosmological theory; hence I may ignore this question when trying to use eternal recurrence to further explicate the experience of immanence involved in *amor fati.*

you have to become to yourself and to life *to crave nothing more fervently* than this ultimate eternal confirmation and seal? (GS 341; I used Magnus' slight corrections)

This is the utmost affirmation of immanence. By craving that every moment, every passing "joy and sigh" be repeated forever, I recognize the closed horizon of immanence as the totality of existence, and also, in *amor fati,* transform this recognition from a burden into a celebration. It is not resignation, but the active joy of the self-created man, liberated from the external yoke of transcendent religion, morality, utopia, or metaphysics.

It should be noticed that what I wish to be endlessly repeated is not only the content of every moment but its very momentariness. Immanence is here identified with the present, with what exists now as merely transitory; and in wishing it to recur time and again I equally wish it to *pass away;* or rather, I recognize and accept the mode of being in which transience is the rule.

Herein lies also Nietzsche's alternative to Goethe's Faust. Faust craves being able to say to the moment: "stay forever!"; he wants eternity to be placed in this-worldly moments. So also does Nietzsche, but to him this-worldly moments contain their passing away within themselves; hence Nietzsche cannot tell the moment to *stay* forever but only to *repeat itself* forever. In this way he both adheres to the moment and affirms and accepts its inevitable transience.

Significantly, Nietzsche attributes eternal recurrence to Heraclitus, his master in matters of flux and transitoriness. But Nietzsche could also have found this theme — colored in pessimistic and "decadent" tones — in Ecclesiastes' complaint that "there is no new thing under the sun" and "the thing that hath been, it is that which shall be." Ecclesiastes, however, a person of ordinary responses, concludes that "all is vanity" and life is a burden; whereas Zarathustra and his followers are supposed to make this ultimate confirmation of immanence a source of celebration.

That eternal recurrence dramatizes the inescapability of immanence can be seen from the following angle as well: in being prepared to live my life, every moment of it, innumerable times over and again, I renounce any claim or hope for a "next world" or an afterlife. Even my hope for the future does not refer to a better state of this world (as in Kant, Hegel, Marx — and as in Christian and Jewish eschatology), but to the same kind of existence taken over and over again. What is to replace my present life for me is this same life again — that is, *nothing* is to replace my present life; and this means: immanent life is all there is; in calling for its identical repetition I only assume the weight of immanence as my only horizon.

But what kind of immanence? Certainly very different from that of Hegel or Spinoza. In Hegel, the historical progress toward freedom and self-knowledge offers a perspective in which the human race, and through it, Being itself, is to be actualized. Although the immanent world is all there is, it has, so to speak, a transcendent dimension within itself: the *telos* (goal) it has to realize and become. This also gives time a qualitative character in Hegel, as the medium of historical novelty and advancement. Spinoza admits of no such teleology, and like Nietzsche, he views time (or better: duration)[12] as qualitatively neutral. At best, the notion of progress can have in Spinoza a merely subjective meaning, relative to *conatus* and personal desire: an individual may indeed attain a rational way of life, but this will occur by purely mechanistic causes and will not manifest any inherent structure or goal of the world-substance as such. In other words: God (the universe) is utterly indifferent to the human lot and to human ethical and rational achievements.

This view of course makes Spinoza much more appealing to Nietzsche than Hegel and his followers. But Spinoza too must be perceived by Nietzsche as having his own — eternalistic, rather than historical — form of "transcendence within immanence," because he accepts the eternal substance and laws of nature as underlying the world of change and as reflecting the inherent rationality and timelessness of God. Even what Spinoza calls *natura naturata*, the world of finite and transitory things, is not really in flux, because it is eternally shaped by *natura naturans* and because, thereby, the transient particulars have *self-identity* while they last.

Moreover, in the "third kind of knowledge" and its accompanying experience of *amor dei intellectualis,* the transcendent element of timelessness is even said to enter the immanent particular — the knowing mind — and transform it in such a way as to abolish its finitude and make it allegedly infinite. Here, the penetration of eternity into the domain of transience has not only scientific, but semi-mystical connotations.

Nietzsche's eternal recurrence excludes both these forms of (what he considers) transcendence: the historicist and the eternalistic.[13] The only eternity Nietzsche admits is the endless recurrence of transitory states, in which his Dionysian philosopher places all the worth which tradition has attributed to

---

[12] "Duration" is Spinoza's term for the temporal process as a *real* mode of being, before its continuity is broken by limits and measurements. The latter is called *tempus* and is considered unreal, a mere (though necessary) "auxiliary of the imagination."

[13] Hegel, incidentally, unites them both in the same *telos*. The goal of historical progress in Hegel is the super-historical (or eternalistic) standpoint which is to emerge from it. After this occurs, there will be a kind of "eternal recurrence of the same" in Hegel's world too — namely, the same *rational and timeless* principle maintaining itself as actualized throughout the empirical varieties in time. (Time again will lose its qualitative nature; there will be only chronological time, but not a strictly historical one.)

permanence. This is not passive resignation but the active joy and vigor of a person delivered from the grip of transcendent religion. But this is an immensely difficult task, which calls for a new type of psychology — and of a person.

It is indeed essential to see that *amor fati,* with its celebrating assumption of immanence, goes counter to the normal human psychology. Ordinary people, Nietzsche expects, will experience pure immanence as a yoke and an oppression; their natural response to it (and to recurrence) will be pessimism and world-weariness, the depression of their vital powers — or the various forms of escape and self-deception current in religion and traditional philosophy (Spinoza not excepted). It takes a powerful act of defiant affirmation, a supreme "nevertheless," to transform the oppression of immanence into its opposite — joy and celebrating power; and this requires a new and rare kind of psychology — the one which constitutes and expresses the *Übermensch.*

To make this transformation feasible, the individual needs support from a new *culture,* based upon the "revaluation of all values," of which *amor fati* and recurrence are the cornerstone: "No longer joy in certainty but in uncertainty; no longer 'cause and effect' but the continually creative; no longer will to preservation but to power" (WP 1059). While these new values are diametrically opposed to Spinoza's teaching, there are others on which Spinoza himself had insisted, like "freedom from morality;... the abolition of the 'will'; the abolition of 'knowledge-in-itself'" (WP 1060).

Amor fati thus differs from Spinoza's *amor dei* not only in content and mood but also in its mental structure. Spinoza's *amor dei* expresses a harmonious agreement with the universe, whereas *amor fati* involves an inner rupture and distance, bridged by an act of defying affirmation. This has several further implications.

First, the structure of defiant affirmation endows the Nietzschean *Übermensch* with a greater share of agency than can be credited to his Spinozean counterpart. In Spinoza, any progress of the mind is determined by the continuous, semi-mechanistic line of logical inference and psychological determinism; even liberation, when attained, is not caused by us, rather it may be said to have "occurred" to us. In Nietzsche, however, a person attains *amor fati* through an act of defying assent by which he or she introduces a break into the ordinary course of events, negating its normal (and continuous) outcome and producing its opposite instead; thus, even without admitting free will, the person may here be credited with more agency and, indeed, freedom in bringing about the ethical state he values.

Secondly, the moment of rupture and defiance precludes all mystical connotations from *amor fati.* There can be no form of *unio mystica* here, as in

Spinoza, because the defiant posture entails a distance between the affirming person and the universe he affirms and loves. *Amor fati* bridges over this distance but does not abolish it; on the contrary, it maintains the tension of "nevertheless" as a constant feature of itself. Thus Dionysus, although he bears a mystical name, actually stands for a non-mystical attitude.

Finally, *amor fati* is an overcoming of Christianity — even in its atheistic cover. *Pessimistic* atheism remains at bottom a Christian frame of mind, because it denies all value to the immanent world as such. What indeed is more Christian than feeling miserable and oppressed in a Godless universe? It is only when the temptation of pessimism is resisted and the world *as* divested of all "shadows of God" is accepted and experienced as a source of joy, that man becomes his own creator and, for the first time, Christianity is overcome and *Dionysos* takes over from *Christos*.[14]

In summary, *amor fati* differs from Spinoza's *amor dei* as *causa sui* differs from Nietzsche's universe, and for the same reasons. Whatever liberation they foresee involves in both the rejoicing acceptance of necessity, but the meaning of necessity is not the same. Necessity in Spinoza expresses the rational essence of the nature-God and of the infinity of things that follows from God according to the laws of cause and effect, which are taken as *logical* laws based on the link of antecedent and consequent. In recognizing the eminent rationality involved in necessity we alleviate its image of coercion; thus *amor dei* depends upon rational knowledge and is mediated by the intellect. In Nietzsche, necessity cannot be explicated in terms of cause and effect, let alone of logical links; it is an *opaque* necessity — the resistance and flux of dis-identical things within an inexplicable world of immanence from which there is no escape; and accepting it in *amor fati* is not an act of the intellect but involves the person's whole life and will to power and includes an act of defiance.

Spinoza as a Genealogical Scandal

To conclude, let me return to the personal level and place it within the philosophical context.

Perhaps because of their striking "dualitude," the person of Spinoza had

---

[14] One can, however, argue whether this overcoming of Christianity is essential to the Dionysian posture or only a necessary historical condition for us; but Nietzsche writes for his contemporaries. Even if the future *Übermensch* will celebrate immediately in immanence, Zarathustra, his precursor, can only do so by overcoming Christianity.

always haunted Nietzsche. "Solitary one, have I sufficiently recognized [i.e., unmasked] you?" Nietzsche asks in his poem "To Spinoza." Has he indeed?

Some of Nietzsche's comments on Spinoza would equally apply to himself. A "sick hermit" Nietzsche calls Spinoza (BGE 5), a "shy" and "vulnerable" man who has put on a "masquerade" (his geometrical method) in order to shield his most *personal* philosophy from a prying, vulgar world. Shifting metaphors, Nietzsche also calls Spinoza's mask a "chastity belt" and his personal philosophy "a virgin" (*ibid.*): the erotic allusion again applies to *both* these bachelor-philosophers (a kinship Nietzsche highlights elsewhere, GM III: 7) and sheds more light on the term "hermit."

Yet these similitudes cease when Nietzsche comes to the core-issue: the love of permanence and eternity. Here the enemy-brothers pattern takes its full force. Spinoza is denounced as the symbol of weakness and decadence, a man oppressed by his own existence, fearful of the Dionysian truth and unable to cope with the trying implications of his own discovery that immanent existence is *all* there is.

Sketching a "psychology of metaphysics" that should apply to *all* rationalists since Plato, Nietzsche singles out Spinoza as his prime example of those who "have feared change, transitoriness," a stand which he says betrays "a straightened soul full of mistrust and evil experiences" (WP 576). Even the *conatus*, Spinoza's most naturalistic principle, is exposed as "the symptom of a condition of distress," because in stressing self-preservation it puts an unhealthy limitation on will to power, the actual principle of life (GS 439). No wonder, Nietzsche speculates, that the survival principle has been advanced by sick philosophers "such as the tuberculosis-stricken Spinoza," since these people "indeed suffered distress" (*ibid.*).

This is not all. Nietzsche goes on (as he is bound) to attribute rancor and subtle vengefulness to Spinoza, even as the psychological essence of his work:

> ... these outcasts of society, these long-pursued, wickedly persecuted one — also the compulsory recluses, the Spinozas and Giordano Brunos — always become in the end, even under the most spiritual masquerade, and perhaps without being themselves aware of it, sophisticated vengeance-seekers and poison brewers (let someone lay bare the foundations of Spinoza's ethics and theology!) (BGE 25)

The context is Nietzsche's attack on the philosopher-martyrs who are supposed to have suffered "for truth's sake"; but with minor differences, it is also a form of *ressentiment* which Nietzsche sees at the root of Spinoza's ethics and metaphysics.[15] In diagnosing the "poison" of *ressentiment* in Spinoza's

---

[15] *Ressentiment* is the dominant attitude of the weak and decadent person, who cannot be sure of himself unless he negates others; it is the genealogical source of the morality

philosophy, Nietzsche does not only burden Spinoza with the ills of rationalism but, paradoxically, also with the ills of his forefathers, the Jewish priests, through whom Christianity had taken over the world!

Here we start to notice the incongruence in the portrait which Nietzsche is *bound* to draw of Spinoza. On Nietzsche's genealogy, Spinoza's philosophy must be seen as expressing and reinforcing the kind of person and life which has the following characteristics: He is the lover of permanence, *hence* a decadent and weak person, who, oppressed by the burden of immanence and by his own existence, escapes the painful perspective of Dionysian truth toward illusory metaphysical comfort. In addition, he is also petty, full of rancor and mistrust, the man of the *ressentiment* who can assert himself only by negating others and who transforms (or sublimates) his vengefulness into the creation of inverted values and theories. Such a person is also bound to glorify suffering and pity, to inspire (and submit to) guilt-feelings and *morsus conscientiae* — in short, *he is bound to be exactly the kind of petty "slave" moralist that Nietzsche abhorred and was exhilarated to discover that Spinoza was not!*

Thus Spinoza upsets Nietzsche's genealogical scheme. Although a lover of permanence and eternity, he is, like Nietzsche himself, a philosopher of power and joy, rejecting the moralism of good and evil, guilt and pity, and trying to expurge the mind of the negative and self-poisonous emotions of envy, hate rancor and *ressentiment,* which he sees as a form of *suffering* that depresses the vigor of life.

Thus something had gone wrong in Nietzsche's genealogy. Spinoza, his enemy-brother, presents him with a singular counter-example. He is both a "Nietzschean" and yet a lover of reason and permanence. Spinoza is thereby a genealogical scandal for Nietzsche — impossible, unthinkable, yet embarrassingly real.

The Hebrew University of Jerusalem

---

of good and evil, whereby the psychological "slaves" take subtle vengeance on their betters by subduing them to their inverted values.

Eugen Biser

Nietzsche und Heine. Kritik des christlichen Gottesbegriffs

Wer fragt, ob Nietzsche eine 'positive Doktrin' vertrat, kann eine fundierte Antwort nur von der richtigen Auffassung von Nietzsches Nihilismus-Prognose erwarten. Wenn Nihilismus, wie der Nachlaß versichert, "die zu Ende gedachte Logik unserer großen Werte und Ideale ist," und wenn diese 'Logik' darin besteht, daß sich gerade die "obersten Werte" entwerten, ist die Antwort zuletzt an den Sinn seiner Kritik des Gottesbegriffs gebunden. Denn Nietzsche sieht das eigentliche Verhängnis im "Glauben an die Realität der höchsten moralischen Qualitäten als Gott," also darin, daß die höchsten Wertvorstellungen an den Gottesgedanken geknüpft waren, der seither als "kategorischer Imperator" über allem steht. Somit sind es die bisherigen Werte selbst, die in seinem Verfall "ihre letzte Folgerung ziehen." Umgekehrt wird erst von diesem Verfall her deutlich, was es mit dem von Nietzsche angekündigten Nihilismus auf sich hat. Doch wie ist das konkret zu verstehen?

Der funktionale Sinn der Gotteskritik

Wer Nietzsches antitheistische Äußerungen durchmustert, wird rasch auf eine Differenzierung stoßen, die ihn schon vor jeder Einsicht in ihre Gründe aufhorchen läßt. So notiert er etwa im Nachlaß unter dem Stichwort 'Die Widerlegung Gottes': eigentlich sei "nur der moralische Gott widerlegt." Und eine dialogisch gehaltene Nachlaß-Aufzeichnung aus der Zarathustra-Zeit versichert geradezu:

Ihr nennt es die Selbstzersetzung Gottes: es ist aber nur seine Häutung: — er zieht seine moralische Haut aus! Und ihr sollt ihn bald wiedersehen, jenseits von Gut und Böse.

Auf derselben Linie liegt eine mit flüchtigen Schriftzeichen hingeworfene

Notiz, die nach einer von Mazzino Montinari im Kommentarband (14) zur Kritischen Studienausgabe veröffentlichten Vorstufe (zu *Scherz, List und Rache*) aus der Zeit der *Fröhlichen Wissenschaft,* also aus den Herbstmonaten des Jahres 1881 stammt:

> *Gott*
> Wir haben ihn mehr geliebt als uns und ihm nicht nur unseren "eingeborenen Sohn" zum Opfer gebracht. Ihr macht es euch zu leicht, ihr Gottlosen! Gut, es mag so sein, wie ihr sagt: die Menschen haben Gott geschaffen — ist dies ein Grund, sich nicht mehr um ihn zu kümmern? Wir haben bisher umgekehrt geschlossen...[1]

Das genügt aber schon, um in Nietzsches Kritik des Gottesbegriffs eine eindeutig funktionale Strategie zu erkennen. Bei aller verbalen Richtigkeit behält Hans Küng somit unrecht, wenn er schon in einer geistesgeschichtlichen Einordnung von Nietzsches Gotteskritik eine Abschwächung vermutet und mit pathetischer Gebärde dekretiert:

> Nein, auch und gerade Nietzsches Atheismus ist theologisch voll ernstzunehmen: Nietzsche leugnet Gott — jeden Gott und besonders den christlichen! Er will nicht noch nachträglich als 'Gottsucher' vereinnahmt werden.[2]

Von dieser pauschalen These hätte ihn schon das sorgfältig abwägende Urteil Franz Overbecks bewahren müssen, der als der Extremfall eines atheistisch denkenden Theologen seine Aufgabe darin erblickte, am Christentum "ein jüngstes Gericht zu vollziehen," und insofern keine Veranlassung hatte, die Wucht von Nietzsches Kritik in irgendeiner Hinsicht abzumildern. Doch gerade er unterscheidet zwischen einem 'menschenmöglichen' und einem 'übermenschlichen' Atheismus, der über Sein oder Nichtsein Gottes zu befinden wagt, während sich die erste Form lediglich auf das menschliche Gottesbewußtsein bezieht; und von diesem versichert er aufgrund seines jahrzehntelangen Umgangs mit Nietzsche:

---

[1] Der Satz bricht nach wenigen weiteren Worten, die keinen rekonstruierbaren Sinn ergeben, ab: KSA 9: 611. Demgegenüber lautet die Vorstufe: "Ich liebe Gott weil (er mich) ich ihn schuf / Und ihr — ihr wollt ihn darum verneinen?? / Der Schluß steht schlecht auf seinen Beinen / Er hinkt: das macht sein Teufelshuf" (KSA 14: 236); ferner: "Die Menschen haben Gott geschaffen, es ist kein Zweifel: sollen wir deshalb nicht an ihn glauben?" (KSA 9: 635)

[2] Hans Küng, *Existiert Gott? Antwort auf die Gottesfrage der Neuzeit* (München, 1978), 413; aus dem Anmerkungsapparat (810) ergibt sich, daß die Attacke gegen die von mir schon in meiner Untersuchung, *Gott ist tot — Nietzsches Destruktion des christlichen Bewußtseins* (München, 1962) und dann noch nachdrücklicher in meinem Beitrag, "Nietzsches Kritik des christlichen Gottesbegriffs und ihre theologischen Konsequenzen," *Philosophisches Jahrbuch* 78 (1971): 34-65; 295-305, vertretene These gerichtet ist.

Nietzsche hat gesagt: Gott ist tot! und das ist etwas anderes als: Gott ist nicht! Das heißt er kann nicht sein, ist nicht, wird nicht sein und ist nie gewesen! Vielmehr: Er ist gewesen! Und dies ist wenigstens der allein menschenmögliche Atheismus, die einzig für Menschen mögliche, ihnen allein zugängliche Form des Atheismus. Die andere Form wäre die übermenschliche, und wie Nietzsche zu dieser stand, steht dahin und hängt vollkommen an der Zweideutigkeit seines Übermenschen-Begriffes. Ein Bekenntnis Nietzsches zu dieser übermenschlichen Form des Atheismus gibt es auf jeden Fall nicht, und von ihr läßt sich allerdings behaupten, daß es sie gar nicht geben kann, wenigstens nicht in seinen zurechnungsfähigen Tagen.[3]

Im übrigen muß die Explikation zeigen, ob die funktionale Deutung tatsächlich, wie Küng behauptet, auf eine Abschwächung der Intention Nietzsches hinausläuft; oder ob in diesem Vorwurf nicht ein Fehlverständnis des Kritikers zum Vorschein kommt. Aber was ist mit dem Ausdruck 'funktional' konkret gemeint?

Nur dies: Nietzsche attackiert Gott nicht um Gottes willen, sondern im Zug seines Angriffs auf Religion und Christentum, wobei er beides im Angriff vielfach gleichsetzt. Seine Gotteskritik ist somit nicht Selbstzweck, sondern Mittel im Kampf gegen die christliche Religion, in der er den Inbegriff der Lebensverneinung erblickt und gegen die sich deshalb sein Frontalangriff richtet. Sie will er insgesamt zum Einsturz bringen, indem er mit seiner Kritik des Gottesbegriffs den tragenden Pfeiler untergräbt. Denn das Christentum ist für ihn ein System, das in seiner Konsistenz vom Gottesbegriff zusammengehalten wird. Gelingt es, diesen Zentralbegriff aus dem dogmatischen und zumal aus dem moralischen Systemgebäude herauszubrechen, so gilt, mit dem Wortlaut des *Antichrist* gesprochen:

Ein Begriff hier weg, eine einzige Realität an dessen Stelle — und das ganze Christentum rollt ins Nichts! (§39)

So entspricht es auch der religiösen Entwicklung Nietzsches, für den Gott nicht nur im öffentlichen Bewußtsein, sondern auch — wohl schon seit Ende seiner Schulzeit — für sein persönliches Erleben 'gestorben' war. Was ihn umtrieb, war darum nicht die klassische Frage, "ob ein Gott sei," die noch die Frage Beethovens gewesen war, sondern lediglich noch das, was er im Eingangsaphorismus zum dritten Buch der *Fröhlichen Wissenschaft* den "Schatten Gottes" nannte: die Vielfalt der vom jüdisch-christlichen Gottesglauben zurückgebliebenen Relikte, durch die er das Menschenleben verdüstert, verkleinert und beschwert sah. Dagegen — und nur dagegen — richtete sich sein Kampf.

---
[3] Carl Albrecht Bernoulli, *Franz Overbeck und Friedrich Nietzsche. Eine Freundschaft* (Jena, 1908), I: 216.

Die hermeneutische Perspektive

Nietzsche ist, wie kaum ein anderer Denker, vielgesichtig, vieldeutig, hintergründig. Das bringt es mit sich, daß man ihn nicht, wie es heute vielfach geschieht, 'eindimensional' angehen und mit Geschick oder Gewalt auf eine Formel bringen kann. Ein angemessenes Verständnis seiner Aussagen muß sich vielmehr am Leitfaden der Nachlaßnotiz orientieren:

> Das Verständlichste an der Sprache ist nicht das Wort selber, sondern Ton, Stärke, Modulation, Tempo, mit denen eine Reihe von Worten gesprochen wird — kurz die Musik hinter den Worten, die Leidenschaft hinter dieser Musik, die Person hinter dieser Leidenschaft: alles das also, was nicht geschrieben werden kann. Deshalb ist es nichts mit der Schriftstellerei.

In eine wissenschaftliche Sprache übersetzt, kommt das der Forderung nach einer Nietzsche-Hermeneutik gleich.[4] Sie muß, um Nietzsches sprachlichem Selbstverständnis zu genügen, wenigstens drei Ebenen berücksichtigen: die lexikalische, die sich auf die von ihm behandelten Begriffe und Motive bezieht; die grammatische, die sich mit der Organisation der Texte befaßt, und die stilistische, die der Frage nach seinen Quellen und ihrer 'Lesart' nachgeht.

Unter diesem dreifachen Gesichtspunkt soll im vorliegenden Zusammenhang lediglich ein Text untersucht werden, der aber schon deshalb eine Antwort auf die thematische Ausgangsfrage erwarten läßt, weil er nach allgemeiner Einschätzung als der Schlüsseltext zu Nietzsches Gotteskritik anzusehen ist: die Parabel 'Der tolle Mensch' aus dem dritten Buch der *Fröhlichen Wissenschaft* (§125). Nicht zuletzt bestätigt das die Tatsache, daß der Text auch außerhalb der wissenschaftlichen Diskussion immer wieder angeführt wird, wenn von Nietzsches Atheismus die Rede ist. Diesen Stellenwert erlangte er nicht zuletzt dadurch, daß er die eindrucksvollste, wenn auch keineswegs einzige Proklamation der Parole "Gott ist tot" enthält. Wie kam diese Parabel zustande, und was ist mit ihr gesagt?

Die 'lexikalische' Ebene

Ein textgeschichtlicher Glücksfall bringt es mit sich, daß die Frage nach den tragenden Motiven und nach der Organisation des Textes weitgehend durch

---

[4] Dazu die Skizze dieses Konzepts in meinem Beitrag "Das Desiderat einer Nietzsche-Hermeneutik," *Nietzsche-Studien* 9 (1980): 1-37.

eine Rekonstruktion der Textgeschichte von ihren Anfängen an beantwortet werden kann. Als sich Nietzsche im Sommer des Jahres 1881 mit dem Plan zu einem 'Zarathustrawerk' trug, notierte er in ein Taschenbuch, das er auf seinen Spaziergängen im Oberengadin mit sich zu führen pflegte: "Wohin ist Gott? Haben wir denn das Meer ausgetrunken?"[5]

Weitere Notizen entwickeln den Gedanken von einem — durch Menschenhände verübten — Selbstmord Gottes, der in der Folge völlig fallengelassen wird, aber auch, zusammen mit dem Ausruf "Gott ist tot" das für den weiteren Aufbau des Textes wichtige Motiv von der Größe der Tat des Gottesmordes, die den Tätern erst noch zu Bewußtsein gebracht werden muß.

Die nächste Stufe bringt eine Erweiterung des Ausgangsbilds vom ausgetrunkenen Meer, das jetzt durch die Frage ergänzt wird:

Was war das für ein Schwamm, mit dem wir den ganzen Horizont um uns auslöschten? Wie brachten wir dies zustande, diese ewige feste Linie wegzuwischen, auf die bisher alle Linien und Maße sich zurückbezogen, nach der bisher alle Baumeister des Lebens bauten, ohne die es überhaupt keine Perspektiven, keine Ordnung, keine Baukunst zu geben schien?

Daraus ergibt sich der Gedanke eines allumfassenden Absturzes, den der Verlust des umgreifenden und sichernden Horizonts nach sich zog. Erst daran kann sich nun der jetzt etwas breiter ausgeführte Gedanke von der unfaßlichen Größe der begangenen Untat anschließen, der jetzt um die Vorstellung von der 'Unzeitigkeit' dieses "ungeheuren Ereignisses" vermehrt wird und in dem Ausruf "Gott ist tot! Und wir haben ihn getötet!" gipfelt:

Es ist noch zu früh, das ungeheure Ereignis ist noch nicht zu den Ohren und Herzen der Menschen gedrungen — große Nachrichten brauchen lange Zeit, um verstanden zu werden, während die kleinen Neuigkeiten vom Tage eine laute Stimme und eine Allverständlichkeit des Augenblicks haben. Gott ist tot! Und wir haben ihn getötet! Dies Gefühl, das mächtigste und heiligste, was die Welt bisher besaß, getötet zu haben, wird noch über die Menschen kommen, es ist ein ungeheuer neues Gefühl! Wie tröstet sich einmal der Mörder aller Mörder? Wie wird er sich reinigen?

Die dritte Stufe ist durch eine dramatische Einkleidung des zunächst eher reflexionsartig gehaltenen Textes gekennzeichnet; damit gewinnt er auch fast schon seine definitive Gestalt. Doch ist er, wie die Eingangswendung erkennen läßt, immer noch dem Zarathustra-Komplex zugeordnet:

---

[5] Nähere Auskünfte über die Entstehungsgeschichte des Textes im Rahmen von Nietzsches Vorarbeiten zum *Zarathustra* gibt der Kommentarband zur Kritischen Studienausgabe 14: 256f; 279ff; 654; dazu ferner Mazzino Montinari "Zarathustra vor *Also sprach Zarathustra,*" in: *Nietzsche Lesen* (Berlin, 1982), 79-91.

> Einmal zündete Z. am hellen Vormittage eine Laterne an, lief auf den Markt und schrie: ich suche Gott! ich suche Gott![6]

Das ändert sich auf der vierten Stufe, auf der mit der Figur des 'Tollen Menschen' auch der endgültige Titel gefunden ist. Mit der Anfügung des epilogartigen Schlusses, in dem der 'tolle Mensch' die Kirchen als die 'Grüfte und Grabmäler Gottes' bezeichnet, ist die Textentwicklung an ihren Abschluß gelangt — bis auf eine Stelle, die Nietzsche erst während des Diktats des Druckmanuskripts, das nach Auskunft der Schwester in Naumburg entstand, änderte. Lautete die zentrale Frage bisher fast unverändert in sämtlichen Fassungen:

> Wie vermochten wir das Meer auszutrinken? Wer gab uns den Schwamm, um den ganzen Horizont wegzuwischen? Ohne diese Linie — was wird nun noch unsere Baukunst sein! Werden unsere Häuser noch fürderhin fest stehn? Stehen wir selber noch fest? —

so ersetzt Nietzsche jetzt die Fortführung des zweiten Bildes durch ein drittes, so daß die Fragen des 'tollen Menschen' nunmehr folgende Fassung erhalten:

> Wie vermochten wir das Meer auszutrinken? Wer gab uns den Schwamm, um den ganzen Horizont wegzuwischen? Was taten wir, als wir diese Erde von ihrer Sonne losketteten? Wohin bewegt sie sich nun? Wohin bewegen wir uns? Fort von allen Sonnen?

Damit hat Nietzsche dem Text — buchstäblich im letzten Augenblick — ein neues Glanzlicht aufgesetzt, doch so, daß darunter, von der Textgeschichte her, die für seine Gedankenführung wichtigste Metapher weiterhin erkennbar bleibt: das Bild vom weggewischten Horizont. Ihm muß im Zusammenhang mit der Motiventwicklung etwas genauer nachgegangen werden.

Die grammatische Ebene

In seiner Spätschrift *Götzen-Dämmerung* äußert Nietzsche die Befürchtung, wir würden Gott solange nicht los, wie wir "noch an die Grammatik glauben." Wenn man unter 'Grammatik' nicht nur die Regeln des richtigen Satzbaus, sondern das 'Organisationsprinzip' eines Textes versteht, trifft diese Bemerkung auf keinen Text so vollgültig zu wie auf die Erzählung vom 'tollen Menschen.' Denn sie ist auf dem Gedanken vom allumgreifenden Horizont und der "ewig festen Linie" aufgebaut, ohne die es keine Denk- und

---

[6] Über die wichtigsten Züge der Entstehungsgeschichte und die ursprüngliche Zuordnung zum 'Zarathustrawerk' informiert eingehend Mazzino Montinari, KSA 14: 256; 279ff.

Lebensordnung gibt. In Nietzsches Bibliothek erhielt sich die Übersetzung einer kommentierten Ausgabe der Werke des altchristlichen Schriftstellers Arnobius, in welchem er sich ein Tertullian-Zitat unterstrich, das Gott die ewige Linie des Alls (*universitatis extrema linea*) nannte.[7] Auch wenn hier von Gott ausdrücklich gar nicht die Rede ist: solange sich Menschen in ihrem Denken und Handeln von der Idee eines ewigen Richtmaßes leiten lassen, halten sie für Nietzsche am Gottesglauben fest. Deshalb kommt es für ihn entscheidend darauf an, den in diesem unausdrücklich gewordenen Gottesbewußtsein Befangenen vor Augen zu führen, daß mit Gott, den sie längst aus ihrem Lebenskonzept gestrichen haben, auch jede Ordnungsperspektive gefallen ist. Wo für sie noch feste Normen und Maße zu bestehen scheinen, herrschen tatsächlich Willkür und Chaos. Davon spricht der 'tolle Mensch.' Mehr noch: er stürzt seine Zuhörer mit seinen Worten geradezu in den durch die Tilgung des umgreifenden Horizonts entstandenen Abgrund hinein. Aber er will — wie Goethes Faust — in diesem Nichts "das Sein gewinnen." Deshalb fragt er, ungeachtet der Unzeitigkeit seiner Botschaft, mit der er zunächst nur Gelächter und Bestürzung erntet:

Ist nicht die Größe dieser Tat zu groß für uns? Müssen wir nicht selber zu Göttern werden, um nur ihrer würdig zu erscheinen?

Und er steigert diese Fragen sogar noch zu der These:

Es gab nie eine größere Tat — und wer nur immer nach uns geboren wird, gehört um dieser Tat willen in eine höhere Geschichte, als alle Geschichte bisher war!

Das liegt zwar durchaus im Vorstellungskreis des Zarathustra-Wortes: "Wenn es Götter gäbe, wie hielte ich es aus, kein Gott zu sein!" Nimmt man jedoch den Gedanken hinzu, daß der Gottesmord die Täter in eine höhere Geschichte versetzt, so entsteht doch der Eindruck, daß mit alledem noch nicht das letzte Wort gesprochen ist. Denn wie konnte es zu einer so verblüffenden Umkehr der Verhältnisse kommen? Wie konnte die Erfahrung des äußersten Verlustes in eine so überraschende Positivität umschlagen?

Die 'stilistische' Ebene

Unter 'grammatischem' Gesichtspunkt besehen ist die Parabel vom 'tollen Menschen' die Geschichte vom Verlust des letztlich umgreifenden Horizonts

---

[7] Näheres dazu in meiner Schrift *Gottsucher oder Antichrist? Nietzsches provokative Kritik des Christentums* (Salzburg, 1982), 67; 70.

und den durch diesen Verlust erzielten Gewinn. Mit 'Stilistik' ist demgegenüber jene Ebene gemeint, auf der diese Geschichte auf neue Weise lesbar wird. Zur vollen Meisterschaft derartiger 'Lektüren' wird es Nietzsche zwar erst in seinem späten Lebensrückblick *Ecce homo* bringen, wenn er, mit einem Wort dieser Schrift gesprochen, die eigene Person als 'Vergrößerungsglas' benutzt, um zu einer neuen Lesart seiner bisherigen Werke und seiner Denkwelt insgesamt zu gelangen. Tatsächlich ist das an die augustinischen *Retractationes* erinnernde Mittelstück des Werkes weit mehr als ein geistvolles Resümee des darin Gesagten; denn es setzt den früheren Schriften immer wieder derartige Glanzlichter auf, daß bisher unsichtbare Züge in ihnen zum Vorschein kommen. Selbstverständlich ist auch der Meister dieser Lesekunst nicht vom Himmel gefallen; vielmehr kündet sie sich schon früher, nicht zuletzt in der Parabel vom 'tollen Menschen' an. Das ist schon daran zu ersehen, daß von ihr eine direkte Linie zu *Ecce homo* hinüberführt, die, bezeichnend dafür, Nietzsches Selbstverständnis betrifft. Während er in den fulminanten Schlußpassagen des Lebensrückblicks seine Befürchtung eingesteht, eines Tages heiliggesprochen zu werden, und diesen erschrecklichen Gedanken mit dem Ausruf zurückweist: "Ich will kein Heiliger sein, lieber noch ein Hanswurst..!" — nimmt der Titel der Parabel diese Narrenrolle bereits beziehungsreich vorweg. Indessen hat der 'tolle Mensch' nicht nur eine Endgeschichte in Nietzsches Selbststilisierung zum Hanswurst, sondern auch eine Vorgeschichte, die jedoch weniger, als man meinen könnte, die heiligen Gaukler und Narren, um so mehr jedoch die negative Bezugsfigur im Proslogion-Argument des heiligen Anselm von Canterbury betrifft. Bekanntlich entwickelte dieser seinen einzigartigen Gottesbeweis, der die Existenz Gottes aus dem Vollbegriff des 'Unübersteiglich-Größten' herzuleiten sucht, im Blick auf die Gestalt des Insipiens, des 'Toren,' der (nach Psalm 14,1) in seinem Herzen spricht: "Es gibt keinen Gott!"

Das ist der kürzeste Weg, um den Nietzsche-Text in jener 'Lesart' erscheinen zu lassen, der auch auf dem mühevolleren Umweg einer Strukturanalyse gefunden werden könnte. Durch sie tritt die Parabel in eine verblüffende Beziehung zu jenem Argument, das seit Kant als der 'ontologische Gottesbeweis' bezeichnet wird. Mehr noch: sie erweckt jetzt den Eindruck, diesen Beweisgang dadurch auf den Kopf zu stellen, daß sie im Unterschied zu ihm nicht gegen, sondern für und durch den Toren entwickelt wird. Insofern erinnert sie unmittelbar an die erste Gegenschrift zu Anselm, die der zum Mönch gewordene Ritter Gaunilo von Marmoutier in seinem *Liber pro insipiente* vorlegte. Doch ist Nietzsches Parabel nicht nur ein Buch zugunsten des Toren, sondern eine durch dessen Mund erzählte Bildgeschichte, die anstatt eines Beweisgrundes für das Dasein Gottes die Proklamation von dessen Tod zum Inhalt hat. Wenn man hinzunimmt, daß von einer 'Parabel' im strikten Sinn des Wortes gesprochen werden muß, könnte man den Nietzsche-Text somit einen gleichnishaften Widerruf des ontologischen Arguments nennen, sofern nur auf einen jeden dieser Begriffe ein voller Akzent gelegt würde.

Dennoch wirkt die Ableitung noch immer zu konstruiert, um voll überzeugen zu können. Indessen kommt der Interpretation auch hier der Glücksfall zu Hilfe, daß nach jahrzehntelangem Suchen die vermutliche 'Quelle' Nietzsches ausfindig gemacht werden konnte. Nachdem bereits der prominente Vertreter der *Nouvelle Théologie,* Henri de Lubac, in seiner *Tragödie des Humanismus ohne Gott* die Ansicht vertrat, daß sich Nietzsche insgeheim an einer Stelle aus Heinrich Heines Essay *Zur Geschichte der Religion und Philosophie in Deutschland* (von 1834) orientierte, verdichtete sich in der Folge, vor allem aufgrund von Forschungen Hanna Spencers, der Eindruck, daß die Ausführungen Heines im näheren Kontext der von Lubac vermuteten Stelle als die von Nietzsche benutzte 'Quelle' zu gelten haben.[8] Während Heine an der von de Lubac anvisierten Stelle vom Sterben des sich immer mehr vergeistigenden Juden- und Christengottes spricht, unternimmt er es im weiteren Verlauf des Essays, seinen französischen Lesern, wenn schon nicht einen Begriff, so doch eine plastische Vorstellung von Kants Destruktion der klassischen Gottesbeweise zu vermitteln. Kant habe, so schreibt er auf dem Höhepunkt seines persiflierenden Berichts, in diesen Passagen seiner *Kritik der reinen Vernunft* den Himmel gestürmt, er habe

die ganze Besatzung über die Klinge springen lassen, (verröchelnd lägen am Boden die ontologischen, kosmologischen und physikotheologischen Leibgarden Gottes), der Oberherr der Welt schwimme unbewiesen in seinem Blute, es gebe keine Allbarmherzigkeit mehr, keine Vatergüte, keine jenseitige Belohnung für diesseitige Enthaltsamkeit, die Unsterblichkeit der Seele liege in den letzten Zügen.[9]

Indessen fällt bei der Durchsicht des Autographs auf, daß Heine die spezielle Kennzeichnung der einzelnen Gottesbeweise wieder gestrichen hat, vermutlich in Erinnerung an die kühne These, die er kurz zuvor aufgestellt hatte:

---

[8] De Lubac, *Die Tragödie des Humanismus ohne Gott* (Originaltitel: *Le drame de l'humanisme athée*), Salzburg, 1966, pp.44, 336; ferner Spencer, "Heine und Nietzsche," *Heine-Jahrbuch* 11 (1972): 126-161 und Sternberger, *Heinrich Heine und die Abschaffung der Sünde,* Hamburg und Düsseldorf 1976 (vor allem der "Nachtrag 1975").

[9] Einen weiteren Beweis für die Abhängigkeit Nietzsches von diesem Heine-Text bietet der Aphorismus "Excelsior!" (*Die fröhliche Wissenschaft* §285), wo es heißt: "es gibt für dich keinen Vergelter, keinen Verbesserer letzter Hand mehr — es gibt keine Vernunft in dem mehr, was geschieht, keine Liebe in dem, was geschehen wird...").

Bemerken muß ich, daß Kant, indem er die drei Hauptbeweisarten für das Dasein Gottes, nämlich den ontologischen, den kosmologischen und den physikotheologischen Beweis angreift, nach meiner Meinung nur die zwei letzteren, aber nicht den ersteren zugrunde richten kann.

In der Folge schwächt Heine diese 'Bemerkung' freilich dahin ab, daß die "Rettung des ontologischen Beweises" dem überlieferten Gottesglauben keineswegs zustatten käme, weil dieser Beweis "ebenfalls für den Pantheismus zu gebrauchen" sei. Dem fügt er die von erstaunlichen Kenntnissen über die Herkunft des Arguments zeugende Erklärung an:

Zu näherem Verständnis bemerke ich, daß der ontologische Beweis derjenige ist, den Descartes aufstellt und der schon lange vorher im Mittelalter, durch Anselm von Canterbury, in einer rührenden Gebetform ausgesprochen worden. Ja, man kann sagen, daß der heilige Augustin schon im zweiten Buche 'De libero arbitrio' den ontologischen Beweis aufgestellt hat.[10]

Wenn es jemals eine Behauptung gab, die Nietzsche als seine ureigene Provokation empfinden mußte, dann dieses 'kritische Referat' der kantischen Kritik. Denn wenn der — auch nach Ansicht Kants — zentrale Pfeiler des Gottesglaubens den gegen die "drei Beweisarten vom Dasein Gottes" gerichteten Vernichtungsschlag überdauerte, mußte alles darangesetzt werden, um ihn endlich doch noch zum Einsturz zu bringen. Und dies um so mehr, als sich gerade mit dem ontologischen Beweis die Gottesvorstellung verband, die mehr als jede andere geeignet war, das Denken selbst dann noch im Sinn des Gottesgedankens zu strukturieren, nachden der Glaube an den von diesem Gedanken Bezeichneten längst erloschen war. Denn im Zentrum des Arguments stand der Formalbegriff des 'Unüberdenklich-Größten,' oder, wie Nietzsche es der Tertullian-Formel entnommen hatte, der *universitatis extrema linea*. Das aber entspricht genau dem, was in bildhafter Umschreibung Gegenstand der zweiten Frage des 'tollen Menschen' ist:

Was war das für ein Schwamm, mit dem wir den ganzen Horizont um uns auslöschten? Wie brachten wir dies zu Stande, diese ewige feste Linie wegzuwischen, auf die bisher alle Linien und Maße sich zurückbezogen...?

Schon diese Annäherung in der Zentralmetapher zeigt, daß die Vermutung, zu der die Rollenfigur des 'tollen Menschen' führte, auch vom Sachgehalt der Parabel her gerechtfertigt ist. Durch die Figur des 'tollen Menschen' rückt Nietzsche seine Reflexion über die Folgen des Gottestodes in eine Beleuchtung, die sie als eine 'Widerlegung' des ontologischen Arguments lesbar

---

[10] Nach Ausweis des Autographs schrieb Heine eindeutig "in einer rührenden Gebetform" und nicht, wie in einer Reihe von Ausgaben unsinnigerweise zu lesen ist, "in einer ruhenden Gebetform."

macht. Daß diese Widerlegung nicht wie bei Kant in argumentativer Form geschieht, kann nicht verwundern. Denn einmal war der 'Alleszermalmer' in dieser Hinsicht nicht zu übertreffen; sodann bedurfte es nach Nietzsches Verständnis auch gar keiner kämpferischen Anstrengung. Der Gottesglaube — und mit ihm alle seine argumentativen Stützen — waren vielmehr bereits durch den Gang der Geistesgeschichte aus den Angeln gehoben worden. Die 'Tat,' deren es nach Kant noch bedurfte, war im Grunde längst schon geschehen; sie war nur noch nicht zu bewußtseinsbildender Effizienz gelangt. Das Attentat auf Gott war noch nicht zu den Ohren und Herzen derer gedrungen, die es durch ihre Hände verübt hatten. So mußte die von Heine her geforderte 'Widerlegung' den Charakter eines 'Widerrufs' annehmen. Der aber konnte gar nicht effektiver geschehen als in der Sprache, in welcher Jesus seine Reich-Gottes-Verkündigung ausgerichtet und so den Gottesglauben im Bewußtsein seiner Hörer verankert hatte: in der Sprache der Gleichnisse.[11]

Die Frage nach der Positivität

Doch gibt es, um auf die Ausgangsfrage zurückzukommen, in diesem auf Abbruch und Widerruf ausgerichteten Unternehmen die Spur einer Positivität? Für Nietzsches unmittelbare Intentionen liegen die Dinge klar. Denn für ihn mußte der Zentralbegriff aus dem christlichen Systemgebäude herausgebrochen werden, damit mit diesem Inbegriff der Lebensverneinung endlich reiner Tisch gemacht werden konnte. Das aber kam bereits dem größten Dienst gleich, der dem Leben überhaupt erwiesen werden konnte. Der mit der Widerlegung Gottes gegen das Christentum geführte Schlag war gleichbedeutend mit der entscheidenden Zusage an die diesseitige Lebenswirklichkeit; er war bereits der Elementarakt der Lebensbejahung, ein Akt höchster Positivität. Wie sehr sich Nietzsche mit dieser Aufgabe identifizierte, erhellt aus der durch Mazzino Montinari bekannt gemachten Nachlaßnotiz, in der er versichert, daß in ihm das Christentum sich selbst überwinde. Er hat das geschichtlich verhängte Ende des Christentums in seinen Wesenswillen aufgenommen und so zu seinem Lebens- und Sterbensgesetz gemacht. Noch deutlicher wird das, wenn man von da auf seine Gotteskritik zurückblendet und sich im Zusammenhang mit zahlreichen Äußerungen des Nachlasses vergegenwär-

---

[11] Daß die Gleichnissprache nicht nachträglich zur Thematik des Gottesreichs hinzukommt, sondern im Interesse ihrer Verkündigung eigens dafür entwickelt wurde, versuchte ich bereits in meiner Schrift *Die Gleichnisse Jesu* (München, 1965), vor allem aber in meiner *Theologischen Sprachtheorie und Hermeneutik* (München, 1970) zu begründen.

tigt, daß sich sein Kampf gegen Gott, oder genauer gesagt, gegen die Relikte des Gottesglaubens darauf richtete, die von der Menschheit in einem Akt grenzenloser Selbstverschwendung an Gott abgetretenen Attribute für sie zurückzugewinnen, um dadurch den Menschen, wie er in dem bekannten Aphorismus 'Excelsior!' sagt, einer vordem noch nie erreichten Höhe entgegenzuführen. Das hat auch der 'tolle Mensch' im Sinn, wenn er sich zu dem Ausruf steigert:

Ist nicht die Größe dieser Tat zu groß für uns? Müssen wir nicht selber zu Göttern werden, um nur ihrer würdig zu erscheinen? Es gab nie eine größere Tat — und wer nur immer nach uns geboren wird, gehört um dieser Tat willen in eine höhere Geschichte, als alle Geschichte bisher war!

An Nietzsches Willen zur Positivität ist somit nicht zu zweifeln, sehr wohl dagegen an seiner Befähigung dazu. Zwar fühlen sich die freien Geister, wie der Aphorismus 'Was es mit unserer Heiterkeit auf sich hat' ausführt, "bei der Nachricht, daß der 'alte Gott tot' ist, wie von einer neuen Morgenröte angestrahlt," weil der vor ihnen liegende "Horizont wieder frei" und jedes kognitive Wagnis wieder erlaubt ist; doch müßte der Vorausverkünder dieser Zukunft zugleich der Prophet einer Verdüsterung und Sonnenfinsternis sein, "derengleichen es wahrscheinlich noch nicht auf Erden gegeben hat." So wird mit dem Tod Gottes zwar der unvollständige — und unbegriffene — Nihilismus, dem die abendländische Denk- und Lebenswelt längst schon verfallen ist, in den vollständigen überführt; doch ist nicht abzusehen, ob der damit heraufbeschworenen Sturmflut jemals Einhalt geboten werden kann. Zwar lebt Nietzsche, gestützt auf seine Lehre von der ewigen Wiederkunft des Gleichen, im utopischen Glauben an einen dialektischen Umschlag des nihilistischen Geschichtstrends in sein positives Gegenteil; doch vermag er die 'Logik' dieses Umschlags nicht glaubhaft zu machen. Dasselbe gilt für seinen Versuch, die an Gott verschwendete "Schönheit und Erhabenheit" für den Menschen zurückzufordern: als seine "schönste Apologie" (KSA 9:582). Denn so sehr die dafür geschaffene Formel des 'Übermenschen' den Willen zu einer letzten Steigerung des Menschseins erkennen läßt, fehlt ihr doch zugleich jedes humane Maß, das sie schon als Formel negiert. So ist zu vermuten, daß der Wille zu einer äußersten Steigerung des Menschen-Möglichen zuletzt doch nur den alten *Grundtext homo natura* zum Vorschein bringt, und daß dieser, mit einer Nachlaß-Notiz gesprochen, in nichts anderem besteht als im Willen zur Macht. Wenn aber das die letzte Konsequenz ist, zu der die "zu Ende gedachte Logik" der bisherigen Werte und Ideale führt, kann man mit Karl Löwith begreifen, daß Nietzsche bisweilen fast neidvoll auf Dante und Spinoza blickte, weil sie in ihrer Einsamkeit immer noch "einen 'Gott' zur Gesellschaft hatten," ja daß ihm das Leben bisweilen in dem Wunsch bestand, daß es "mit allen Dingen anders stehn möge," als sie sich ihm darstellten, und daß ihm jemand seine "Wahrheiten unglaubwürdig mache."[12]

Aber wird es bei dieser Anwandlung geblieben sein? Schlug bei Nietzsche nicht vielmehr die nostalgische Sehnsucht nach dem verlorenen Gott und der durch ihn gewährleisteten Ordnung alsbald wieder um in den Willen zum Extrem, dessen 'Zauber' ihn fortriß, in den Willen zum Wagnis und zur Erkenntnis um jeden Preis, auch um den Preis der Selbstzerstörung? Wenn es sich mit ihm aber so verhält, verliert sich die Frage nach der Positivität seines Denkens im Halbdunkel, in welchem noch zu viel Licht herrscht, als daß man sie verneinen dürfte, aber doch zu wenig, um sie uneingeschränkt bejahen zu können.

Ludwig Maximilians Universität
München

---

[12] Brief an Franz Overbeck (vom 2. Juli 1885); dazu auch die von Montinari erstellte Nietzsche-Chronik, in: KSA 15:151.

Nietzsches Gotteskritik 217

Synopse der Übereinstimmungen

zwischen Heines *Zur Geschichte der Religion und Philosophie in Deutschland* und Nietzsches Aphorismus 'Der tolle Mensch'

Heine	*Nietzsche*
Ich enthalte mich, wie gesagt, aller popularisierender Erörterung der Kanteschen Polemik gegen jene Beweise. Ich begnüge mich zu versichern, daß der Deismus seitdem im Reiche der spekulativen Vernunft erblichen ist.	Der tolle Mensch sprang mitten unter sie und durchbohrte sie mit seinen Blicken. "Wohin ist Gott? rief er, ich will es euch sagen! *Wir haben ihn getödtet* — ihr und ich! Wir alle sind seine Mörder!"
Diese betrübende Todesnachricht bedarf vielleicht einiger Jahrhunderte, ehe sie sich allgemein verbreitet hat	Dies ungeheure Ereigniß ist noch unterwegs und wandert — es ist noch nicht bis zu den Ohren der Menschen gedrungen.
wir aber haben längst Trauer angelegt. De profundis!	Man erzählt noch, daß der tolle Mensch desselbigen Tages in verschiedene Kirchen eingedrungen sei und darin sein Requiem aeternam deo angestimmt habe.
Immanuel Kant hat bis hier den unerbittlichen Philosophen traciert, er hat den Himmel gestürmt, er hat die ganze (gestrichen: ontologische, kosmologische und physikotheologische) Besatzung über die Klinge springen lassen (gestrichen: verröchelnd liegen am Boden die ontologischen, kosmologischen und physikotheologischen Leibgarden Gottes), der Oberherr der Welt schwimmt (nachträglich eingefügt: unbewiesen) in seinem Blute... (gestrichen ist außerdem das Wort, "mausetodt" vor "liegen am Boden").	Gott ist todt! Gott bleibt todt! Und wir haben ihn getödtet! Wie trösten wir uns, die Mörder aller Mörder? Das Heiligste und Mächtigste, was die Welt bisher besaß, es ist unter unsern Messern verblutet — wer wischt dies Blut von uns ab?

Hat er eben dadurch, daß er alle Beweise für das Daseyn Gottes zerstörte, uns recht zeigen wollen, wie mißlich es ist, wenn wir nichts von der Existenz Gottes wissen können? Er handelte da fast ebenso weise wie mein westfälischer Freund, welcher alle Laternen auf der Grohnderstraße zu Göttingen zerschlagen hatte und uns nun dort, im Dunkeln stehend, eine lange Rede hielt über die praktische Nothwendigkeit der Laternen, welche er nur deshalb theoretisch zerschlagen habe, um uns zu zeigen, wie wir ohne dieselben nicht sehen können.

Hier schwieg der tolle Mensch und sah wieder seine Zuhörer an: auch sie schwiegen und blickten befremdet auf ihn. Endlich warf er seine Laterne zu Boden, daß sie in Stücke sprang und erlosch. "Ich komme zu früh," sagte er dann, "ich bin noch nicht an der Zeit..."

Mazzino Montinari

Nietzsche — Wagner im Sommer 1878*

1. Am 1. August 1878 bekam Nietzsche — auf Urlaub im Berner Oberland — folgende Meldung von seinem wendigen Verleger Ernst Schmeitzner: "Dann erlaube ich mir Sie im Voraus auf die nächste (August-)Nummer der Bayr [euther] Blätter aufmerksam zu machen. Wagners Artikel Publikum und Popularität ist die Antwort auf Ihr letztes Werk (Menschliches und Unmenschliches, wie es Wagner nennt. Den Verfasser führt er nicht an.) Er kann die 'historische Schule' nicht leiden, nur Darwin getraut er sich nicht rundheraus zu verwerfen. Das Seciren ist ihm, dem Künstler, überaus verhaßt." Darauf antwortete Nietzsche, am 25. August: "Daß Wagner gegen mich Einwendungen öffentlich macht, ist mir sehr erwünscht, ich hasse alle Dunkelei und Munkelei der Gegnerschaft; anderseits wünsche ich um Alles nicht mit den Tendenzen der Bayreuther Blätter verwechselt zu werden." Anfang September las Nietzsche Wagners Aufsatz, darüber schrieb er: "Gestern las ich W[agner]'s bitterböse, fast rachsüchtige Seiten gegen mich. [...]" So an Schmeitzner, und an Overbeck: "[...] es that mir wehe, aber *nicht an der Stelle,* wo W. wollte." Eine Woche später verbat er sich die Zusendung der *Bayreuther Blätter* durch Schmeitzner: "Wozu sollte ich mich verpflichten, Monatsdosen Wagner'schen Ärger-Geifer's einzunehmen! Ich möchte auch fürderhin über ihn und seine Größe rein und klar empfinden: da muß ich mir sein Allzumenschliches etwas vom Leibe halten."

Was hatte Wagner gegen Nietzsche geschrieben? Die beiden ersten Folgen seines Aufsatzes waren der Beschaffenheit des modernen Publikums gewidmet. Wagner hatte sich mit dem Problem der damaligen Massenmedien, am Beispiel der 400.000 Abonnenten der *Gartenlaube,* der sechzig Auflagen des *Trompeter von Säckingen,* und der vielbesuchten Theateraufführungen (also Zeitung, Verlag, Theater), auseinandergesetzt. Sein Schluß war: "Was durch unsere Theater gegenwärtig zu einem Eigenthum ihrer Abon-

---

* The paper first appeared in *Nietzsche-Studien* 14 (1985):13-21; it is reprinted here with their permission.

nenten und Extrabesucher geworden ist, kann mir durch diesen Aneignungsakt noch nicht als volksthümlich, will sagen: dem Volke eigenthümlich gelten. Erst die höchste Reinheit im Verkehr eines Kunstwerkes mit seinem Publikum kann die nöthige Grundlage zu seiner edlen Popularität bilden." Die dritte und letzte Folge von *Publikum und Popularität* war dem "akademischen Publikum" gewidmet. Wagner nahm sie zu Anlaß für seinen Angriff auf die "Schüler der Wissenschaft," die Professoren. Er meinte damit *seinen* ehemaligen Professor Friedrich Nietzsche, dem er nun vorwarf: "sein Leben bringt er vor und hinter dem Katheder zu; ein weiterer Spielraum, als dieser Wechsel des Sitzplatzes zuläßt, steht ihm für die Kenntniß des Lebens nicht zu Gebote. Die Anschauung alles dessen, was er denkt, ist ihm meistens von früher Jugend her versagt, und seine Berührung mit der sogenannten Wirklichkeit des Daseins ist ein Tappen ohne Fühlen." Auch noch persönlichere Anspielungen fehlten nicht, den kurzsichtigen Nietzsche ließ er z. B. wissen: "Die Brillen scheinen für dieses Unterrichtssystem besonders erfunden zu sein, und warum die Leute in früheren Zeiten offenbar hellere Köpfe hatten, kam gewiß daher, daß sie mit ihren Augen auch heller sahen und der Brillen nicht bedurften." Doch uns interessieren Wagners persönliche Ausfälle gegen Nietzsche so wenig wie des letzteren Bosheiten gegen Wagner, die er anscheinend in einige Aphorismen von *Menschliches, Allzumenschliches* versteckt hatte. Wir werden vielmehr sehen, und gerade Nietzsches Kurzsichtigkeit wird uns gleichsam die Gelegenheit dazu bieten, daß die Gegnerschaft zwischen Nietzsche und Wagner auf eine philosophische Basis, sowie früher ihr Bündnis auf prinzipielle Übereinstimmung, gründete.

2. Wagners Angriff gegen Nietzsche war so verfaßt, daß keiner, der nicht ganz eingeweiht wäre, etwas hätte merken können. Der von ihm am Schluß entwickelte Gegengedanke ist der einer Offenbarung Christi "ohne jehovistische Subtilitäten," dann würde der Heiland...wiederkehren. Ganz folgerichtig wird in knapp zehn Seiten durch Wagner die obskurantistische Bayreuther Ideologie bis zu dem ebenso unhistorischen und phrasenhaften wie verworrenen und unheilvollen Konzept eines reinmenschlichen (lies: antisemitischen) Christentums variiert. Cosima Wagner fand denn auch das Motto dazu: "Erlösung dem Erlöser!" Das sind bekanntlich die letzten Worte aus dem *Parsifal,* an dessen musikalischer Komposition damals Wagner arbeitete. Dieser fand die Interpretation seines Aufsatzes und des *Parsifal* in der Zusammenfassung seiner Frau gewagt: "Du bist kühn, Weibchen." Doch bemerkte er gleich darauf: "Ja, Schopenhauer und andere hatten es schon ausgesprochen, daß es ein Unglück sei, daß das Christentum auf das Judentum aufgepfropft sei, keiner aber hat noch gesagt, das ist Gott!" Ich zitiere

aus Cosimas *Tagebüchern,* in denen man die Entstehungsgeschichte der dritten Folge von *Publikum und Popularität* von der Ankunft von Nietzsches *Menschliches, Allzumenschliches,* am 25. April 1878, bis zur Vorlesung jenes fertigen Gegenaufsatzes, am 25. Juli, verfolgen kann.

"Jeder deutsche Professor muß einmal ein Buch geschrieben haben, welches ihn zum berühmten Manne macht: nun ist ein naturgemäß Neues aufzufinden nicht Jedem beschieden; somit hilft man sich, um das nöthige Aufsehen zu machen, gern damit, die Ansichten eines Vorgängers als grundfalsch darzustellen, was dann um so mehr Wirkung hervorbringt, je bedeutender und größtentheils unverstandener der jetzt Verhöhnte war," in dieser verklausulierten Form spielt Wagner auf Nietzsche (den deutschen Professor), *Menschliches, Allzumenschliches* (das Buch) und auf Schopenhauer (den bedeutenden und größtenteils unverstandenen Vorgänger) an. Die Wissenschaft blickt stolz "auf uns Künstler, Dichter und Musiker, als die Spätgeburten einer verrotteten Weltanschauungsmethode" herab; "Philologen und Philosophen erhalten aber, namentlich wo sie sich auf dem Felde der Ästhetik begegnen, durch die Physik im Allgemeinen, noch ganz besondere Ermunterungen, ja Verpflichtungen, zu einem, noch gar nicht zu begrenzenden Fortschreiten auf dem Gebiete der Kritik alles Menschlichen und Unmenschlichen." Die Experimente jener Wissenschaft geben ihnen die Berechtigung zu "einer ganz besonderen Skepsis." Die "edelsten Opfer" weden dabei "abgeschlachtet und auf dem Altar der Skepsis dargebracht." Die neueste Methode der Wissenschaft, welche sich die historische Schule nennt, besteht darin, jede Größe, namentlich das "Genie" als verderblich, ja als ganz irrtümlich über Bord zu werfen. Jede Nötigung zu einer metaphysischen Erklärungsweise der Erscheinungen, die der rein physikalischen Erkenntniß unverständlich bleiben, wird verworfen: kein intuitives Erkennen wird zugelassen, nur die abstrakt wissenschaftliche Erkenntnis, und als "würdige Erscheinung am Schlusse der Welt-Tragödie" bleibt allein das rein erkennende Subjekt, auf dem Katheder sitzend, als existenzberechtigt übrig. Das Volk aber lernt auf einem Weg lernen, welcher dem des "historisch-wissenschaftlichen Erkennenden" gänzlich entgegengesetzt ist, d.h. im Sinne des rein Erkennenden lernt es gar nichts, aber es kennt seine großen Männer und es liebt das Genie. Endlich verehrt das Volk das Göttliche. Werden ihm die Theologen helfen können? Gewiß nicht, so lange eine "der schrecklichsten Verwirrungen der Weltgeschichte" — daß nämlich "der Gott unseres Heilandes uns aus dem Stammgotte Israel's erklärt werden sollte" — bestehen bleibt. Wer kennt aber Jesus? "Vielleicht die historische Kritik?" fragt Wagner, um Nietzsche wiederum zitieren und verhöhnen zu können. "Sie steht mitten unter dem Judenthum und verwundert sich, daß heute des

Sonntags früh noch die Glocken für einen vor zweitausend Jahren gekreuzigten Juden läuten, ganz wie dieß jeder Jude auch thut." Man lese dazu den Aphorismus 113 aus *Menschliches, Allzumenschliches*. Wagner wünscht sich eine Kritik, die alles andere als eine historische sein darf, eine dichterisch und künstlerisch inspirierte Kritik, eine Kritik, die — da sie ihr Resultat im voraus kennen muß, welches ihr von Wagner diktiert wird — vollends keine ist: "Sollte es der Theologie so ganz unmöglich sein, den großen Schritt zu thun, welcher des Wissenschaft ihre unbestreitbare Wahrheit durch Auslieferung des Jehova, der christlichen Welt aber ihren rein offenbarten Gott in Jesus dem Einzigen zugestatte?"

Was sich damals in Wagner vollzog, war die letzte künstlerische Ausformung des schopenhauerisch-buddhistisch-christlichen Mythos der Erlösung. Letzterer aber ist nur als bewußtes Festhalten an der metaphysischen Illusion möglich: somit fehlt ihm jede Ursprünglichkeit des Glaubens und er ist eher Ideologie denn Mythos. Indem Wagner nach allen Kunstmitteln der Mystifikation zur Erschaffung des Mythos greift, wird ihm der sogenannte Mythos zum bloßen Vorwand und Anlaß seine "Kunst"-werks. Im *Parsifal* werden alle bisherigen antithetischen Tendenzen seiner Ideologie, seines falschen Bewußtseins, ja auch deren menschlich-allzumenschliche und *unmenschliche* Ingredienzien (wie der Antisemitismus) aufgehoben: sie konnten ihm, dem Künstler letzten Endes doch nicht Ernst sein. Nur die metaphysische Grundposition, die Annihilation des Willens, die Verneinung des Lebens als der Sünde an sich bleibt übrig, als der existentielle Kern des Ganzen. Die ungeheure Faszination, die berückende Schönheit der Parsifal-Musik kann uns nicht darüber hinwegtäuschen, daß sich hier die ganze deutsche Romantik, in ihrer spätesten, reifsten, zermürbten, ja dekadentesten Inkarnation, der Sehnsucht nach dem Tode, nach dem Nichts total ergibt.

Die weltgeschichtliche Vision am Schluß von *Publikum und Popularität,* steht im Zeichen der Rückkehr der Menschheit zur Barbarei "etwa um die Mitte des nächsten Jahrtausends"(!). "Denn das Eine müssen wir — schreibt Wagner — bei einem denkbaren dereinstigen gänzlichen Verfalle unserer Kultur in Barbarei annehmen, daß es auch mit unserer historischen Wissenschaft, Kritik und Erkenntniß-Chemie zu Ende ist." Zu hoffen wäre dann, daß die Theologie "schließlich mit dem Evangelium in das Reine gekommen, und die freie Erkenntniß der Offenbarung...uns erschlossen wäre." Der "Heiland" würde uns gemäß seiner Verheißung wiederkommen... Dagegen opponierte Nietzsche ein paar Jahre später in einem seiner bedeutendsten Aphorismen (429) aus der *Morgenröthe*: "Ja, wir hassen die Barbarei, — wir wollen Alle lieber den Untergang der Menschheit, als den Rückgang der Erkenntniss!"

3. Über die Bayreuther Reaktion auf *Menschliches, Allzumenschliches* schrieb Nietzsche an seinen Verleger (30. Juni): "Ihre Erfahrungen sind bitter, aber nicht wahr, wir Beide wollen ehrlich darnach streben, dabei selber 'süss' zu bleiben, als gute Früchte, denen böse Nächte nicht allzu sehr zusetzen dürfen? Die Sonne wird schon wieder scheinen — wenn auch nicht die Bayreuther Sonne. Wer kann jetzt sagen, wo Aufgang, wo Niedergang ist und dürfte sich vor Irrthum sicher fühlen? Verhehlen will ich aber nicht, dass ich von ganzem Herzen das Erscheinen meines freigeisterischen Licht-Buches in einem Augenblicke segne, wo die Wolken sich schwarz über Europa's Culturhimmel sammeln und die Verdunkelungs-Absicht fast als Moralität angerechnet wird." Während der enttäuschte, wegen der Bosheit seines einstigen Freundes verbitterte Wagner in Bayreuth über seinen Gegenangriff sinnierte, weilte Nietzsche auf den Bergen der Schweiz und notierte sich zahlreiche Gedanken zu Wagner und seiner eigenen neuen Einstellung ihm gegenüber. Er arbeitete an seinem nächsten Buch, das den Wagnerschen Titel einer *Mittheilung an meine Freunde* erhalten sollte. An die Wagnerianerin Mathilde Maier in Mainz, hatte er sich brieflich inzwischen mit aller nur wünschbaren Deutlichkeit über die Absichten seines Werks *Menschliches, Allzumenschliches* mitgeteilt, freilich zu großer Bestürzung dieser enttäuschten Freundin. Nietzsches Brief an sie enthält alle theoretischen und biographischen Hauptmotive seines Bruchs mit Wagner in einer Weise, die für ihn geradezu kanonisch bis zu dem 10 Jahre später, am Schluß seiner geistigen Peripetie, verfaßten *Ecce homo* bleiben wird.

[...] es ist nicht zu ändern: ich muß allen meinen Freunden Noth machen — eben dadurch daß ich endlich ausspreche, wodurch ich mir selber *aus* der Noth geholfen habe. Jene metaphysische Vernebelung alles Wahren und Einfachen, der Kampf *mit* der Vernunft *gegen* die Vernunft, welcher in Allem und Jedem ein Wunder und Unding sehen will — dazu eine ganz entsprechende Barockkunst der Überspannung und der verherrlichten Maßlosigkeit — ich meine die Kunst Wagner's — dies Beides war es, was mich endlich krank und kränker machte und mich fast meinem guten Temperamente und meiner Begabung entfremdet hätte. Könnten Sie mir nachfühlen, in welcher reinen *Höhen*luft, in welcher milden Stimmung gegen die Menschen die noch im Dunst der Thäler wohnen ich *jetzt* hinlebe, mehr als je entschlossen zu allem Guten und Tüchtigen, den Griechen um hundert Schritt näher als vordem: wie ich jetzt *selber*, bis in's Kleinste, nach Weisheit strebend *lebe,* während ich früher nur *die Weisen* verehrte und anschwärmte — kurz wenn Sie diese Wandelung und Krisis mir nachempfinden können, oh so *müßten* Sie wünschen, etwas Ähnliches zu erleben! Im Bayreuther Sommer [1876, bei Gelegenheit der ersten Festspiele] wurde ich mir dessen völlig bewußt: ich flüchtete nach den ersten Aufführungen denen ich beiwohnte, fort in's Gebirge, und dort in einem kleinen Walddorfe, entstand die erste Skizze, ungefähr ein Drittel meines Buches, damals unter dem Titel 'die Pflugschaar.' (15. Juli 1878)

Aus der "Mittheilung an die Freunde" wurde nichts, ein Teil der Aufzeichnungen wurde in die nächste Schrift (*Vermischte Meinungen und Sprüche*, erschienen Anfang 1879) aufgenommen, der größte Teil davon, entstanden zwischen Anfang August und Mitte September 1878, während der Sommerferien im Berner Oberland, ist Nachlaß geblieben. Welchen Inhalts waren diese Aufzeichnungen?

In einem Plan der aufgegebenen Mitteilung an die Freunde resümiert Nietzsche die Etappen seiner bisherigen Entwicklung. Die Kultur schien ihm gefährdet durch den Krieg von 1870/71, durch die Entfesselung von kulturfeindlichen Kräften, so bei Gelegenheit des (angeblichen) Brandes des Louvre durch die Kommunarden. Der Kulturbegriff wurde geschwächt durch den nationalen Hochmut der Bildungsphilister, durch die historische Krankheit. Dagegen rekurrierte er auf Schopenhauers Metaphysik als überhistorisch, den er als heldenhaften Denker, von einem fast religiösen Standpunkt auffaßte; sowie auch auf Wagners Kunst, der seine Kunst gegen den Zeitgeschmack verteidigte. Die vier *Unzeitgemäßen Betrachtungen* entsprechen den hier gezeichneten Motiven. Aber aus dieser Einstellung entstanden neue Gefahren: "[...] das Metaphysische treibt zur Verachtung des *Wirklichen*: insofern zuletzt *culturfeindlich* und fast gefährlicher." Der Genius wurde von ihm überschätzt. Die anderen Gefahren: "Die Cultur der Musik lehnt die Wissenschaft, die Kritik ab; vieles Beschränkte aus Wagner's Wesen kommt hinzu. Roheit neben überreizter Sensibilität. Das Deuten und Symbolisieren nimmt überhand bei den Wagnerianern. Ich entfremdete mich der Kunst, der Dichtung (lernte das Alterthum mißverstehen) und der Natur, verlor fast mein gutes Temperament. Dabei das schlechte Gewissen des Metaphysikers. Bedeutung von Bayreuth für mich. Flucht. Kaltwasser-Bad. Die Kunst, die Natur, die Milde kommt wieder. Zweck der Mittheilung: Freunde" (30[166], KSA 8: 552).

Das alles sah Nietzsche ein, "mit Betrübniss, manches sogar mit plötzlichem Erschrecken." Endlich aber fühlte er, daß er gegen sich und seine Vorliebe Partei ergreifend, den Zuspruch und Trost der Wahrheit vernahm: "ein viel grösseres Glück kam dadurch über mich, als das war, welchem ich jetzt freiwillig den Rücken wandte" (30[190], KSA 8: 556f).

Auch eine Vorrede an seine früheren Leser hatte Nietzsche entworfen: "Es giebt Leser, welche den etwas hochtrabenden und unsicheren Gang und Klang meiner früheren Schriften dem vorziehen, was ich gegenwärtig anstrebe — möglichste Bestimmtheit der Bezeichnung und Geschmeidigkeit aller Bewegung, vorsichtigste Mäßigung im Gebrauch aller pathetischen und ironischen Kunstmittel" (30[72], KSA 8: 543).

Zu Wagner selbst notiert sich Nietzsche: wenn er, um den *Parsifal* schaffen zu können, genötigt ist aus der religiösen Quelle her neue Kräfte zu pumpen, so ist dies kein Vorbild sondern eine Gefahr. Er selber, Nietzsche, hatte gehofft, durch die Kunst, z. B. den *Ring des Nibelungen,* könne den Deutschen das abgestandene Christentum völlig verleidet werden, die deutsche Mythologie könne sie an Polytheismus gewöhnen: welchen Schrecken empfand er dagegen über die restaurativen Strömungen! "Mein Fehler war der, dass ich nach Bayreuth mit einem Ideal kam: so musste ich die bitterste Enttäuschung erleben. Die Überfülle des Hässlichen Verzerrten Überwürzten stieß mich heftig zurück" (30[1], KSA 8: 522).

So wünscht er jetzt, daß sein Buch als eine Art Sühne dafür gelte, daß er früher einer gefährlichen Ästhetik Vorschub leistete, deren Bemühen war, alle ästhetischen Phänomene zu Wundern zu machen: dadurch habe er Schaden angestiftet, unter den Anhängern Wagners und vielleicht bei Wagner selbst, der alles gelten läßt, was seiner Kunst höhern Rang verleiht (vgl. 30[56], KSA 8: 531). Er bemüht sich andererseits Wagner Gerechtigkeit widerfahren zu lassen: "Es ist schwer, im Einzelnen Wagner angreifen und nicht Recht zu behalten; seine Kunstart Leben Character, seine Meinungen, seine Neigungen und Abneigungen, alles hat wunde Stellen. Aber als Ganzes ist die Erscheinung jedem Angriff gewachsen" (30[80], KSA 8: 536), und: "Man wird es Wagner nie vergessen dürfen dass er in der zweiten Hälfte des 19. Jahrhunderts in seiner Weise — die freilich nicht gerade die Weise guter und einsichtiger Menschen ist — die Kunst als eine wichtige und grossartige Sache ins Gedächtniss brachte" (30[90], KSA 8: 536). Das Motiv des Barockstils als des Stils von Wagners Musik, das Nietzsche — wie wir sahen — schon in dem Brief an Mathilde Maier angedeutet hat — wird in einigen Aphorismen der *Vermischten Meinungen und Sprüche* ausgeführt. Im Aph. 144 geht Nietzsche unter Burckhardts und Stendhals Suggestion den historischen Gründen des Barockstils nach: "[...] es hat von den griechischen Zeiten ab schon oftmals einen Barockstil gegeben, in der Poesie, Beredtsamkeit, im Prosastile, in der Sculptur eben so wohl als bekanntermaassen in der Architektur," der Barockstil "entsteht jedesmal beim Abblühen jeder grossen Kunst, wenn die Anforderungen in der Kunst des classischen Ausdrucks allzugross geworden sind, als ein Natur-Ereigniss, dem man wohl mit Schwermuth — weil es der Nacht voranläuft — zusehen wird, aber zugleich mit Bewunderung für die ihm eigenthümlichen Ersatzkünste des Ausdrucks und der Erzählung." Deshalb ist es anmaßend, "[ihn] ohne Weiteres [...] abschätzig zu beurtheilen, so sehr sich Jeder glücklich preisen darf, dessen Empfindung, durch ihn nicht für den reineren und grösseren Stil unempfänglich gemacht wird." In der endgültigen Fassung erwähnt Nietzsche Wagner nicht, in der Vorstufe aber schreibt er mit voller Deutlichkeit: "Wir können das Phänomen der Barockkunst jetzt sehr schön studieren, falls wir unser genug Herr sind: denn die letzte der Künste, die Musik, ist gegenwärtig, durch die Einwirkung Richard Wagners, in dieses Stadium getreten, und zwar in außerordentlicher Pracht der Erscheinung, ganz und gar seelen- und sinnesverwirrend." Dazu endlich ein resümierendes Aperçu, als Vorstufe zu Aph. 131: "Barockkunst. Es ist als ob man die ungemeine *Spannung* der Besonnenheit (die Freiheit unter dem Gesetz) bei den Classikern nicht mehr aushielte — eine Art Schwindel erfasst den Zuschauer. Der Bogen bricht."

In diesen Aufzeichnungen radikalisiert Nietzsche seine historische, antimetaphysische Stellung gerade zur Musik; sie ist jetzt gemäß Aph. 144: "das allerletzte *Austönen* und Nachläuten einer *Cultur,* einer Summe von Empfindungen welche unter bestimmten sociales politischen Verhältnissen, in einem bestimmten Bogen gewachsen; nicht eine allgemeine überzeitliche menschliche Sprache, wie man glauben möchte, sondern genau den inneren Zuständen entsprechend, welche eine Cultur im Gefolge hat. [...] Wagner's Leben und Walten im germanischen Mythus und seine Beseelung desselben durch den christ(lichen) mittelalterlichen Zug zur Erlösung erscheint als Reaktion gegen den Geist der Aufklärung und die übernationalen Gedanken der Revolution" (Vs zu VM 171, KSA 14: 173). An dieser streng historischen Betrachtung der Dinge hielt Nietzsche von nun an fest.

Jede psychologisierende, psychiatrisierende, hin und her ärztelnde Deutung von Nietzsches Bruch mit Wagner interpretiert am Kern der Sache vorbei, da sie immer nur auf biographische, d.h. höchst ungewisse Argumente angewiesen ist.

Im Herbst 1980 erschien die große Wagner-Biographie von Martin Gregor-Dellin. Dieser veröffentlichte zum erstenmal den vollständigen Text des Briefwechsels, den Richard Wagner über Nietzsches Krankheit mit dem Frankfurter Arzt Otto Eiser im Hebst 1877 geführt hatte. Otto Eiser, ein Freund Nietzsches und überzeugter Wagnerianer, gab in seinen Briefen nach Bayreuth allerlei Auskunft über Nietzsches sexuelles Leben, weil Wagner, in seiner Sorge um den jungen Freund, eine Vermutung über die Ursachen von Nietzsches Kurzsichtigkeit und Kopfschmerzen geäußert hatte, die sehr bezeichnend für die Mentalität der damaligen Zeit ist. Er fragte, ob Nietzsches Leiden durch Onanie könne verursacht sein? Er, Wagner, habe ähnliche traurige Schicksale an anderen jungen Freunden erleben müssen. Eiser widerlegte Wagners Vermutung dadurch, daß er Nietzsches sexuelles Leben als ganz normal bezeichnete: Nietzsche habe z. B. den Coitus noch im vergangenen Jahr 1876 in Sorrent aus therapeutischen Gründen, d.h. auf Anraten der Ärzte gegen Kopfschmerzen mehrmals praktiziert. Die ganze Sache kam später auf Umwegen und entstellt zu Nietzsches Ohren. So schrieb er im

Sommer 1878 in seine Notizbücher: "Der weiss noch nichts von der Bosheit, der nicht erlebt hat, wie die niederträchtigste Verleumdung und der giftigste Neid sich als Mitleid geberden" (30[37], KSA 8: 528). "Unter dem scheinheiligen Namen des Mitleidens die niederträchtigsten Verleumdungen hinter dem Rücken aussprengen" (28[59], KSA 8: 512). Noch im Winter 1882/83 und später mußte Nietzsche in seinen Briefen, von Wagners "Perfidie" zu reden. Wagner starb. Kurz darauf richtet Nietzsche einen erschütternden Brief an Franz Overbeck, in welchem er unter anderem auf eine "tödtliche Beleidigung" anspielte, die zwischen ihm (Nietzsche) und Wagner bestanden hätte, ohne sich allerdings weiter darüber auszulassen.

Nietzsche- und Wagner-Forscher haben sich die Frage gestellt, was Nietzsche wohl damit gemeint haben mochte. Sowohl Gregor-Dellin als auch Curt Paul Janz, Nietzsches neuester Biograph, identifizieren die "tödtliche Beleidigung" mit der Hypothese über das nicht normale sexuelle Leben Nietzsches, die Wagner in seinem Briefwechsel mit Otto Eiser formuliert hatte und die Nietzsche beleidigen mußte, zumal sie ihm als eine Anspielung auf sexuelle Ausschweifungen, auf Pederastie, zu Ohren kam. Die an sich belanglose Frage, "was meinte Nietzsche, wenn er von einer tödtlichen Beleidigung sprach?" hat Nietzsche zum Glück selber beantwortet, und zwar durch einen Janz und Gregor-Dellin noch nicht bekannten Brief vom 21. Februar 1883 an Malwida von Meysenbug — eine Woche nach Wagners Tod, und gleichzeitig mit dem schon erwähnten an Franz Overbeck — den ich zuerst 1980 in meiner Chronik zur Kritischen Studienausgabe und 1981 in Nietzsches Briefwechsel veröffentlicht habe.

W[agner]s Tod hat mir fürchterlich zugesetzt; und ich bin zwar wieder aus dem Bett, aber keineswegs aus der Nachwirkung heraus. — Trotzdem glaube ich, daß dies Ereigniß, auf die Länge hin gesehn, eine Erleichterung für mich ist. Es war hart, sehr hart, sechs Jahre lang Jemandem Gegner sein zu müssen, den man so verehrt und geliebt hat, wie ich W[agner] geliebt habe; ja, und selbst als Gegner sich zum Schweigen verurtheilen müssen — um der Verehrung willen, die der Mann als *Ganzes* verdient. W[agner] hat mich auf eine *tödtliche* Weise beleidigt — ich will es Ihnen doch sagen! — sein langsames Zurückgehn und -Schleichen zum Christenthum und zur Kirche habe ich als einen persönlichen Schimpf für mich empfunden: meine ganze Jugend und ihre Richtung schien mir befleckt, insofern ich einem Geiste, der *dieses* Schrittes fähig war, gehuldigt hatte.

Dies so stark zu empfinden — dazu bin ich durch unausgesprochne Ziele und Aufgaben gedrängt.

Jetzt sehe ich jenen Schritt als den Schritt des *alt* werdenden Wagner an; es ist schwer, zur rechten Zeit zu sterben.

Hätte er noch länger gelebt, oh *was* hätte noch zwischen uns entstehen können! Ich habe furchtbare Pfeile auf meinem Bogen, und W[agner] gehörte zu der Art Menschen, welche man durch *Worte tödten* kann.

4. Dieser Nietzsche aus dem Sommer 1878, der Nietzsche der freigeisterischen Bücher ist bekanntlich nicht der ganze, nicht der letzte Nietzsche. In seiner unermüdlich versuchenden Philosophie wird er noch zehn Jahre lang viele Wege, Umwege und Holzwege gehen; keiner dieser Wege jedoch wird ihn hinter die damals überschrittene Schwelle zurückführen. "Eines Tages — es war im Sommer 1876 — kam mir eine plötzliche Verachtung und Einsicht in mich: unbarmherzig schritt ich über die schönen Wünschbarkeiten und Träume hinweg, wie sie bis dahin meine Jugend geliebt hatte, unbarmherzig ging ich meines Wegs weiter, eines Weges der 'Erkenntnis um jeden Preis'." Dies sollten wir Nietzsche endlich glauben.

Index

aesthetics 220
affirmation 200 203
   style of 132ff
affirmative ethics 69ff
affirmative philosophy 31 81 110 132ff 144ff 204
amor dei 189 191 197 200
amor fati 185ff 196ff 200ff
Anti-Christ 47 162 206
Apel, K.O. 67
Aristotelian ethics 73ff 80ff 86ff 89
art 3 4 99 102 221 222
atheism 205

Baeumler, A. 59
being 135 142 145 146
Beyond Good and Evil 48 80 90 91 93 94 98 100 101 102 103 107 108 153 165
The Birth of Tragedy 92 160

Christianity 46ff 71 77 83 88 94 100ff 133 136 138 156ff 162 193 201 206 214 220
community 86
conatus 190-194
conscience 12 13
contradictions in Nietzsche's thought 64ff
creativity 115
critical thought 110
culture 224 226
   critique of 66

Danto, A. 20 98n
Dawn 30 87 222
death of God 51 65 133 142 146 160 175 185 208 211 213 215 217
deconstruction 40 58
Derrida, J. 36 40 57 70
Descartes, R. 193
digestion 143
Dionysus 165 193 195 197 202
Dostoevsky, F. 71 148 149

Ecce Homo 55 69 91 142 153 165 174 211
ecstatic identification of man with God 112 114ff
education 119 123 124 128 130 131
   concept of 123-130
   genuine 124ff 128ff
   manipulative 123ff
   Schopenhauerian 124
eternal recurrence 53 54 61 64 66 163 197ff
ethics
   Aristotelian 74ff 80 82ff 86ff 89
   egalitarian 85
   Hegelian, *Sittlichkeit* 79
   Humean 73
   Kantian 24 26 30 73ff 77ff 85
   vs. morality 72

facts 5 6 33
falsification 99ff
flux 64 186 194 196
Foot, P. 82
Foucault, M. 23 36 57 58
freedom 127ff 154-159
   Pauline notion of 157ff
free spirits 103 159 181 190
Freud, S. 167 173 189
friendship 86
functionalism 83

Gadamer, H.G. 61 66 67
gaiety 15 70 91 198
Gast, P. 148
Gay Science 15 23 37 59 64 94 98 113 185
genealogy 22ff 80 113 135 142 203
   British 21 22
   Humean 21 22
   methodology of 22 23 24
Genealogy of Morals 21 23 94 101 154
God 65 186 195 197 205ff 208ff
genuine philosophers 125ff
German heroic past 224
Goethe, J.W. von 83 183 184

Gordon, H. 164
Granier, J. 28
great style 115ff
Gregor-Dellin, M. 226

Hare, R. 84
Hegel, G.W.F. 73 74 79 185 187 193 198
Heidegger, M. 57 58 60ff 66ff 147 189 193
Heine, H. 188 212 213 215 217 218
Heraclitus 9 64 181 183n 198
hermeneutics 29 66 67 207
historicism 63f
history 5 62 209
Homer 76 82
Human All-Too-Human 59 63ff 150 222ff
Hume, D. 21 22 29ff 37
   ethics of 73
Husserl, E. 61 168 175ff
   phenomenology of 175ff

ideals 55
innocence of becoming 103
instinct 109
instrumentalism 41
interpretation 1-8 15 19 24 26 29 32 34ff
   43 52 60ff 138 194
   first and second order 35ff
   healthy and sick 36ff
introspective psychology 148ff

James, W. 37 57
Jesus 45f 162 222
Judaism 220
Judeo-Christian tradition 40 77 87 220

Kant, I. 24 26 29 30 32 74 81ff 152 211 214
Kantian morality 24 26 30 74 77ff 85
Kaufmann, W. 40n 69 88 161n 168
knowledge 6 7 9 14 16 18 19 27 53 92 95ff
   110 175 185
   joyful knowledge 185
Kofman, S. 28 34ff 60
Küng, H. 205

language 41ff 136ff 146
life 10 16 98 110
   enhancement of 2 14 191f

logos 67
Löwith, K. 60
Lukács, G. 60

MacIntyre, A. 73 82 83 86 87 88
madman 213ff 217
Magnus, B. 163n 198
Maier, M. 223 225
Maimonides 151 158
masks 63 65 126 165 188
mass media 220
meta-phora 134 135 140 143 145 209
metaphysical realism 27
metaphysical speculation 45 222
metaphysicians 91 103 105
misologism 136
Montinari, M. 205 208n 209n 214 216n
morality 21 27 30 45 47 51 71 72 74ff 91 94
   100 137 168ff 179ff 189
   Kantian 24 26 30
   master 48 49 80 87 172
   slave 48 49 156 157 172 203
   vs. ethics 72
moral philosophy 41 44 74
   psychology 175
   types 80
music 223 224ff
mysticism 220 224

naturalism 41 185
Nazi interpretation of Nietzsche 59
Nehamas, A. 84n
Nietzsche
   affinities to Spinoza 150ff 158
   affirmative ethics of 69-89
   concept of education 110-131
   contradictions in thought 62 64 66
   critical thought of 110
   and Freud 167 173 189
   and Heine 204-218
   illness of 226
   interpretations of 59 60 61 64 66
   new values of 76 78
   phenomenology of 169 171 175
   as philosopher 4ff
   positive doctrine of 31 81 110 204
   as psychologist 4ff

psychology of power 160-182
scepticism of 26 109 113 177 221
sexuality in life of 226
Socratic 109-118
and Spinoza 183-203
style of affirmation 132-146
and Wagner 219-228
nihilism 5 6 12 51 54 62 71 72 107 109 114 117 129 131 204

objectivity 7 8 14 95
Of the Use and Disadvantage of History for Life 63 116
On the Future of our Educational Institutions 119f 124
Overbeck, F. 148 157 158 184 205 216n 227

Parmenides 9 198
Parsifal 220 222 224ff
Paul 46 156ff
permanence vs. flux 194
perspectivism 7 8 24 27 28 35 43 52 56 92 96 115 176 177 179 180 194 208
phenomenology
 of Husserl 175ff
 of Nietzsche 169 171 175ff
 of power 165 171 176
 view of history 173
philology 3 23 35 135ff 144
philosophers 9 11ff 44 70 115ff 165
 genuine 110 112 113 125 126
 new 103 150 161 181
 sly 120ff
philosophical therapy 37ff 168 180ff
philosophy 1 5 8 9 34 40 44 46 57 70 166
 of immanence 190ff 196 199
 moral 41 44 74
Philosophy in the Tragic Age of the Greeks 9
physiology 135-142
Plato 5 53 123 128 129 152
pluralism 35 36
politics 143
power 116 143 164 166 167 170 172 176 179
 negative 162 171 173 174
 positive 161 162 165 169 171 173 175 176 177 181

psychologism 179ff
psychology 134 147 153 161 165 166 168 170 177 178ff
 moral 175
 of power 160 162
public art 222

realism 99 137
reality 110 112 113 115 116
reason 42 74 111 112 117
revaluation of values 15 173 177 200
Rée, P. 20 21 29
relativism 1 109
religion 45
ressentiment 31 48 49 120ff 193 202f
Rorty, R. 57 58
Rosen, S. 72

Salomé, L.A. 70 88
Sartre, J.-P. 159
scepticism 26 109 113 166 177 221
Schacht, R. 69 197n
Schmeitzner, E. 219
Schopenhauer, A. 9 10 21 22 26 137n
 Wagner on 220ff
Schopenhauer as Educator 124 172
science 5 7 9 12 14 27 91 92
Searle, J. 106 106n
self-overcoming 113ff 117 173 176 190ff
self-preservation vs. self-transcendence 191ff
sin 45 49
slave 121 122ff 156ff 172
social practices 80
Socrates 74 109ff 118
Spencer, H. 20 23
Spinoza, B. 88 150 151 158 184-208
spirit 190
struggle for power vs. struggle for existence 150
style 99 139 163ff 211
 great 115ff
subject 42 187
subjectivism 1
subjectivity 66 67
sublimation 65
suffering 112 114 115

teachers 165 182
theory of knowledge 52
therapeutic philosophy 168 180ff
Thus Spoke Zarathustra 83 104 124
truth 3 6 7 9 11 14 15ff 43 52ff 65ff 93 111 117 145 159 181 194
Twilight of the Idols 66 74 87 209

Übermensch 51 54 56 65 66 83ff 153 164 169 172ff 184 190 191 200ff
Untimely Meditations 38 62ff 65 224
utilitarianism 30 32 73

Value 2 3 11 13 21 91 101 169 171
  new 76 78
  transfiguration of all 15 173 177 200
Versuchung and *Verführung* 162
virtue 31 49 72 85
vitalistic interpretation of Nietzsche 61

Wagner, R. 219-227
  against the metaphysicians 220
  on art 220ff
  conflict with Nietzsche over *Parsifal* 220ff
  last communication with Nietzsche 226
  Nietzsche against 223ff
  Nietzsche's reasons in favor 224
  role of genius in art 221
Will
  to ignorance 90 93ff
  to power 13 35 41 44 61 66 84 86 104 105 108 113 125 132 190ff 215
  to truth 90 94 105
Will to Power 44 64 129 132 138
world 4 7 10 18 186
Wurzer, W.S. 183n

Zarathustra 2 15 70 71 87 91 104 107 124 125ff 130ff 153 164n 181 201n 204 208

MARTINUS NIJHOFF PHILOSOPHY LIBRARY

1. D. Lamb, Hegel – From Foundation to System. 1980. ISBN 90-247-2359-0
2. I.N. Bulhof, Wilhelm Dilthey: A Hermeneutic Approach to the Study of History and Culture. 1980. ISBN 90-247-2360-4
3. W.J. van der Dussen, History as a Science. The Philosophy of R.G. Collingwood. 1981. ISBN 90-247-2453-8
4. M. Chatterjee, The Language of Philosophy. 1981. ISBN 90-247-2372-8
5. E.-H.W. Kluge, The Metaphysics of Gottlob Frege. An Essay in Ontological Reconstruction. 1980. ISBN 90-247-2422-8
6. D. Dutton and M. Krausz (eds.), The Concept of Creativity in Science and Art. 1981. ISBN 90-247-2418-X
7. F.R. Ankersmit, Narrative Logic. A Semantic Analysis of the Historian's Language. 1983. ISBN 90-247-2731-6
8. T.P. Hohler, Imagination and Reflection: Intersubjectivity. Fichte's *Grundlage* of 1794. 1982. ISBN 90-247-2732-4
9. F.J. Adelmann (ed.), Contemporary Chinese Philosophy. 1982. ISBN 90-247-3057-0
10. E.N. Ostenfeld, Forms, Matter and Mind. Three Strands in Plato's Metaphysics. 1982. ISBN 90-247-3051-1
11. J.T.J. Srzednicki, The Place of Space and Other Themes. Variations on Kant's First Critique. 1983. ISBN 90-247-2844-4
12. D. Boucher, Texts in Context. Revisionist Methods for Studying the History of Ideas. 1985. ISBN 90-247-3121-6
13. Y. Yovel, Nietzsche as Affirmative Thinker. 1986. ISBN 90-247-3269-7

Series ISBN 90-247-2344-2